S0-BIF-432

U.S. Strategy Against
Global Terrorism

U.S. Strategy Against Global Terrorism

How It Evolved, Why It Failed, and Where It is Headed

Andrew T H Tan

U.S. STRATEGY AGAINST GLOBAL TERRORISM
Copyright © Andrew T H Tan, 2009.

All rights reserved.

First published in 2009 by
PALGRAVE MACMILLAN®
in the United States—a division of St. Martin's Press LLC,
175 Fifth Avenue, New York, NY 10010.

Where this book is distributed in the UK, Europe and the rest of the world,
this is by Palgrave Macmillan, a division of Macmillan Publishers Limited,
registered in England, company number 785998, of Houndmills,
Basingstoke, Hampshire RG21 6XS.

Palgrave Macmillan is the global academic imprint of the above companies
and has companies and representatives throughout the world.

Palgrave® and Macmillan® are registered trademarks in the United States,
the United Kingdom, Europe and other countries.

ISBN: 978–0–230–61997–5

Library of Congress Cataloging-in-Publication Data

Tan, Andrew T H (Andrew Tian Huat)
    US strategy against global terrorism : how it evolved, why it failed, and
where it is headed / Andrew T H Tan.
        p. cm.
    ISBN 978–0–230–61997–5 (alk. paper)
        1. Terrorism—Government policy—United States. 2. War on
Terrorism, 2001– I. Title. II. Title: United States strategy against global
terrorism.

HV6432.T36 2009
363.325′15610973—dc22   2009008648

A catalogue record of the book is available from the British Library.

Design by Newgen Imaging Systems (P) Ltd., Chennai, India.

First edition: November 2009

10 9 8 7 6 5 4 3 2 1

Printed in the United States of America.

CONTENTS

Acknowledgments   vii

One   The United States and Global Terrorism   1

Two   The Failure of the GWOT   19

Three   The U.S. Invasion of Iraq   45

Four   The Iraq Conundrum and Its Implications   71

Five   The Continuing Threat and Why
the United States Failed   97

Six   The Evolution of U.S. Counterterrorism
Strategy: From GWOT to COIN   117

Seven   The Evolution of U.S. Counterterrorism
Strategy: From COIN to Global
Counterinsurgency   139

Eight   The Future for Counterterrorism   177

Notes   193

Biography   219

Bibliography   221

Index   231

ACKNOWLEDGMENTS

The author wishes to thank Palgrave Macmillan, particularly Farideh Koohi-Kamali for supporting this project. The research support provided by the University of New South Wales (UNSW), through the award from the Strategic Priority Fund, is also particularly appreciated. A special thanks goes to the following at the UNSW: Vice-Chancellor Fred Hilmer, Professor Mark Wainwright (former Vice-Chancellor), Professor James Donald (Dean, Faculty of Arts), Emeritus Professor Roger Bell, Associate Professor Rogelia Pe-Pua (Head of School), and Professor Terry Walter (now at University of Technology, Sydney).

Further, the author wishes to thank Professor Rohan Gunaratna (author of Inside Al Qaeda), who encouraged the author to have the work published in the United States. Special thanks also to the following for their support and encouragement for this work: Emeritus Professor David Rapoport (University of California at Los Angeles), Professor James Lutz (Indiana University-Purdue University at Fort Wayne), Professor Michael Rainsborough (War Studies, King's College, London), Associate Professor Jeffrey Kaplan (University of Wisconsin), and Associate Professor James Veitch (Victoria University of Wellington, New Zealand).

The author wishes to thank his wife, Angela, for her encouragement, love, and support, his mother, Mary, and sister, Lily, for their many years of love and perseverance.

CHAPTER ONE

The United States and Global Terrorism

The Attacks on September 11, 2001

The seminal terrorist attacks in the United States on September 11, 2001 (or 9/11) were carried out by 19 members of a hitherto unknown, shadowy organization known as Al Qaeda. Four commercial airliners on domestic flights in the United States were hijacked by the group, which was divided into four teams. Two of the aircraft, American Airlines Flight 11 and United Airlines Flight 175, were deliberately crashed into the World Trade Center in New York causing both towers of the center to collapse. A third aircraft, American Airlines Flight 77, crashed into the Department of Defense headquarters (known as the Pentagon) in Washington. A fourth aircraft, United Airlines Flight 93, which was en route to another target, crashed in a field in Pennsylvania after passengers heroically attempted to retake the aircraft from the hijackers. This fourth aircraft was intended for either the U.S. Congress on Capitol Hill or the White House. In all, 2,986 people of some 80 nationalities died, including those on the four aircraft.

The attacks were a huge shock to the United States, as this was the first major foreign attack on the U.S. homeland since the surprise attack by Japanese forces on Pearl Harbor in 1941 that killed some 2,400 people. There was initial confusion and panic, which resulted in restrictions on flying and other security measures that halted aviation traffic for several days. On September 12, 2001, the United Nations condemned the terrorist attacks and affirmed the right of self-defense when states come under attack. President George Bush declared a "war on terror" after the attack. The United States also swiftly mobilized international support against terrorist groups, including the perpetuator, Al Qaeda.[1]

Although Al Qaeda initially denied involvement, it claimed responsibility in a videotape aired on the Arab broadcaster, Al Jazeera, a year later in September 2002, in which Osama bin Laden eulogized the 9/11 attackers as "great men who deepened the roots of faith in the hearts of the faithful, reaffirmed allegiance to God and torpedoed the schemes of the crusaders and their stooges, the rulers of the region."[2]

The 9/11 attacks were unprecedented. Until then, the most lethal single act of contemporary terrorism was the Abadan theater attack in Iran that killed over 400 people in 1978.[3] The high number of casualties and the huge political, economic, and social impacts also marked 9/11 as different from previous contemporary terrorist attacks. More significantly, the attacks appeared to mark the emergence of a new form of lethal, mass casualty terrorism that would forever change the nature of terrorism. The attacks seemed to validate the assertions of Bruce Hoffman and others, who argued that a new form of globalized, religious, millenarian terrorism had arisen since the 1990s, one that was different from the ethnopolitical terrorist groups that appeared after the end of World War II.[4]

The Evolution of U.S. Grand Strategy

A day after the attack, on September 12, 2001, President Bush had this to say to the U.S. public:

> This enemy attacked not just our people, but all freedom-loving people everywhere in the world. The United States of America will use all our resources to conquer this enemy. We will rally the world. We will be patient, we will be focused, and we will be steadfast in our determination. This battle will take time and resolve. But make no mistake about it: we will win.[5]

On September 15, 2001, in a radio address to the U.S. public, President Bush vowed "a broad and sustained campaign to secure our country and eradicate the evil of terrorism."[6] The Global War on Terror (GWOT) was thus launched. Numerous arrests took place all over the world as governments hunted down radical Islamists linked to Al Qaeda. In late 2001, U.S.-led forces joined with the opposition Northern Alliance in Afghanistan in Operation Enduring Freedom to topple the Taliban regime that had supported Al Qaeda training camps and given it sanctuary. However, Al Qaeda's leader, Osama bin Laden, as well as the

Taliban leader, Mohammed Omar, escaped capture and are believed to have fled across the Afghan–Pakistan border, where sympathetic Pashtun tribes in the lawless northwest provinces of Pakistan have provided sanctuary.

The U.S. attack on Afghanistan, which had the broad support of the international community, was followed by the controversial U.S. invasion and occupation of Iraq in 2003, an action that the rest of the world opposed. Although the United States achieved a swift victory in Iraq, it dissipated much of the international goodwill and sympathy that it had gained in the immediate aftermath of 9/11, especially when it became obvious that Saddam Hussein had neither weapons of mass destruction (WMDs) nor links with Al Qaeda, as the Bush administration had claimed.

The audacious terrorist attacks on September 11 also exposed fundamental weaknesses in U.S. counterterrorism, intelligence, immigration controls, and airport security. It spurred action on dramatically improving homeland security, leading to the creation of the Department of Homeland Security. The Patriot Act was also passed. It gave law enforcement agencies extraordinary powers of surveillance, search, and arrest in order to root out the danger of terrorism, leading to concerns over its possible abuse as well as the erosion of civil liberties.

After lengthy deliberations, the National Commission on Terrorist Attacks (or the 9/11 Commission), an independent commission created by congressional legislation, released its report on July 22, 2004. The commission was critical of intelligence failures that led to 9/11. It concluded that the emergence of Al Qaeda in the late 1990s presented challenges to U.S. governmental institutions that they were not well designed to meet, and it specifically cited the "failure of imagination" that prevented the government from understanding the nature of the terrorist threat posed by Al Qaeda before the 9/11 attacks.[7] The commission concluded that the attacks were indeed carried out by Al Qaeda operatives. However, it also confirmed that while there were contacts between Al Qaeda and Saddam Hussein, there was no collaborative relationship between them, thus undermining one of the key reasons for attacking Iraq.[8]

The first coherent response in terms of strategy by the Bush administration to 9/11 came in the form of the National Security Strategy released a year later, in September 2002. The document acknowledged that the United States faced threats by "catastrophic technologies in the hands of the embittered few." However, it also asserted that the United States had "unprecedented and unequalled strength and influence" and thus it was also a time of opportunity for America. The document then laid out the goals of the United States, which are to "champion aspirations for human dignity," strengthen alliances to defeat global terrorism, work with others to defuse regional conflicts, prevent states threatening the United States with WMDs, and transform national security institutions to meet the challenges of the twenty-first century. Interestingly, the document also stated as U.S. objectives the promotion of free markets and free trade, development, and democracy.[9]

As a statement of intent, it was useful in indicating the general direction of U.S. defense and foreign policies in the post-9/11 era. Significantly, it recognized the enormous power the United States possessed after the end of the cold war and appeared to strongly advocate the use of that power in dealing with emerging security threats such as global terrorism, while using that power to spread American values. The strategy thus hinted strongly at the perceived need to consolidate or even impose such values that would underpin the global power and influence of the United States. In turn, this would result in a world that would be more amenable to U.S. interests, and one in which global terrorism could also be deterred.

In February 2003, President Bush unveiled a much more specific and focused U.S. National Strategy for Combating Terrorism. Its stated objective was to identify and defuse terrorist threats before they reached U.S. borders; in other words, it advocated a preemptive approach.[10] Thus, the United States "will not hesitate to act alone…including acting pre-emptively against terrorists to prevent them from doing harm to our people and our country."[11] The National Strategy for Combating Terrorism consisted of four D's: defeating terrorist organizations, denying them sanctuary and state sponsorship, diminishing the underlying conditions that terrorists seek to exploit, and defending U.S. citizens and interests at home and abroad.[12] The National Strategy also strongly advocated the promotion of democracy as an antidote to the spread of terrorism, a position that reflected the neoconservative agenda that had become dominant in Washington after 9/11.[13]

Over three years later, an updated National Strategy for Combating Terrorism was released in September 2006.[14] The revised document attempted to counter the many criticisms, domestic and global, of U.S. counterterrorism strategy since 9/11. Thus, the document claimed that the U.S. had "made substantial gains in degrading the Al Qaeda network." The controversial Patriot Act as well as the promotion of democracy was also defended as the best long-term answer to Al Qaeda's agenda. The revised strategy spoke of setting the course of action "for winning the War on Terror."[15] This centered on the following: the prevention of attacks by terrorist networks, denying WMDs to rogue states and terrorist allies who seek to use them, denying terrorists the support and sanctuary of rogue states, and denying terrorists control of any nation that they would use as a base and launchpad for terror attacks.[16] Overall, the revised document was defensive in tone and reflected a defense of neoconservative prescriptions that had come under serious criticism.

Despite its many strategic mistakes in the GWOT since 9/11, however, the United States has also demonstrated a surprising capacity to learn from its own mistakes. By 2008, it had arrived at a much more sophisticated understanding of the changed nature of security challenges in the twenty-first century, particularly the evolution of the asymmetric threat environment. For instance, in May 2008, national security analysts meeting in Washington issued a call for an Integrated National Asymmetric Threat strategy that would address these new global threats to the security of the United States.

According to the analysts, the evolving asymmetric threats can be compared in the following manner:

20th Century	Vs	21st Century
The Good War—WWII		The Longest War—Iraq
MAD Strategy		Undefined Strategy
War/Military		Conflict/Non-Military
Nation-State Wars		Cell Conflicts
Generals'/Admirals' Wars		Sergeants' Wars
Combat Power		Influence the Population
DoD Superior Technology		Will, Time, Determination
Think Order of Battle		Think in Terms of Enemy's Culture/Ideals
Maneuver Space (Battlefield)		Population/Urban Space
Military Victory, Rebuild		Hearts and Minds Victory, Nation-Building
Sequential Process (in Phases)		Parallel Processes (All Phases at Once)
Physical Defeat/Victory		Ideological Defeat/New Ideals
Regulated Warfare		Unregulated Warfare
Unconditional Surrender		Negotiated Peace (Limited Objectives)
One Moral High Ground		Multiple Moral High Grounds
War of Military Might		War of Ideas
Courage, Commitment, Rejection		Fear, Apathy, Support
Ex-Urban Scattered Population		Urban Clustering and Megacities

Source: Appendix B—Describing Evolving Asymmetric Threats, in "Dealing with Today's Asymmetric Threat to US and Global Security," CACI International and National Defense University, Washington, May 2008, http://www.caci.com/announcement/CACI_Asymmetric_Threat_paper.pdf

This much more sophisticated and cogent analysis of the changed strategic environment reflected the spirit of self-criticism and appraisal over the many strategic mistakes in the GWOT since 9/11. Ultimately, the process helped to clear up the confusion and lack of clarity that had characterized U.S. strategy.

In mid-2008, the new U.S. National Defense Strategy demonstrated, seven years after 9/11, that the United States had begun to learn from its many missteps and was now beginning to seriously formulate a coherent grand strategy to deal with global terrorism. Crucially, the new National Defense Strategy was supervised by the new defense secretary, Robert Gates, who took a rational, realistic approach, as opposed to the neoconservative ideological agenda that his predecessor Donald Rumsfeld had followed. Instead of military transformation based on reliance on technology, a military-oriented solution to problems, and the use of unilateral, preemptive measures, the new approach emphasized traditional war-fighting skills in countering insurgencies, a comprehensive approach to problems and a more multilateral approach through working with allies.[17]

The National Defense Strategy incorporated the "best-practice" recommendations of those who had studied the United States' failures and strategic missteps since 9/11. The strategy acknowledged that the U.S. faced a global struggle against extremist ideology characterized by the "struggle for legitimacy and influence over the population."[18] Thus, the nature of the battle is ideological and would involve the winning over of hearts and minds. The strategy also emphasized much greater interagency and international collaboration in pursuing a comprehensive approach.[19] Reflecting much greater sophistication, the strategy also called for the adoption of "approaches tailored to local conditions that will vary considerably across regions."[20] Significantly, the revised strategy acknowledged that the United States could not in fact meet all possible security threats all the time and thus had to make choices with regard to how to use its limited resources to manage and mitigate security challenges—a risk management approach.[21] This keen awareness of the limits of resources available compared with the scale of the complex and evolving security landscape, one that included not only nonstate actors such as terrorist groups but also the emergence of peer competitors such as China, is a departure from the previous triumphalism based on the presumed dominance of the United States on account of its superior military power. Compared with earlier documents, the National Defense Strategy of mid-2008 is an impressive and remarkable document. At last, the United States had the outlines of a coherent grand strategy against new, post–cold war security threats such as global terrorism.

The Analysis of Terrorism

Before 9/11, the study of terrorism had been relegated to an esoteric social science practiced by a small group of terrorism experts who tried to make sense of contemporary terrorism.

Despite the fact that much of the terrorism literature before 9/11 focused on WMDs, there were growing fears in the 1990s of the emerging threat from religiously motivated terrorists, who could use such weapons to commit mass casualty terrorist acts. Thus, Nadine Gurr and Benjamin Cole warned of the growing danger of religious terrorists using WMDs.[22] Similarly, Walter Lacqueur, too, warned of the danger of WMD terrorism from religious fanatics, including such eclectic types as white supremacists and Jewish vigilantes.[23] Despite the fact that the Aum Supreme Truth had failed in its sarin nerve gas attack in Tokyo in 1995 although it had enormous resources, that chemical and biological weapons had proven ineffective in wars, and that such weapons have been costly and difficult to use, the apprehensions raised led to massive counterterrorism budget outlays in the United States since 1994, with much of the money meant to counter a WMD attack even though some analysts had warned that airlines were particularly vulnerable.[24]

On the other hand, other terrorism experts have tried to locate the terrorism phenomenon in historical context. For instance, David Rapoport postulated that terrorism has come in four waves. The first was the anarchist wave, which emerged in the 1880s and continued for some forty years. The second was the anticolonial wave, which began in the 1920s and largely disappeared by the 1960s. This was followed by the New Left, which lasted from the 1960s to the 1990s. Finally, a fourth religious wave began in 1979 with the Iranian revolution.[25] According to Rapoport, "history shows that the inspiration for a terrorist wave may dry out in time, and that resistance can destroy organizations or make them ineffectual."[26] Thus, the latest wave, if it followed the pattern of its predecessors, would also dissipate in time. In other words, since terrorism is a historical social phenomenon, Al Qaeda would turn out to be no different from established, historical patterns of the terrorist problem.

This is in sharp contrast to Bruce Hoffman, who has provided the most cogent exposition of the "new" terrorism through his by-now celebrated book *Inside Terrorism,* which appeared in 1998 (since expanded and revised in a second edition in 2006). Hoffman argued that global-ization and other factors have resulted in a new form of globalized, reli-gious terrorism, one that has made a sharp break from traditional, older forms of terrorism. These "new" terrorist groups differ from traditional terrorist groups in several crucial ways. Instead of ethnonationalist causes, they embrace much more amorphous religious and millenarian objectives. They are less cohesive in their organization, with a more diffused cell–like structure and membership. These "new" terrorists are also potentially far more lethal than traditional terrorist groups given their attempts at mass casualty terrorist acts, that is, acts calculated to kill very large numbers of people by using conventional explosives or WMDs as the sarin nerve gas attack on the Tokyo subway by the Aum Supreme Truth demonstrated in 1995. Increasingly, such groups do not bother to explain or justify their attacks, as their aim appears to be to punish and destroy rather than make political statements. Such groups therefore see violence as an end in itself, not just a means to an end.

Moreover, the internationalization of terrorism has also become more pronounced as terrorist groups, taking advantage of porous bor-ders in a rapidly globalizing world economy, today operate in vari-ous countries. These transnational terrorists are much more difficult to track and have also been able to exploit the new information economy and the Internet to reach out to a much wider base of support than was possible in the past. Thus, instead of obtaining the small, clandestine support as in the past, they could now reach out to millions of potential sympathizers. The new terrorist groups are therefore much less depen-dent on the support of states as they have become much more mobile, flexible, and do not need fixed base areas to operate from. Nonetheless, the ethnic conflicts and disintegration of states in the post–cold war era in various places, such as Afghanistan, Yugoslavia, and the former Soviet Union, have afforded them sanctuary in weak or failed states.[27] Thus, the new-terrorism analysts argue that the improved prospects for terrorism in an age of globalization have made possible new transna-tional actors with new weapons, with the ability to cause widespread panic in society through their capacity for mass casualty terrorist acts.

Following the dramatic events of 9/11, a shocked world searched for answers. Fortuitously, Rohan Gunaratna had just completed his book on Al Qaeda, which he had spent five years researching through extensive fieldwork around the world, including interviewing terror-ists linked with Al Qaeda. His book, which appeared in 2002, was the first in-depth study of Al Qaeda and provided a wealth of hith-erto unknown information of this little-known, secretive network.

The book revealed Al Qaeda's global operational focus and detailed its financial infrastructure and the many terrorist plots that it had carefully planned. The book's revelations came as a shock, as it demonstrated the extent of the Al Qaeda global terrorist threat that had been so dramatically demonstrated in the audacious 9/11 attacks. More presciently, Gunaratna warned that a military response by the United States would be effective only in the short term. In the long run, dealing with Al Qaeda would require a "multi-pronged, multi-agency, and multidimensional response by the international community," a lesson that the United States would begin to learn only in 2008 with the appearance of a new National Defense Strategy.[28] In concluding his seminal work, Gunaratna also warned that "a vital component of the US-led anti-terrorist coalition must be the discrediting of Al Qaeda's leadership, ideology, strategies and tactics in the very countries where Muslims live and work," a prescription that took years for the United States to acknowledge should be a priority over purely military security responses.[29] Following the events of 9/11, Gunaratna achieved celebrity status as he appeared on U.S. and global news networks as he explained the nature of the threat and its implications.

There have also been a number of journalistic accounts of Al Qaeda as the mass media tried to uncover its trail. Of these, Jason Burke's *Al Qaeda* is acknowledged to be one of the most accurate and readable accounts available on the complex nature of the radical Islamist threat. Despite being posited as an alternative to Gunaratna (by many of Gunaratna's detractors, particularly those on the neo-left), Burke offers much the same view. Like Gunaratna, Burke recognizes that there must be a military component to counter terrorism. Similarly, he argues for strategies that must be broader and more sophisticated; military power must be only one tool among many. We must, according to him, "eliminate our enemies without creating new ones."[30] He identified the nature of the war as a battle not for global supremacy but for the hearts and minds of the Muslim world.[31] Similar to Gunaratna, he points out that "long term success in the war on terror will depend on successfully countering the growing sympathy for the militants...an important first step will be a single, substantial paradigmatic shift in the way the threat facing us all is currently understood and addressed...the threat is not from one man or one organization."[32]

The U.S. invasion of Iraq in 2003 and the subsequent insurgency there led to a publishing boom as the terrorism studies literature focused on the Iraq question. Attention was focused on the controversial decisions to go to war (based ultimately on the discredited conflation of global terrorism with Iraq), the many mistakes the United States made that led to the civil conflict and insurgency there, and the geopolitical implications arising from the dismembering of a secular, Sunni-dominated bulwark against Iran.

For instance, in *Insurgency and Counterinsurgency in Iraq*, Ahmed S. Hashim explained the complexities of the ethnic and religious divisions of the country that the United States blundered into in 2003. In the light of U.S. blunders in Iraq, Hashim concluded that Iraq's future is bleak, observing that "the various Iraqi interests seem incapable of resolving...their differences or even reduce their maximalist demands vis-à-vis one another for the sake of the greater good...the only reason that they have not fallen upon each other in an orgy of violence is the presence of the Coalition."[33] Similarly, in the self-explanatory title of the volume *The Occupation of Iraq: Winning the War, Losing the Peace,* Ali Allawi, who served as the first post–Saddam minister of defense, observed that as a result of many mistakes, "America's civilising mission in Iraq stumbled, and then quickly vanished, leaving a trail of slogans and an incomplete reconstruction plan." For Iraqis, life now revolved around daily chaos, confusion, shortages, and the lack of security. Thus, the corroded and corrupt state of Saddam had now been replaced by "the corroded, inefficient and corrupt state of the new order." Allawi thus concluded that President Bush "may well go down in history as presiding over one of America's great strategic blunders."[34]

Other excellent accounts of the U.S. invasion and occupation of Iraq include Peter W. Galbraith's *The End of Iraq: How American Incompetence Created a War without End* and Thomas E. Ricks's *Fiasco: The American Military Adventure in Iraq*, both titles being self-explanatory in their focus on the strategic mistakes that led to the United States invading, then failing to competently govern the country, resulting in civil conflict and insurgency.[35]

The difficulties that the U.S. military encountered in dealing with the burgeoning insurgency in Iraq after 2003 led to much debate over how counterinsurgency could be better carried out. Cogent critiques emerged from within the ranks of the U.S. military itself. For instance, Isaiah Wilson, the official U.S. Army historian for the 2003 invasion of Iraq, has been critical of the lack of Phase 4 postconflict stabilization planning. Wilson thus describes Iraq as "the poster-child of America's failures at winning the peace in its war-fights abroad."[36] The focus on better and more comprehensive approaches to counterinsurgency has also been the subject of several RAND studies. Austin Long, in summing up some fifty years of counterinsurgency study at RAND, argued that traditional counterinsurgency (COIN) continues to be relevant since defeat of terrorists within a state's borders will by definition mean that transnational terrorism will be impossible.[37] Other recent RAND studies have focused specifically on COIN in Iraq and Afghanistan.[38] In such studies, the focus is on how the military could perform better against insurgent adversaries, particularly in more competently applying COIN principles in dealing with insurgencies. For instance, James Corum, in *Fighting the War on Terror: A Counterinsurgency Strategy,* advocates updating COIN strategies through an emphasis on training allies and local forces to fight insurgents, focusing on winning hearts and minds, and establishing good intelligence.[39] On a more practical note, David Kilcullen's succinct and readable short article "Twenty-Eight Articles: Fundamentals of Company-Level Counterinsurgency" has been adopted by U.S. forces as a guide to the operational art of counterinsurgency.[40] The soul searching culminated in the revised U.S. Army Counterinsurgency Field Manual, which was adopted in 2006. The revised manual advocates a much more comprehensive approach as well as an emphasis on the winning of hearts and minds. Kilcullen, who had contributed to this revision, has acknowledged that the new COIN approach is really an updated British Commonwealth approach.[41]

However, the realization that better COIN in Iraq could not substitute for a grand strategy to counter the threat of global terrorism led to attempts to formulate such a grand strategy. Thus, Daniel Byman advocates a "Five Front War," focusing on a more effective military that can help allies fight insurgents rather than doing so directly, a war on ideas, better intelligence, homeland defense, and democratic reform throughout the Muslim world while recognizing the limits of such an approach.[42] Rohan Gunaratna and Michael Chandler argue in *Countering Terrorism* that defeating global terrorism requires a coordinated, collaborative effort from the international community, preferably led by the UN. They also advocate a "multi-pronged approach against a multi-dimensional threat," that is, a comprehensive approach.[43] Audrey Cronin, in *Ending Terrorism: Lessons for Defeating Al-Qaeda,* advocates a strategy of countermobilization in which ideological war is waged to discredit and erode Al Qaeda's appeal.[44]

A more promising approach has been the adoption of COIN principles on a global scale. Thus, Thomas Mockaitis argued for a global counterinsurgency (GCOIN) strategy to replace the GWOT in which there is a change in emphasis from a direct to an indirect military approach, with the military taking a more supporting role in a predominantly ideological, political, and diplomatic response.[45] This global counterinsurgency strategy should focus on a comprehensive strategy designed to win hearts and minds, the same strategy that was used to defeat communist guerrillas during the Malayan Emergency.[46]

But how would GCOIN actually work? The most cogent and best articulated version of GCOIN has come from David Kilcullen, who has advocated a strategy of "disaggregation." According to Kilcullen, disaggregation focuses on "interdicting links between theatres, denying the ability of regional and global actors to link and exploit local actors, disrupting flows between and within *jihad* theatres, denying sanctuary areas, isolating Islamists from local populations and disrupting inputs from sources of Islamism in the greater Middle East."[47] He thus defined disaggregation as delinking or dismantling, the objective of which is to prevent the dispersed and disparate elements of the *jihad* movement from functioning as a global system. Just as containment strategy was central to the cold war, this new, updated global COIN strategy, Kilcullen argued, would provide a "unifying strategic conception," or grand strategy, which has been lacking in the war on global terrorism.[48]

What is immediately striking in the evolution of the terrorism studies literature is the fascination of some analysts with adapting classical counterinsurgency strategy to meeting present-day threats. This conflation of insurgency and global terrorism should come as no surprise, given that after 2003, insurgency and terrorism became conflated in the way global terrorism and Iraq somehow became conflated. Though Iraq and global terrorism had no linkages, U.S. actions in Iraq had succeeded in making this a self-fulfilling prophecy. Thus, fighting local insurgencies and fighting Al Qaeda at the global level have become intertwined. But has the new COIN strategy, as encapsulated in the revised U.S. Army Counterinsurgency Field Manual, really worked? The situation in Iraq remains fragile and problematic, and the situation in Afghanistan has worsened. Globally, it is unclear how the United States could lead a grand strategic approach based around GCOIN, given legitimate questions over the dearth in leadership, resources, and moral legitimacy on its part.

Another serious shortcoming in the literature thus far has been the failure to consider the broader picture, given its narrow focus on "winning" the war on terror. The events of 9/11 and the subsequent U.S. response have led to a chain of events that have resulted in important, even fundamental, changes to the international system. September 11 did not just mark the emergence of a new form of globalized, mass casualty, religiously inspired terrorism (even if one accepts the Hoffman thesis). It has also helped clarify the shape of the evolving post-cold war international order as well as the nature of conflict in a rapidly globalizing and changing world. While the fall of the Berlin Wall and the end of the cold war appeared to give way to the unipolar superpower hegemony of the United States, the events of 9/11 and after have seen the limits of U.S. power, painfully demonstrated when dealing with asymmetric terrorist and insurgent challenges in Iraq and Afghanistan and its impotence in the face of North Korea's nuclear test in 2006. More seriously, Linda Bilmes and Joseph Stiglitz have estimated that the economic cost of the invasion and insurgency in Iraq will eventually top $3 trillion. This includes costs hidden in the defense budget, money needed to help future veterans, and resources needed to refurbish depleted military equipment. They concluded that the Bush administration will bequeath to the next administration deep economic problems that have been seriously exacerbated by reckless war financing.[49] These warnings coincided with the unexpected problems in the U.S. banking industry due to the subprime lending crisis in late 2008, a crisis which has severe implications for the U.S. economy and its ability to find the resources to meet the security challenges that it faces in Afghanistan from a resurgent Taliban.

In addition, the U.S. has squandered the one commodity that could have ensured U.S. power and influence for a long time to come, in the manner that Britain retained its influence long after its relative decline and the end of empire—its soft power and legitimacy. This has come about through the Bush administration's unilateral, military-oriented approach and controversial actions, such as the invasion of Iraq. Throughout the Muslim world, in Europe, and among even the United States' closest allies, U.S. actions, including the use of torture, renditions, Guantanamo Bay, and, crucially, the invasion of Iraq, have alienated many and diminished the standing and moral legitimacy of the United States.

Yet, the Bush administration was reported to have seriously considered attacking Iran in 2006, with suggestions that tactical nuclear weapons could be used in a preemptive strike.[50] The consequences of such a course of action would have been tremendous, not for Iran but for the United States. Not only would Europe disassociate itself from the United States, such an action would probably result in the end of NATO and the trans-Atlantic alliance. It would also result in a realignment of powers, including Russia and China, to contain a "rogue" power whose ready use of military force is becoming a major cause of instability in the international system.[51]

The strategic failures and missteps of the United States can be traced not just to its imperial hubris at the end of the cold war and the failure of leadership in the Bush administration, but to the failure in strategic clarity arising from seeing the world through an ideological neoconservative prism. All this have led to the conflation of the global war on terror with a mix of other security challenges and foreign policy objectives, such as geopolitics, "rogue states" and WMD proliferation, and the need for energy security (since Iraq does have one of the world's largest reserves of oil). Not surprisingly, the United States has found itself stretched and bewildered, for no state, no matter how powerful, could have the resources to deal with so many challenges all at once.

The events of 9/11 have thus led to a series of events that have diminished the global power of the United States. More importantly, 9/11 and its aftermath have also strengthened the agency of the state, rather than global norms and international institutions. Subsequent events appeared to prove that the institutions and agencies of states matter much more than multilateral bodies such as the UN in the global war on terror. But the cumulative effect of the United States' unilateralism has been to diminish the UN's standing and the many international regimes that govern international relations.

The United States would still be a power of note, but in the evolving post-9/11 era where the international system is in a state of flux, it would only be one among equals. The post–cold war world order is gradually becoming clear. According to Coral Bell, it would not be one dominated by a single superpower hegemon but is evolving toward a multipolarity dominated by several regions or states, such as the United States, China, India, Russia, the European Union, and Japan.[52]

However, the international system as it is evolving is not likely to resemble entirely the concert of powers of nineteenth-century Europe. The current globalization (there having been many globalizations in contemporary history) has resulted in the emergence of a global interlinked economy and the free flow of technology and resources that have also led to the emergence of nonstate actors. In particular, armed groups (including terrorist and insurgent groups) enabled by globalization are posing a serious challenge not only to security and stability in weak and failed states but also to global society because of the transnational nature of their activities.[53]

The Objectives of This Book

The brief survey above of the evolution of the terrorism studies literature points to the need for a critical assessment of the evolution and development of U.S. strategy against global terrorism since the seminal events of 9/11. Instead of the rational unfolding of a coherent and well-thought-out grand strategy, the United States has not developed a unifying strategic conception. Instead, it used blunt military force in a unilateral fashion on the assumption that targeting specific individuals and organizations would solve the problem of global terrorism. Even this simplistic approach toward countering global terrorism became intertwined with numerous objectives, such as exporting democracy, removing Saddam Hussein from power in Iraq, dealing with the proliferation of WMDs, countering "rogue" states, containing local Muslim insurgencies all over the world, and ensuring homeland security, among a host of terrorism- and non-terrorism-related issues. This lack of clarity and coherence has cost the United States dearly.

However, the United States has demonstrated a remarkable ability to learn from even its worst mistakes. The evolution of U.S. grand strategy against global terrorism is a story that is worth telling, as it has evolved and developed in the midst of various strategic mistakes and missteps, to culminate in the recently released National Defense Strategy in 2008. There has also been a substantial literature on the failures of U.S. grand strategy and the reasons for those failures, but what has been lacking is its relation to the evolution of this grand strategy as the United States began painfully to learn from its mistakes. Finally, there is a need to understand better the problems and prospects for U.S. grand strategy and where it is heading, given that despite the failures and mistakes of the Bush administration, it has bequeathed to the Obama administration in Washington a more rational and coherent grand strategy than it had started out with in the wake of 9/11. Thus, three key questions can be posed: How has U.S. grand strategy against global terrorism evolved? What explains the failures in U.S. strategy? What are the prospects for U.S. grand strategy?

This book is divided into eight chapters. Chapter 2 examines the failure of the GWOT. It traces the initial successes in the GWOT as the seminal events of 9/11 with its many non-U.S. casualties had such a huge impact that the United States received the sympathy and support of its allies and the international community. But initial successes in Afghanistan against Al Qaeda and its Taliban supporters soon gave way to terrorist attacks across the world, most of which have been carried out not by Al Qaeda itself but by its local regional affiliates. Thus, while Al Qaeda suffered tactical battlefield losses in Afghanistan and worldwide security action led to many of its operatives being captured or killed, it has, conversely, reconstituted itself to pose an even greater strategic threat through its evolution into an international franchise and a global ideological threat.

Chapter 3 examines the U.S. invasion of Iraq. It examines the reasons that led to the U.S. attack on Iraq, despite the opposition of many of its allies and the international community. While the military offensive in 2003 proved to be a walkover, the United States soon encountered unexpected challenges because of its failure to plan adequately for postconflict stabilization. Thus, the United States ended up facing a growing insurgency as well as civil conflict between different groups in Iraq.

Chapter 4 assesses the Iraq conundrum. Iraq had little to do with the GWOT, given that Saddam Hussein had little, if any, contact with Al Qaeda. Nor did he possess WMDs. Yet, the decision to invade and occupy Iraq later came to haunt the United States. The conflation of Iraq with global terrorism led to very negative outcomes for the GWOT. It gave Al Qaeda's cause a huge boost as the United States lost its legitimacy within the Muslim world. The invasion also destabilized the Middle East, as Iraq could no longer serve as a bulwark against Iran (and greater Shiite influence) in a region of great strategic importance to the United States. The invasion of Iraq also isolated the United States internationally and fractured its domestic body politic as the cost in human and economic terms of countering the insurgency mounted.

Chapter 5 examines the question of why the United States failed in its grand strategy against global terrorism. It explains the reasons for U.S. failures, such as the U.S. predisposition to substitute military force as an easy solution to problems rather than construct a meaningful political strategy. This has been attributed to the so-called American Way of War, which was strengthened during the Bush administration by Donald Rumsfeld's strong advocacy of a New American Way of War based on the use of technological and informational superiority that were supposed to fundamentally transform U.S. conventional military power. But U.S. power in Iraq and Afghanistan has proven illusory, as stunning battlefield successes have not translated into meeting political objectives. Instead, the much-vaunted U.S. military proved vulnerable to asymmetric challenges such as terrorism and insurgent attacks.

Chapter 6 discusses the development of U.S. grand strategy in the global war on terror. It examines the National Strategy for Combating Terrorism in 2003 and the revised version in 2006. From the criticisms of the unilateral, military-oriented approach of the GWOT strategy under the Bush administration, alternative strategies have emerged.

Some advocated better COIN, while others argued for the application of classical COIN principles to a global grand strategic approach, dubbed "global counterinsurgency", or GCOIN. However, the blurring of lines between counterterrorism and counterinsurgency is the result of the conflation of terrorism and insurgency in the aftermath of the U.S. invasion of Iraq and the outbreak of the Iraqi insurgency. The COIN approach to countering global terrorism is thus problematic for a number of reasons.

Chapter 7 explains and assesses the evolution of U.S. counterterrorism strategy from its attempt to revise COIN strategy to fit present-day realities, to the use of classical COIN principles as the basis for a GCOIN grand strategy. This is epitomized firstly by the revised U.S. Army Counterinsurgency Field Manual, which adopted a comprehensive, hearts and minds approach to COIN, a departure from the application of kinetic military force as a first resort. This was followed in 2008 by the National Defense Strategy, which also took a comprehensive approach based on interagency cooperation, multilateralism, and the use of nonmilitary instruments such as economic development and political measures.

Chapter 8 concludes with an assessment of the future for counterterrorism. It examines the present challenges in countering a global terrorist threat that has now become a long-term ideological challenge. There is now some consensus in the United States on the contours of what should constitute a coherent, comprehensive grand strategy against terrorism. The new U.S. National Defense Strategy released in mid-2008 is indeed an impressive document, demonstrating the ability of the United States to learn from its previous missteps. In the final analysis, however, the vicissitudes of U.S. strategy since the pivotal events of 9/11 have been overtaken by fundamental changes in the international system. It is this context that has been missing in the debates about Iraq and the GWOT.

CHAPTER TWO

The Failure of the GWOT

Initial Successes

The seminal events on September 11, 2001 (9/11) led to a forceful response from the United States, resulting in a U.S.-led Global War on Terror (GWOT). Shocked by the high number of casualties and the fact that citizens of some 80 nations had been among the victims, U.S. allies and the international community were swift to condemn the attacks. The United States was thus able to successfully mobilize international support against Al Qaeda and other groups linked to Al Qaeda.

On September 12, 2001, NATO invoked its collective obligation to self-defense under Article 5 of the Washington Treaty for the first time in its history. NATO also pledged to "undertake all efforts to combat the scourge of terrorism."[1] By doing so, NATO also mandated itself to make combating terrorism an enduring NATO mission.[2] On the same day, the United Nations also condemned the terrorist attacks and called for "international cooperation to bring to justice the perpetrators, organizers, and sponsors of the outrages of 11 September 2001."[3] Article 4 of the hitherto moribund ANZUS Treaty between Australia, New Zealand, and United States was invoked and the 9/11 attacks were declared to be an attack on Australia as well.[4] On September 28, 2001, the UN Security Council adopted Resolution 1373, which called on states to criminalize assistance for terrorist activities, deny financial support and safe haven to terrorists, and share information about groups planning terrorist attacks. The resolution also urged states to become parties to all international conventions and protocols relating to terrorism.[5] Soon after this, the United Nations established the Counter Terrorism Committee (CTC). Comprising the 15 members of the Security Council, the CTC is charged with monitoring the implementation of Resolution 1373.[6]

Resolutions were backed by actions, as governments around the world took action against Al Qaeda. Numerous arrests were made worldwide as governments hunted down radical Islamists linked to Al Qaeda. Arrests were made in Europe, the Middle East, the Indian subcontinent, and Southeast Asia.

Pakistan turned out to be a key ally in the GWOT, as several hundred Al Qaeda operatives, including some key leaders, were apprehended and turned over to the United States. Among the top Al Qaeda leaders captured were Khalid Sheikh Mohammed, Ramzi bin Al-Shibh, and Mustafa Ahmed Hawsawi, all of whom had been involved in the planning of the 9/11 attacks. Khalid turned out to be the key mastermind of those attacks. Other important Al Qaeda arrests in Pakistan included Abu Zubaydah, who was Al Qaeda's chief of operations; Ahmed Kahalfan Ghailani, an Al Qaeda computer expert; and Abu Faraj Al-Libbi, who headed Al Qaeda's external operations.[7] In Southeast Asia, the arrests of key Al Qaeda operative Omar Al-Farouq in Indonesia, and Hambali (or Riduan Hishamuddin), who had organized the deadly Bali bombings in 2002, in Thailand, were also major successes.[8]

A number of key Al Qaeda figures were also arrested in the Middle East. They included Mohammed Haydar Zammar, who was arrested in Morocco and had a role in the 9/11 attacks; Mohamedou Ould Slahi, who was arrested in Mauritania and allegedly plotted to attack Los Angeles airport in 2000; Abu Issa Al-Hindi, an Al Qaeda operative who was captured in Britain; Abd Al-Rahim Al-Nashiri, who was arrested in the United Arab Emirates and is believed to be Al Qaeda's chief of operations in the Persian Gulf; and Mounir Al-Motassadek who was arrested in Germany for his role in the 9/11 attacks.[9] These arrests led to the uncovering of other planned terrorist attacks as well as the further arrest of other members of Al Qaeda. They also demonstrated the efficacy of transnational security cooperation as U.S. security agencies had worked closely with other governments in all these cases.

Apart from arrests, the United States took direct action, including copying the Israeli tactic of targeted assassinations. Mohammad Atef, Al Qaeda's operations commander, was killed by a U.S. missile fired from a unmanned aerial vehicle (UAV) in Kabul, in Afghanistan in November 2001.[10] Qaed Salim Sinan Al-Harethi, who was linked to the bombing of the *USS Cole* in 2000 in Yemen, was also killed by a U.S. missile fired from a UAV in Yemen in November 2002.[11]

The United States also obtained broad international support from both the international community and its allies to intervene in Afghanistan, where Al Qaeda was sheltering under the protection of the Taliban regime. The austere, fundamentalist Taliban regime had seized power in Kabul in 1996 at the end of the civil war that followed the withdrawal of Soviet troops in 1989. The United Nations needed little prompting, as the Security Council had already imposed sanctions on the Taliban regime in October 1999. After the 9/11 attacks, the Security Council demanded that the Taliban hand over Osama bin Laden and close Al Qaeda training camps. When it refused, the United Nations imposed new sanctions in January 2002.[12]

The United States itself delivered an ultimatum to the Taliban regime on September 20, 2001, demanding that it surrender all Al Qaeda leaders and closed all terrorist training camps.[13] When it refused, the United States intervened militarily through Operation Enduring Freedom, justifying it as a response to the 9/11 attacks masterminded by Al Qaeda and abetted by its Taliban ally in Kabul. According to President Bush, the objectives of Operation Enduring Freedom were "to disrupt the use of Afghanistan as a terrorist base of operations, and to attack the military capability of the Taliban regime." Bush welcomed the military participation of Britain, Canada, Australia, Germany, and France, as well as the support of over 40 countries, which gave landing or transit rights and shared intelligence. Bush was thus able to speak of being "supported by the collective will of the world."[14] From October 7, 2001, U.S. air strikes involved heavy bombers such as the B1 Lancer, B2 Spirit, and B52 Stratofortress, carrier-based fighter-bombers such as the F-18 Hornet, and cruise missiles launched from naval vessels.

Air strikes alone did not have the desired political effect on the ground, which was the toppling of the Taliban regime. This required a ground offensive. However, the United States was able to exploit the internal political and tribal differences within Afghanistan. The anti-Pashtun Northern Alliance, comprising Tajiks and Uzbeks, had been battling the Taliban through its toehold in the north. It was led by the charismatic Ahmad Shah Masoud, the so-called "Lion of the Panjhir Valley," given his heroic role in battling the Soviets during the 1980s. Masoud was assassinated by Al Qaeda on September 9, 2001 when a suicide team disguised as a television film crew succeeded in getting close enough to kill him with explosives hidden in a film camera.[15] Despite this setback, Northern Alliance forces were able to take on the Taliban with the help of U.S. Special Forces and air support.

On its part, the U.S. approach had been unconventional and innovative, comprising special forces operating deep in enemy territory, the massive use of precision-guided air attacks, and the assistance of local allies familiar with the local terrain and conditions. As U.S. Secretary of Defense Donald Rumsfeld noted approvingly, the special forces involved in the seminal battle of Mazar-I-Sharif "sported beards and traditional scarves and rode horses trained to run into machine gun fire."[16] Success came swiftly as the Taliban regime collapsed in the face of the onslaught. By December 2001, the last Taliban stronghold, Kandahar in the south, had fallen. In the Battle of Tora Bora, the last of the Taliban and Al Qaeda strongholds too fell, although Mullah Mohammed Omar, the leader of the Taliban, and the senior Al Qaeda leadership, including Osama bin Laden, fled across the border to shelter among sympathetic Pashtun tribes in northwestern Pakistan, a lawless zone which the central government in Pakistan has never managed to control.

While there was Muslim disquiet and some outrage at the U.S. attack on Afghanistan, there was general approval and support for the U.S. action as it appeared to be a just response to the deadly 9/11 attacks. At the UN conference in Bonn in December 2001, the preferred U.S. candidate, Hamid Karzai, was installed as Afghanistan's new interim leader.[17] In December 2001, the Security Council established the International Security Assistance Force (ISAF) to maintain security in Afghanistan.[18] In March 2002, the United Nations also established the United Nations Assistance Mission for Afghanistan (UNAMA) to manage the country's reconstruction.[19] ISAF is, however, not a UN force and was initially led by Britain and other U.S. allies. In August 2003, NATO took over to lead ISAF. In October 2003, the Security Council passed Resolution 1510, which authorized the force to operate beyond Kabul.[20] This was deemed necessary due to the continuing security problems and massive political and economic challenges in Afghanistan. The fall of the Taliban regime did not unite the country but had brought into power a disparate coalition of warlords. Although Karzai won the October 2004 presidential elections, the diffusion of military power limited the authority of the national government headed by Karzai in the capital Kabul. Indeed, Karzai's authority has not extended much beyond Kabul and has been decidedly shaky in the southern provinces, which are populated by Pashtun tribes hostile to the United States and its allies.

Despite strong criticism voiced by a number of European governments with the United States over its invasion of Iraq in 2003, the commitment of NATO and Europe to ISAF has endured.[21] By May 2007, there were 35,500 NATO and non-NATO troops from 37 countries in ISAF.[22] Yet, major challenges remained. Despite the setback in late 2001, the Taliban was able to regroup by the beginning of 2004, aided by assistance and sanctuary from across the porous boundary between Afghanistan and Pakistan, where the Taliban was able to obtain help from sympathetic Pashtun tribes in Pakistan's lawless northwest provinces. There, the Pakistan government's military offensives to deal with the fundamentalists have so far failed, with the army suffering heavy casualties. This led to ceasefires and attempts to negotiate with the militants, thus leaving the provinces as a safe haven for the Taliban and Al Qaeda. The Taliban's resurgence has also been attributed to the booming drugs trade and the dissatisfaction, particularly among Pashtuns in the southern provinces, with the Karzai government due to the slow pace of reconstruction.[23]

The Taliban has thus become bolder and have been able to carry out suicide terrorist attacks in Kabul, and has also been involved in major battles in the south. The increased level of violence has led to rising casualties amongst international troops. By January 2009, 1,055 international troops, including 637 U.S., 142 British, and 107 Canadian soldiers, had been killed.[24] To make matters worse, a number of key NATO countries such as Germany, France, and Italy are not prepared to participate in the actual fighting, garrisoning their troops in the comparative safety of the north.[25] An amnesty program begun by Karzai in 2005 has had limited success and while the Taliban resurgence is not sufficient to threaten the Kabul government, it has posed very serious tactical challenges for the international force. Indeed, a key Taliban commander stated that the Taliban had 12,000 fighters and boasted of its close ties with Al Qaeda.[26] Taliban leader Mullah Omar also proclaimed his belief that the Taliban will prevail as the *mujahideen* had during the 1980s against the Soviets. His strategy is to ensure that Afghanistan remains ungovernable and that Kabul cannot secure the entire country, a classic insurgent strategy of winning by not losing.[27] The key to a return to stability in Afghanistan clearly lies in the ability to win the support of the Pashtuns in the southern provinces. Winning hearts and minds that would keep Taliban fundamentalism at bay requires development programs that can deliver real benefits to the people. The problem, however, is that reconstruction efforts have failed to deliver due to the lack of security amid constant attacks on aid and development workers.

There is also clearly the need to remove the safe havens for the Taliban in the northwest provinces of Pakistan. Following the assassination of

Benazir Bhutto in 2007 and the election results in Pakistan, which resulted in the routing of Islamist parties in the northwest, the Pakistan army thus began a major offensive in Waziristan province in early 2008. The objective of the offensive was to clear the area of militants associated with Al Qaeda, such as Baitullah Mehsud who is suspected to have masterminded Bhutto's death and whose followers have carried out a number of suicide attacks across Pakistan.[28] This, however, proved to be a very difficult undertaking given the terrain, the local support for the Taliban, and the sheer determination of the militants in opposing the military offensive.

The End of Al Qaeda, or Not?

In sum, the United States has been able to call upon its allies from around the world to help it pursue Al Qaeda leaders and operatives, freeze its assets, and destroy its sanctuaries. By September 2003, two years after 9/11, the United States claimed to have killed or captured 3,000 Al Qaeda members, or two-thirds of its membership, and destroyed all its sanctuaries in Afghanistan.[29] Despite the fact that the top two leaders, Osama bin Laden and Ayman Al-Zawahiri, remained at large, it appeared that the concerted security, intelligence, and military efforts had paid off. In carrying out the 9/11 attacks, Al Qaeda had miscalculated the U.S. response, and had not expected it to so quickly and successfully invade and occupy Afghanistan, where it had safe haven. Al Qaeda also did not expect the rapid worldwide security action that, in a relatively short time, was able to cripple its operational capabilities. As an organization, Al Qaeda has been put under immense pressure, with its safe havens destroyed, leaders and operatives arrested and killed, and many of its planned operations disrupted. Al Qaeda's leadership and operational capabilities have thus been in significant decline since 9/11.

Because of this, it has been argued that Al Qaeda no longer posed a strategic threat to the U.S. homeland since an attack on the scale of 9/11 requires a transnational financial network, highly trained operatives, undetected surveillance of targets, and safe haven territory to plan such attacks.[30] Such an assessment is based on the fact that Al Qaeda has failed to carry out a major attack on the U.S. homeland since 9/11. In addition, except for attacks in Saudi Arabia, no major terrorist operation around the world since 9/11 can be directly attributed to Al Qaeda.

Thus, in November 2008, a U.S. National Intelligence Council report, *Global Trends 2025*, citing the four waves of terrorism theory developed by David Rapoport, argued that Al Qaeda's terrorism wave might be breaking up. The report pointed out that "in relying almost exclusively on terrorism as a means to achieve its strategic objectives, rather than transforming into a political movement like Hizbollah or Hamas, Al Qaeda is using a stratagem that rarely is successful." The report thus concluded that Al Qaeda's weaknesses, such as its unachievable strategic objectives, inability to attract broad-based support, and self-destructive actions, would cause it to decay.[31]

The report indirectly alluded to a key debate in terrorism studies: How "new" is the new terrorism epitomized by Al Qaeda? On the one hand, there are those such as David Rapoport in his four waves of terrorism theory, who argue that terrorism is an historical social phenomenon, the implication being that Al Qaeda is no different from established, historical patterns of the terrorist problem, and that it will wane wax and wane accordingly.[32] On the other hand, there are the "new" terrorism analysts such as Bruce Hoffman, who argue that globalization and other factors have resulted in a new form of globalized, religious terrorism that marks a sharp break from traditional, older forms of terrorism. The new terrorism, Hoffman has argued, contains features that are totally new, such as the apocalyptic nature of its message, the globalized networked structure, ability to exploit the opportunities afforded by the global communications and information technology (IT) revolution, much reduced reliance on state sponsors due to the emergence of the global economy, and the resort to mass casualty terrorist attacks potentially involving weapons of mass destruction.[33] These "new" features underpin the argument by the "new" terrorism advocates that the GWOT will be a "long war."

So which school of thought is right? Is the post-9/11 global terrorism a continuity of historical trends, or does it represent a radical change? The answer is perhaps not straightforward, given the complexities of the global terrorist threat. Thus, the same National Intelligence Council report, *Global Trends 2025*, noted that "because history suggests that the global Islamic terrorist movement will outlast Al Qaeda as a group, strategic counterterrorism efforts will need to focus on how and why a successor terrorist group might evolve during the remaining years of the Islamic terrorist wave."[34] Looking ahead, the report also warned that "for those terrorist groups active in 2025, the diffusion of technologies and scientific knowledge will place some of the world's most dangerous capabilities within their reach."[35] Thus, the threat of catastrophic mass casualty terrorism, begun by Al Qaeda, will remain a feature of global society for the foreseeable future. In other words, while there has been continuity in terrorism patterns, there has also been change.

Thus, despite the decline of Al Qaeda the organization, there remains considerable unease and apprehension over the continuing threat of global terrorism. Just where the threat is coming from is suggested, for instance, by Marc Sageman, who has argued that it now emanates from the grassroots, such as radicalized individuals and groups who meet and plot in their neighborhoods and on the Internet.[36] Thus, while Al Qaeda the organization has been crippled, the global terrorist threat has been replaced by a much deadlier one—Al Qaeda's radical ideology. Enabled by the Internet, improved communications, and the border-less global economy, and galvanized by U.S. strategic mistakes as well as fundamental grievances felt by Muslims everywhere, the emerging challenge is the radicalization of local groups and individuals with few if any direct connections to Al Qaeda. This is epitomized, for instance, by the London bombings in 2005, carried out by self-radicalized British Muslims, as well as regional affiliates carrying out terrorist and insurgent attacks in the name of Al Qaeda. Indeed, the main radical Islamist group in Iraq is called "Al Qaeda in Iraq," while the militant Islamist faction of the Al Qaeda–linked Jemaah Islamiah (JI), which has been carrying out attacks in Southeast Asia is the self-styled "Al Qaeda in the Malay Archipelago."

This assessment of a global ideological war is contained in the U.S. Homeland Security Threat Assessment for 2008–2013, which predicts that the pool of radical Islamists within the United States will increase over the next five years partly due to the ease of online recruitment. The report foresees "a wave of young, self-identified Muslim 'terrorist wannabes' who aspire to carry out violent acts." While these "terrorist wannabes" are more aspirational at this point given the lack of sophisticated operational capabilities, they would learn very quickly and get better over time. The report thus warns that the United States could face a destructive biological attack in the next five years.[37]

Yet, there continues to be a debate over whether Al Qaeda the organization continues to pose a threat to United States and global security. A U.S. National Intelligence Estimate in July 2007, for instance, warned that:

Al Qaeda is and will remain the most serious terrorist threat to the Homeland, as its central leadership continues to plan high-impact plots, while pushing others in extremist Sunni communities to mimic its efforts and to supplement its capabilities. We assess the group has protected or regenerated key elements of its Homeland attack capability, including: a safe haven in the Pakistan Federally Administered Tribal Areas (FATA), operational lieutenants, and its top leadership.[38]

Hoffman thus warned, in reference to claims of Al Qaeda's demise as an organization, that "if we believe we are safe, we may face the most consequential terrorist attack yet." He warned that Al Qaeda has demonstrated a remarkable ability to survive in the face of the concerted U.S.-led onslaught and asserted that "despite the comparatively far more modest amenities and confining nature of Pakistan's Federally Administered Tribal Areas (FATA) and surrounding provinces, Al Qaeda has nonetheless been able to reconstitute its global terrorist reach."[39]

Hoffman further asserted in January 2009 that the central front in the GWOT is not Iraq but the lawless border region between Afghanistan and Pakistan. He argued that:

> If 9/11 has taught us anything, it is that Al Qaeda is most dangerous when it has a sanctuary or safe haven from which to operate—as it now indisputably does. Indeed, virtually every major terrorist attack or plot of the past four years has emanated from Al Qaeda's reconstituted sanctuary in Pakistan's Federally Administered Tribal Areas (FATA) or Northwest Frontier Province (NWFP). Perhaps most important, however, is that the broader movement's ability to continue to appeal to its hardcore, political base and thus guarantee a flow of recruits into its ranks, money into its coffers, and support for its aims and objectives, ensures that this struggle will neither abate on its own accord nor be easily—and quickly—defeated.[40]

Thus, Hoffman's view is that although Al Qaeda has evolved into a global ideological threat, the Al Qaeda core is still dangerous. Defeating Al Qaeda in all its respects will take a very long time as well as much effort—hence the "long war." It is also noteworthy that this line of argument, that Al Qaeda the organization in fact remains dangerous as it is regrouping in Northwest Pakistan with the help of its Taliban sympathizers and that the United States therefore has to refocus the GWOT from Iraq to Afghanistan and Pakistan, seems to have been embraced by the Obama administration, which took office in January 2009.

Terrorist Plots in the U.S. Homeland

The persistence of the theme of a continuing threat from Al Qaeda has its roots in the sense of insecurity stemming from the threat of catastrophic mass casualty terrorism, which was begun by Al Qaeda with the 9/11 attacks and which many believe will remain a feature of global society. Another reason is the sense of strategic failure since 9/11. This stems from the many terrorist attacks around the world since then, which appear to indicate that the global terrorist problem has expanded manifold, even though no further major terrorist attack has taken place in the United States itself. There is consensus that the worldwide terrorist attacks since 9/11 have been heavily influenced or inspired by Al Qaeda's radical ideology as well as enabled by U.S. strategic mistakes.

Since the early successes against the new global terrorism, such as the arrest of Al Qaeda operatives throughout the world and the ouster of Al Qaeda and its Taliban allies from its sanctuaries in Afghanistan in late 2001, there has been growing doubts and criticism of the evolving U.S. strategy. Any criticism would have been muted had the GWOT demonstrated that the problem of global terrorism had been brought under control. Instead, the global terrorist problem appears to have grown exponentially, despite U.S. and international counterterrorism actions.

One of the key reasons is the transformation of Al Qaeda into a global insurgency, with a much greater geographical footprint and much greater support for its radical and violent agenda than in the past by local regional groups and individuals around the world, a stunning strategic success considering the tactical losses suffered by Al Qaeda since 9/11. Despite the deaths and arrests of many of its leaders and operatives, the Al Qaeda radical agenda has survived and outgrown the organization itself. The proof lies in the many deadly Al Qaeda-linked attacks across the globe since 9/11.

Although no terrorist attack has since taken place since 9/11 in the United States itself, the evidence suggests that a combination of intelligence cooperation, better homeland security measures, the vigilance of security personnel, and just sheer luck has disrupted several planned terrorist plots in the United States. Khalid Shaikh Mohammed, the alleged mastermind of the 9/11 attacks, had planned to use suicide bombers from its Southeast Asian affiliate, the JI, to attack the U.S. Bank Tower, the tallest building in Los Angeles. As revealed by the U.S. Government in 2006, the planning began a month after 9/11 and involved the use of shoe bombs to breach pilot doors and hijack aircraft for the operation.[41] It was also later revealed that U.S. security services had thwarted other plans to bring down iconic symbols in the United States, such as the Brooklyn Bridge, the Statue of Liberty, and the Golden Gate Bridge in San Francisco in a series of coordinated attacks in the months following 9/11.[42]

A plan that almost succeeded was the attempt to bring down an American Airlines Boeing 767 that was flying from Paris to Miami in the United States on December 22, 2001. Alert passengers and crew overpowered a would-be suicide bomber who was trying to light a fuse to a sophisticated bomb packed into his shoe. The now infamous shoe bomber, Richard Reid, turned out to be a homegrown terrorist as he was born in Britain but had later converted and then joined Al Qaeda.[43] In 2005, U.S. Attorney-General Alberto R. Gonzales revealed that the authorities had thwarted several terrorist plots in the United States itself. Some were planned by a cell led by Ahmed Omar Abu Ali, a resident of Virginia, who had received training in weapons, explosives, and document forgery from Al Qaeda in Saudi Arabia. The operations that were planned allegedly included the assassination of President Bush as well as similar attacks to 9/11 with airplanes flying from other countries to the United States.[44] In July 2005, in a routine police investigation into armed robberies, a militant cell that was planning a string of attacks was uncovered. In one suspect's apartment, police found material that indicated that a militant group had planned to attack a number of targets, including Los Angeles International Airport, synagogues, National Guard armories, and U.S. Army recruiting centers.[45]

In June 2006, seven people including two foreigners were charged over a plot to destroy the tallest building in the United States, the Sears Tower in Chicago, as well as the FBI building in North Miami Beach. What was disturbing about the plot was that these were not Al Qaeda members. Although they had pledged allegiance to Al Qaeda, they had no contacts with it. Instead, they were homegrown terrorists who were self-radicalized after being exposed to violent *jihadist* propaganda.[46] This was a disturbing trend, which suggested that the Al Qaeda brand of radical ideology appealed to some Muslims, indicating that the threat was evolving into one emanating not from Al Qaeda the organization but from Al Qaeda's radical ideology.

The threat to the U.S. homeland also came from terrorist plots attempted from outside the United States. In July 2006, three people were arrested in Lebanon in connection with a plan to carry out attacks on trains in the train tunnel under the Hudson River connecting Manhattan with New Jersey using suicide bombers and backpack bombs. If the tunnels collapsed, a huge number of casualties among passenger commuters would have occurred. The chief suspect was a lecturer at a local Lebanese university who had links with Al Qaeda.[47]

In August 2006, cooperation between British and Pakistan authorities led to the arrest of some 24 people involved in an audacious plot to simultaneously blow up ten jets leaving Britain for the United States using liquid explosives. The plot was quite advanced, as they were about to embark on a trial run. Two of the suspects had also earlier traveled to Pakistan and received money to fund the operation. One suspect was a Heathrow Airport worker who had access to all areas of the airport.[48] The abortive plot resulted in new restrictions on the carrying of liquids onto passenger aircraft that have remained in place today. However, the terrorist plan itself was not new. In 1994, a similar plan to use liquid explosives to blow up a dozen airliners in the Asia Pacific was thwarted when Ramzi Yousef, the original World Trade Center bomber in 1993, left behind a laptop containing details of the plot, codenamed Operation Bojinka after a town in Bosnia, following a fire in his flat in Manila in the Philippines.[49]

In May 2007, five foreign-born radical Islamists were charged with conspiring to attack U.S. soldiers with grenades and assault rifles at Fort Dix in New Jersey. The men, part of a homegrown cell of immigrants from Jordan, Turkey, and the former Yugoslavia, had been radicalized by *jihadist* propaganda on the Internet and had trained at a shooting range in Pennsylvania in order to carry out their plan. However, the plan unraveled after an alert store clerk informed the authorities when the group tried to have their training videos copied onto a DVD.[50]

In June 2007, four people were charged with plotting to attack John F. Kennedy Airport in New York, one of the busiest in the United States. The four conducted surveillance of the airport, including videotaping their targets and downloading satellite images from the Internet, but the plan was revealed when they recruited an FBI informant to help with the plot. Had it succeeded, it would have caused major devastation and casualties as the fuel pipelines that were apparently targeted run for 64 km and served two other airports.[51]

Thus, Lee Hamilton, Vice-Chairman of the National Commission on Terrorist Attacks Upon the United States (also known as the 9/11 Commission), stated in an interview in September 2006 that while he agreed with the general assessment that the U.S. homeland was safer than prior to 9/11, "we are not safe," and there remained "much more we need to do to be safer." He concluded that "not only the United

States, but many of our allies as well remain highly vulnerable to a whole range of threats."[52]

Terrorist Attacks Across the World

Indeed, the distinct lack of progress in the GWOT has been reflected in the relentless wave of Al Qaeda-linked or -inspired terrorist attacks worldwide. The first major terrorist attack after 9/11 occurred on October 12, 2002 in Indonesia. On that day, bomb attacks on the popular tourist island of Bali in Indonesia killed 202 people, of whom 164 were foreign nationals, including 88 Australians. In all, citizens from 21 countries were killed, including 38 Indonesians. In this case, Australians, being Western and therefore largely conflated with Americans, were targeted as October is the start of the Australian tourist influx. The attack was carried out by a suicide bomber who detonated himself inside a popular and crowded bar. This first bomb sent large numbers of people out onto the streets, where a second bomb, this time a car bomb, was detonated, causing more casualties. The Indonesian government, which had until then denied there was any terrorist problem in the country, now accepted the assistance of the Australian Federal Police in conducting investigations into the attack. The forensic investigations yielded enough clues to eventually lead to the arrest of more than 30 members of the secretive radical Islamist network known as the JI, which aimed to use violence to establish a pan-Islamic caliphate in Southeast Asia that would cover the Malay Archipelago, home to the world's largest population of Muslims.[53] The captured militants were mostly unrepentant and claimed that they were carrying out *jihad* against the West for its supposed oppression of Muslims. Indeed, a key perpetuator, Amrozi bin Nurhasyim, subsequently became known as the "smiling bomber" who gave the thumbs up upon receiving the death sentence. During his trail, Amrozi stated that he was proud of what he had done, that he welcomed the death penalty and that executing him would turn him into a martyr.[54]

Further investigations revealed that the JI or Al Jama'ah Al-Islamiyyah (Islamic Group) is a radical Islamist terrorist network active in Southeast Asia and Australia with close connections with Al Qaeda. Its origins and development are similar to many Al Qaeda affiliates elsewhere and because it carried out the first successful major attack after 9/11, it is worth noting how it became part of Al Qaeda's global *jihad*. The JI originated in an Islamic boarding school in Indonesia established by two religious clerics, Abu Bakar Bashir and Abdullah Sungkar. After attracting the attention of the authorities due to their fundamentalist teachings, they fled to Malaysia, where they built up a following among Malaysians and Indonesian émigrés. They then established links with the Middle East through ex-Afghan *mujahideen* from Southeast Asia who had fought Soviet forces in Afghanistan in the 1980s. Indeed, all the senior members of the JI central committee trained in Afghanistan in the late 1980s and the 1990s. It was in the camps of the Afghan *mujahideen* leader Abdul Rasul Sayyaf that they developed *jihadist* fervor, international contacts, and deadly terrorist skills.[55] This set the stage for the establishment of the clandestine network, the JI, in around 1993.

However, it has been argued that in fact the real origins of the JI date much further back to the 1950s, since Abu Bakar and Abdullah Sungkar considered themselves the heirs of the Darul Islam, a movement that aimed to establish an Islamic state in Indonesia through an armed rebellion that eventually cost 25,000 lives.[56] The JI, however, established close links with Al Qaeda due to its shared ideology. It received funding from Al Qaeda and adopted its modus operandi, such as a networked organizational structure. However, indicative of the nature of the worldwide Al Qaeda network, the JI operated independently and makes most of its operational decisions locally.[57] The phenomenon of the JI and other similar Al Qaeda affiliates is indicative of the globalized nature of the radical Islamist threat.

The JI was exposed even before the Bali bombing, when initial arrests of 13 of its operatives took place in early 2002 following the discovery of its ultimately abortive Singapore bomb plots. The JI had planned, in conjunction with Al Qaeda, a major series of terrorist attacks in Singapore targeting Western embassies, several key U.S. companies, U.S. ships and military personnel, and local military facilities. The planned operation was exposed in late 2001 after U.S. Special Forces found a surveillance tape in an Al Qaeda house that was bombed in Afghanistan. To date, over 400 alleged JI operatives have been arrested throughout Southeast Asia, including its key operations commander and liaison with Al Qaeda, Hambali, an Indonesian who was arrested in Thailand and is now in U.S. custody.[58]

Within days of the Bali bombing, another major terrorist attack took place, this time in Russia. The Chechen Muslim insurgents battling for independence in Chechnya in Russia had been fighting the authorities before 9/11 and had already carried out a number of deadly attacks. However, their close links with Al Qaeda and the major terrorist attacks they have carried out since 9/11 have attracted much international attention. In October 2002, for instance, a team of 40 armed male and female Chechen terrorists stormed a theatre in Moscow during a performance of the musical *Nord-Ost* and took over 700 people hostage. The attack appeared to be a joint operation between two Chechen groups with Al Qaeda links, namely, the Special Purpose Islamic Regiment, and the Riyadus–Salikhin Reconnaissance and Sabotage Battalion of Shahids.

The Special Purpose Islamic Regiment was a product of Chechnya's war of independence with Russia. Originally led by Arbi Barayev, the group aimed to establish an Islamic state in Chechnya. The small but deadly group has carried out many deadly attacks in the Caucasus and in Russia. After Barayev's death in 2001, he was succeeded by his nephew, Movsar Barayev, who commanded the terrorist team in the Moscow theatre siege.[59] The Riyadus–Salikhin Reconnaissance and Sabotage Battalion of Shahids is another radical Chechen Islamist group, led by Shamil Basayev. Basayev was an ex-Afghan *mujahideen* fighter who had fought in Afghanistan in the 1980s, where he forged a close relationship with Al Qaeda. The aim of the group is the secession of Chechnya from Russia and the establishment of a pan-Islamic Muslim state covering Chechnya as well as other neighboring Muslim areas such as Dagestan. Basayev led many terrorist attacks on Russia as well as in neighboring Dagestan.[60]

The Moscow theater siege ended when Russian commandoes stormed the building and used gas to incapacitate those inside. However, the gas killed 128 of the hostages as well as the 40 terrorists, including its leader, Movsar Barayev.[61] Shamil Basayev publicly claimed responsibility for the audacious attack. The Moscow theater siege was closely followed by a string of other deadly terrorist attacks. In December 2002, three suicide bombers rammed vehicle bombs into the local government headquarters in the provincial capital, Grozny, in Chechnya, killing more than 80 people and injuring 127 others.[62] In May 2003, in Znamenskoye, Chechnya, a truck bomb detonated by three suicide bombers outside a government building located in a residential area killed 60 people.[63] In July 2003, a suicide bomb attack on a rock concert in Moscow killed 15 people and injured more than 50.[64] This was followed by another deadly suicide truck bombing at a military hospital in August 2003 in Mozdok, North Osetia, killing 50 people and injuring more than 100.[65]

Direct action was also carried out by Al Qaeda and its affiliates in the Middle East. In May 2003, terrorist attacks at residential complexes housing Western expatriates were carried out by Al Qaeda operatives in Saudi Arabia. The attack resulted in the deaths of 34 people, including 9 U.S. citizens. Over 200 people were also wounded.[66] In December 2004, five militants attacked the U.S. consulate in Jeddah, killing five consulate employees and injuring 10 others, with security forces killing 4 of the militants. In December 2004, the Ministry of the Interior and a security recruiting center were attacked in a double suicide car bombing. This operation was not, however, considered successful as the three suicide bombers died without killing anyone. Investigations into these attacks by Saudi officials revealed Al Qaeda's methods of operations, such as the renting of houses and cars using stolen identity cards, disguising themselves as women or smart young men, and diverting money it had raised for terrorist operations in Iraq.[67]

Intensive security operations by the Saudi security services beginning in 2004 led to a tapering of attacks but Al Qaeda continued to fund, train, and attempt terrorist attacks. Both Al Qaeda and other Islamist groups have also continued to recruit young Saudis to fight in Iraq, Chechnya, and other *jihadist* theaters. Within Saudi Arabia, Al Qaeda's objective is to bring down the pro-U.S. Saudi government. Indeed, Osama bin Laden has consistently called for the overthrow of the royal family. Saudi Arabia thus remains a prime target for the radical Islamists.[68]

A few days after the attack on the housing complex in Saudi Arabia, Al Qaeda-linked suicide bombers struck in Casablanca, in Morocco in May 2003. The separate but coordinated bomb attacks targeted a Jewish community center, a Spanish restaurant and social club, a hotel, and the Belgian consulate. Forty-one people were killed, half at the Spanish social club, with another 100 were injured. Most of the dead and injured, however, were Moroccans.[69] Later investigations, as well as arrests in France, revealed that the perpetuators were members of the radical Islamist organization, the Moroccan Islamic Combatant Group (Groupe Islamique Combattant Morrocain [GCIM]). This group was formed in the 1990s from veterans of the Afghan conflict as well as those who had trained in Afghanistan under Al Qaeda. The group aims to establish an Islamic state in Morocco but has also joined the global *jihad* led by Al Qaeda against the West, which accounted for the Western and Jewish targets of the Casablanca operation.[70] Indeed, some members are believed to hold dual membership and work closely to assist Al Qaeda. After the Casablanca bombings, four members were executed and 39 sentenced to long jail terms. Led by Taeb Bentizi and Mohamed Guerbouzi, the secretive GCIM has proven itself to be a deadly and effective terrorist organization, with established linkages with other North African radical groups and is believed to maintain sleeper cells in various Western European countries. The United States designated the group a terrorist organization in 2002.[71]

As a result of these attacks, *Time* observed in its edition of May 26, 2003 that the "rash of suicide bombings...kills the idea that the West is winning the terror war."[72] Deadly terrorist attacks continued. In August 2003, a suicide bomber in a car blew himself up prematurely as he was stopped for a security check at the entrance of the U.S.-owned Marriott Hotel in central Jakarta in Indonesia. The premature detonation probably saved many lives but 12 people, mostly Indonesians, were killed, and over 100 were injured.[73] In the same month, in August 2003, the world witnessed the spectacular bombing of the UN Headquarters in Baghdad, in Iraq. At the time, Iraq had just come under U.S. occupation following the U.S. attack on Iraq. The deadly bomb attack claimed the lives of 22 people, including the UN Special Representative Sergio Viera de Mello, who had until then had a distinguished career at the United Nations. More than 100 people were also wounded.[74] The fact that the United Nations is a terrorist target should come as no surprise, given that Al Qaeda has perceived it to be a tool of the West, particularly the United States.

In November 2003, suicide attacks on two synagogues in Istanbul in Turkey killed 25 people. This was followed by two bomb attacks, which targeted the British Consulate and the HSBC Bank in Istanbul.[75] Thirty-two people were killed, including three Britons, one of whom was the British Consul-General. A hitherto unknown Islamist group, the Brigades of the Martyr Abu Hafz al-Masri, claimed responsibility for the deadly attacks.[76]

Another spectacular Al Qaeda-linked attack took place soon after, this time in the Philippines. In February 2004, a television set containing explosives was detonated on a ferry leaving Manila, killing 118 people. The Super Ferry bombing was the worst terrorist attack in Southeast Asia since the Bali bombing in October 2002. Responsibility was claimed by the Al Qaeda-linked Abu Sayaff Group, although this was believed to have been a joint operation with the JI. Although the Abu Sayaff started off as a separatist terrorist organization fighting for Moro independence in the south, it had developed strong links with Al Qaeda through ex-Afghan *mujahideen*.[77]

Spain too was targeted by Al Qaeda. Osama bin Laden issued a public warning in October 2003 that included Spain in the list of countries that Al Qaeda would retaliate for joining the U.S. invasion of Iraq in 2003. In March 2004, a coordinated series of bomb attacks using backpacks on the Madrid subway killed 191 people and injured more than 1,800. The attacks centered on three subway stations in southeast Madrid, viz., Atocha, El Pozo, and Santa Eugenia.[78] Initial suspicions and blame fell on the Basque separatist group, ETA, which had previously been responsible for a number of terrorist attacks in Spain. However, as an editorial in Saudi Arabia's *Arab News* succinctly commented, "Spain, for its part, has an election ahead, and blaming the attacks on ETA may be politically convenient...an Al Qaeda operation in Spain could be embarrassing for a government that to many Spaniards has been too slavish in its support for the US in Iraq."[79] Subsequent investigations, however, revealed that the perpetuators were members of the Al Qaeda-linked GCIM from Morocco, which had also been responsible for the earlier Casablanca bombings in May 2003. A number of suspects, mostly Moroccan, were later arrested, though the alleged leader of the train attacks was from Tunisia. Seven of the suspects, including the alleged leader of attacks, spectacularly blew themselves up when cornered by security forces in their Madrid flat. The Madrid train attacks may have had a political impact in the general elections that took place shortly after, as the elections returned a socialist government, which promptly announced the withdrawal of Spanish troops from Iraq.[80]

In Russia, more attacks attributed to Chechen militants took place. In December 2003, a suicide bombing on a commuter train in Yessentuki in southwest Russia killed 42 people.[81] In August 2004, two Russian passenger airliners that departed from Moscow were destroyed in mid-air by explosives, killing a total of 89 people. Investigations suggested that two female suicide bombers from Dagestan were the probable perpetuators. An Al Qaeda-linked group, known as the Al-Islambouli Brigades of Al-Qaeda later claimed responsibility for the attacks. The group is named after Khaled al-Islambouli, the leader of the group that assassinated President Anwar Sadat of Egypt in 1981.[82]

The most shocking of the militant terror attacks since 9/11, and one of the most deadly terrorist incidences in contemporary times, was the Beslan school siege in September 2004, which ended in the death of 344 people, half of whom were school children. In September 2004, 32 armed Islamists, consisting of Chechens, Ingush, and other ethnic groups from the Caucasus, took 1,300 schoolchildren and adults hostage at a school in Beslan in North Ossetia in Russia. The hostages were herded by their captors into the school gymnasium, which was rigged with tripwires and explosives. The terrorists demanded the withdrawal of Russian troops from Chechnya. On the third day, Russian special forces stormed the building when they heard gunfire. In the ensuing gunfire and explosions, a very large number of the hostages died, as did 31 of the 32 terrorists. Shamil Basayev, leader of the deadly Chechen Islamist group, the Riyadus–Salikhin Reconnaissance and Sabotage Battalion of Shahids, claimed responsibility for the attack.[83] Reportedly, at least 10 of the dead terrorists were foreign Arab *jihadists*.[84]

In Indonesia, more terrorist attacks by the Al Qaeda-linked JI took place. In September 2004, a massive car bomb attack at the Australian High Commission in Jakarta killed 11 people, all Indonesians, and injured 161 others.[85] In October 2005, a second bombing in Bali took place close to the second anniversary of the first bomb attack in 2002. Two coordinated attacks at popular tourist spots, Jimbaran Beach and Kuta, resulted in the killing of 26 people and left 150 wounded.[86] These attacks were again attributed to the JI.

In July 2005, the deadly London bombings took place. Coordinated bomb attacks were carried out by four suicide bombers on trains as well as a double-decker bus during the morning rush hour. Fifty-two people were killed and more than 700 injured in the attacks. Two weeks after this, similar attacks were attempted by four would-be suicide bomb-ers but were aborted when the bombs failed to explode. Investigations revealed the perpetuators were British Muslims, or refugees who had come to live in Britain. They fell prey to radical Islamist ideology while in Britain, and then joined terrorist cells. After the bombings, a hitherto unknown group, known as Al Qaeda in Europe, claimed responsibility and stated that the attacks were in response to Britain's participation in the U.S.-led attacks on Iraq and Afghanistan.[87]

In August 2005, Al Qaeda released a videotape that was aired on Al Jazeera television, in which Ayman Al-Zawahiri, Al Qaeda's deputy commander, blamed the London attacks on British involvement in Iraq, and warned that more attacks would take place unless Britain pulled out of Muslim lands.[88] In September 2005, another video was aired on Al Jazeera, in which British-born Mohammed Siddique Khan, the leader of the first attack in July 2005, justified it on grounds of Britain's role in the invasion of Iraq. Speaking fluent English with a pronounced Yorkshire accent, he stated that "until we feel secure you will be our targets...until you stop the bombing, gassing, imprisonment and tor-ture, we will not stop this fight." Al-Zawahiri also appeared in the same video, in which he claimed responsibility on behalf of Al Qaeda for the attacks.[89]

Terrorist attacks also took place in Egypt, where the government has taken strong action against radical Islamists. In October 2004, attacks at Taba and Nuweiba, both resorts in the Sinai frequented by Israeli and Western tourists, resulted in the deaths of 34 people, including 12 Israelis, and also left 105 people injured.[90] This was followed by a bigger attack in July 2005 at Sharm el-Sheikh, which left 67 people killed and more than 200 wounded.[91] The attacks involved two suicide car bombers and a bomb left in a bag. Although tourists were targeted, most of the dead and wounded were Egyptians.[92] In April 2006, another terrorist attack, this time at the Red Sea resort town of Dahab resulted in the deaths of 23 people, including three Western tourists, and the wounding of 62 others.[93]

Investigations revealed that all three attacks were carried out by a self-radicalized group, which was founded by a dentist, Khaled Mosaed, in northern Sinai in 2002. About 100 people, all natives of the Sinai, joined the group, which called itself Al Tawhid Wal Jihad. Although this group is not believed to have strong links with Al Qaeda, they were clearly inspired by Osama bin Laden and adhered to the same radical ideology. Members of the group were angered by the actions of the United States and also the failure of Arab governments to implement Islamic laws. Mosaed and other members of the group were later either killed or arrested by the authorities, though an undetermined number remain at large.[94]

Jordan, too, was not spared. In November 2005, three coordinated suicide bombings in the capital Amman targeted Western hotels, including the Days Inn, the Grand Hyatt, and the Radisson. At the Radisson, a suicide bomber detonated in the midst of a wedding party. In all, 59 people were killed, of whom 33 were Jordanians. 96 people were also injured. The insurgent group, Al Qaeda in Iraq, claimed responsibility. This group, which has been fighting the U.S. invasion and occupation of Iraq, was led by Abu Musab Zarqawi, a Jordanian.[95] This deadly attack had followed a number of other attacks attributed to Zarqawi, including an audacious plan to use chemical weapons to attack the intelligence headquarters in Amman in 2004.[96]

Attacks also took place in Algeria. While fundamentalist insurgents have been targeting the Algerian government for years, the Algiers bombing in April 2007 had special significance because it was claimed in the name of Al Qaeda. Bombs were detonated outside the prime minister's office and the headquarters of the security services, killing 24 people and wounding 222 others.[97] In December 2007, another bombing took place in Algiers, in which 26 people were reported killed and over 100 injured in two separate car bombings on a UN building and a courthouse. Eleven UN employees were among those killed.[98] An Al Qaeda offshoot, "Al Qaeda in the Islamic Maghreb" claimed responsibility for both attacks. This pan-Islamist group is an umbrella organization of radical Islamist groups in North Africa and formed in an attempt to coordinate the efforts of all radical Islamist groups in the region. The core group of this organization is the Salafist Group for Prayer and Combat (GSPC), a radical Islamist group that has violently opposed the government in Algeria. The umbrella organization brought the GSPC together with the Moroccan Islamic Combat Group, the Libyan Islamic Fighting Group, and the Tunisian Combatant Group under the banner of Al Qaeda and under the overall spiritual leadership of Osama bin Laden. The GSPC pledged its allegiance to Al Qaeda in September 2006 and "Al Qaeda in the Islamic Maghreb" came into existence in January 2007.[99]

Deadly terrorist attacks have taken place in India. In August 2003, two car bomb attacks in Mumbai killed 52 people. In July 2006, seven coordinated bombs went off in trains on Mumbai's busy commuter network, killing 186 people. India accused Pakistan's intelligence services of having planned the attack, although the actual operation was carried out by the militant Pakistani group, Lashkar-e-Toiba.[100] In November 2008, an audacious terrorist attack was carried out by ten militant gunmen who landed on the Mumbai coast in inflatable boats and proceeded to attack a busy railway station as well as the Oberoi and Taj Mahal hotels. At least 195 people, including Western tourists, were killed. Nine of the gunmen were killed and one captured. Subsequent investigations revealed that the attackers were all Pakistanis who had trained for the attack in Pakistan and were allegedly members of the Pakistani militant groups Lashkar-e-Toiba and Jaish-e-Mohammad.[101] Pakistan subsequently arrested some 71 militants, including leaders from the two groups.[102]

The Pakistan Front in the GWOT

Despite the worldwide attacks, Pakistan is emerging as a key target for Al Qaeda. There are several reasons for the strategic significance of Pakistan to Al Qaeda. Not only is it a sizeable Muslim state of 165 million people, it is the only Muslim state today that possesses nuclear weapons. If its radical Islamist allies could destabilize and perhaps take control of the country, it would have a powerful base from which to destabilize the Middle East and challenge the West. The conditions in Pakistan have also become favorable for the radical Islamists. Indeed, they had obtained considerable support from Pakistan's intelligence services in the Afghan war against the Soviets in the 1980s, as well as in the conflict in Kashmir. Nurtured by the intelligence services, the radical Islamist organizations were able to recruit from within Pakistan and *mujahideen* from further afield, carry out terrorist training as well as stockpile arms, and disseminate radical propaganda. They have continued to retain a measure of support from within the security services through sympathizers. Although Islamist parties only managed to obtain 11% of the vote in the elections in 2002, radical Islamists have been aggressive and assertive in pushing their agenda and some groups have used violent terrorist tactics. They have moved into urban areas and have carried out a string of deadly terrorist attacks, directed at the security services, the armed forces, and governmental institutions. The radical Islamists have thus begun to seriously challenge the authority of the government.

They were aided by the fact that the military regime led by General Pervez Musharaff was highly unpopular and considered illegitimate by most Pakistanis. Musharaff seized power in a coup in October 1999 when he deposed the elected civilian government of Nawaz Sharif. After this, Musharaff repressed and marginalized the mainstream democratic parties, thus leaving the ground open for the militants to gain greater support. In order to stay in power, Musharaff courted fundamentalist Muslim groups, although the more extreme ones involved in terrorist activities have been proscribed. However, militant groups were able to continue operating in both cities as well as in the provinces, as Musharaff was reluctant to crack down hard for fear of causing a public backlash. Given his support for the United States in the GWOT after 9/11, however, Al Qaeda targeted him for assassination. In September 2007, Osama bin Laden, through As-Sahad, the propaganda arm of Al Qaeda, issued a religious edict or *fatwa* against Musharaff, stating that "it is obligatory on the Muslims in Pakistan to carry out *jihad* and fighting to remove Perez (Musharaff), his government, his army and those who help him."[103] Indeed, Musharaff escaped a number of attempts to kill him.

Some of Pakistan's many unregulated religious schools or *madrassas* have been conduits for radicalism, providing a steady stream of recruits to the extremist cause. Pakistan has suffered a number of suicide terrorist attacks in recent years, which has been attributed to poverty, unemployment, romantic notions of *jihad*, and the growing influence of radical Islamic groups.[104] More significantly, Pakistan has provided the only relatively safe haven for Al Qaeda and its Taliban allies who were evicted from Afghanistan following 9/11. Al Qaeda operatives and leaders, as well as Taliban fighters, have taken refuge in the northwest frontier region, especially in Waziristan and Baluchistan, where Pashtun tribes who have never been successfully subdued by the central government have offered them sanctuary. Western intelligence agencies believe that Osama bin Laden and his deputy, Ayman Al-Zawahiri, are sheltering in the region. In the 2002 elections, an Islamist alliance, Muttehida Majlis Amal, took control of Waziristan for the first time in 58 years.[105] In 2004, the failure of military offensives against militants in Waziristan led to a truce, which was hailed by the militants as a victory.[106] These events have meant that northwest Pakistan has become a useful sanctuary for Al Qaeda and its Taliban allies to hide and recuperate. The Taliban has been able to regroup and operate across the porous border in southern Afghanistan against NATO-led forces seeking to contain them.

Although there has been a long list of terrorist attacks in Pakistan, two recent attacks have been strategically significant. On October 18, 2007, suicide bombers targeting the opposition leader Benazir Bhutto killed 134 and injured 450 others who were amongst 200,000 people who had turned up in Karachi to welcome her back after eight years in exile.[107] This was followed by the assassination of Bhutto herself on December 28, 2007, plunging Pakistan into deep political crisis as she was a key democratic alternative to Musharaff and the militants.[108] Although it is possible that President Musharaff himself ordered her assassination, he would have little to gain by doing so, given that he would invariably be blamed for the popular leader's death. In any event, Al Qaeda claimed responsibility. In a telephone call to a Pakistani journalist, Mustafa Abu Al-Yazid, Al Qaeda's senior commander in Afghanistan, stated that "we terminated the most precious American asset which vowed to defeat the *mujahideen*," a credible claim given the enormous antipathy she had generated amongst the militants.[109] The elections that were subsequently held in February 2008 were won by the opposition, leading to Musharaff's resignation in August 2008. Bhutto's widower, Asif Ali Zardari, now leader of her party, the Pakistan People's Party (PPP), became the president of Pakistan in September 2008, vowing to lead the fight against the militants.[110]

Al Qaeda and Post-9/11 Terrorist Attacks

Thus, many terrorist attacks have taken place around the world since 9/11. Most of these post-9/11 terrorist attacks bear the hallmarks of

Al Qaeda in several ways. The attacks focused on Western targets such as tourist hotels, restaurants, embassies, international institutions such as the United Nations (which Al Qaeda despises as a tool of the United States), and government facilities or institutions of Muslim allies of the United States. Attacks in Europe, on the other hand, focused on the transportation system, such as subway trains and buses. Many of the techniques and skills required for such terrorist attacks have been imparted by Al Qaeda to its own operatives as well as to many thousands of radical Islamists belonging to affiliate groups sympathetic to its radical ideology, through its training manuals and camps in Afghanistan before 9/11.

The U.S. invasion of Iraq in 2003 has also turned Iraq into a vast training center for terrorists. Though the overwhelming majority of those involved in the anti-U.S. insurgency are local Iraqis, the insurgency there has also attracted *mujahideen* from outside of Iraq, particularly from Saudi Arabia. Iraq has proved to be a very useful training ground for honing all the necessary skills in urban terrorism, such as the use of improvised explosive devices (IEDs), car and truck bombs, suicide attacks, ambushes, assassinations, kidnapping, sniper attacks, and sabotage.

The most common terrorist tactic has been the use of bombings. The technical skills involved in making bombs are not complex, as standard commercial or military explosives could be used. Alternatively, improvised blasting agents can be made from precursors that are easily obtainable following well-known recipes.[111] However, Al Qaeda and its allies have been very innovative, using a range of very effective bombing methods, such as backpack bombs to attack subways and massive truck bombs to attack well-defended targets. Al Qaeda's use of aircraft as missiles in the 9/11 attacks is not a new idea but the organization and execution of such a major operation was flawless.

Suicide bombings have, however, become the ultimate terrorist tactic. The use of suicide bombing is not new and has been a tactic perfected by terrorist groups such as the Tamil Tigers in Sri Lanka, Hezbollah in Lebanon, and Hamas in Palestine. Al Qaeda, however, has played an important role in the spread of this tactic, as it has been instrumental in facilitating its adoption by local groups and radical associates in Pakistan, Afghanistan, Yemen, the Philippines, Saudi Arabia, Turkey, Indonesia, Morocco, Tunisia, Chechnya, Qatar, Iraq, and the United Kingdom.[112] Not only is it Al Qaeda's principal terrorist tactic, it has succeeded in justifying it ideologically and glorifying it to such a degree that there have been many willing volunteers. Suicide bombings, as the above examples demonstrate, are very hard to counter as there is little effective defense against a terrorist determined to die along with the victims. The effectiveness of this tactic has resulted in many deadly terrorist attacks since 9/11.

What the outbreak of radical Islamist attacks across the world since 9/11 demonstrates is that Al Qaeda and its associates worldwide have not only weathered unprecedented security operations by military and security forces all over the world, they have, in fact, adapted, evolved, and grown into an even deadlier global insurgency. This global insurgency does not have any real central directing authority and indeed has none or very tenuous links with Al Qaeda itself, but consists mainly of local groups motivated by the same radical ideology, driven by causes such as the U.S.-led invasion and occupation of Iraq, and fired up by local political, economic, and social grievances.

As Bruce Hoffman noted in his testimony to the U.S. Congress in February 2006:

Al Qaeda's greatest achievement has been the makeover it has given itself since 2001. The current Al Qaeda thus exists more as an ideology than as an identifiable, unitary terrorist organization. It has become a vast enterprise—an international franchise with like-minded local representatives, loosely connected to a central ideological or motivational base, but advancing the remaining centre's goals at once simultaneously and independently of each other...the result is that today there are many Al Qaedas rather than the single Al Qaeda of the past.[113]

In other words, the many terrorist attacks linked to or inspired by Al Qaeda since 9/11 suggests that the GWOT is not really a war against Al Qaeda the organization but a fight against Al Qaeda's brand of radical ideology and its worldwide radical adherents. This represents a stunning strategic achievement in the face of considerable tactical losses.

CHAPTER THREE

The U.S. Invasion of Iraq

The Case Against Iraq

Apart from the wave of Al Qaeda-inspired terrorist attacks around the world since 9/11, Iraq has proven problematic for the Global War on Terror (GWOT). At issue here is how an Iraq, which was initially unrelated to Al Qaeda, became part of the terrorist problem and part of the GWOT. Indeed, from nonrelevance to the GWOT, Iraq has become a focal point in the radical *jihadist* propaganda that is part of the information war being waged for the hearts and minds of the *umma* or worldwide Muslim community. As a result of its invasion of Iraq, as well as its own ineptitude in countering this information war, the United States has thus far lost this battle. The broader strategic implications of Iraq for the GWOT as well as the balance of power in the Middle East are highly negative.

Under President Ronald Reagan, the United States had backed the Saddam regime against Iran during the long and vicious Iran–Iraq war from 1980–1988, a conflict that claimed more than a million lives. The Reagan administration did nothing to stop Iraq from developing weapons of mass destruction (WMDs), including chemical weapons such as nerve gas, which Iraq deployed on the battlefield. The CIA also shared battlefield intelligence with Iraq.[1] The Reagan administration followed this course of action out of realist geopolitical calculations, fearing that if Iran won the war, it would install a religious Shiite regime in power in Iraq, one that would not only give Iran control over the vast oil wealth of the country but would also enable Iran to become the dominant power in the Persian Gulf. Such a scenario would have dire consequences for the stability of the Middle East, as Iran could then destabilize the rest of the Persian Gulf, given the presence of significant numbers of Shiites living in Saudi Arabia and other Gulf states. A Persian Gulf dominated by Iran would be inimical to U.S. interests, given the hostility between the United States and Iran following the Iranian Revolution in 1978 that overthrew the pro-U.S. Shah and brought Ayatollah Khomeini to power. It would also jeopardize Israel's security, given the strong anti-Israel stance taken by the post-Shah government of Iran.[2]

Various reasons have been put forward for the U.S. invasion of Iraq in 2003, such as the need for oil, President Bush's desire to "get even" with Saddam Hussein for having allegedly tried to assassinate his father (Bush Sr.), the desire to "finish the job" left abandoned during the First Gulf War, and the need to remove Saddam as a threat and a danger to the Middle East. Although there appears to be a complex mix of factors, the major impetus stems from the huge psychological impact of 9/11. It forcefully and dramatically brought home the danger that rogue terrorists and rogue states posed to the United States. A sense of alarm over what would have happened had the terrorists used WMDs galvanized the United States into action. It appeared to reinforce the conviction that if terrorist groups and rogue states, which have been developing WMDs, were not forcefully confronted, they could establish alliances of convenience and eventually result in the United States and its allies being subjected to nuclear blackmail or attack.

Within days of the 9/11 terrorist attacks, key neoconservative officials plodded the Bush administration into a radical new strategy. The United States should no longer wait patiently for multilateral diplomacy and sanctions to work. Instead, it should now use its massive military capabilities, preemptively if necessary, to confront states that sponsored terrorism, with the goal of undermining those regimes, overthrowing them, and then imposing democracy.[3] As then Defense Secretary Donald Rumsfeld maintained, "defending the United States requires prevention and sometimes pre-emption...defending against terrorism and other emerging threats requires that we take the war to the enemy."[4] This fitted well with the growing unilateral impulse in the United States, which must be seen in the context of its growing technological and military power, coupled with a growing sense that encumbrances of alliances, international norms and laws, and the United Nations, should not prevent the United States from pursuing and protecting its global national interests.

The rise of the neoconservatives has been a significant political development in the United States since the 1980s, influencing the choice and direction of its defense and foreign policies. The post-9/11 political atmosphere was thus right for neoconservative elements gathered around Deputy Defense Secretary Paul Wolfowitz to push the agenda for regime change, which they had advocated for years. Neoconservatives believed that peace would never come to the Middle East until it truly changed, and until the repressive Arab regimes stopped trying to deflect from their own corruption, repression, and failures by channeling hatred toward Israel. The key to this was a reformed, post–Saddam Iraq. With a middle class, oil, free markets, the rule of law and democracy, Iraq could become a model for the region, sparking democratic change in the rest of the region and paving the way for lasting peace in the Middle East.[5] Although this political scenario was built not on any empirical evidence but on pure fantasy and did not accord with the geopolitical and cultural realities on the ground, it was asserted by neoconservatives as a viable project of change based on their belief in the efficacy of the military power and superior democratic values of the United States.

Wolfowitz was supported by other senior administration figures, such as Defense Secretary Donald Rumsfeld and Vice-President Dick Cheney. They helped to create a shadow agency of Pentagon analysts to compete with the CIA and its military counterpart, the Defense Intelligence Agency. Because of this top-level support, the Office of Special Plans (OSP) was able to push for a justification for war, based on biased misinformation obtained from the Iraqi opposition. The OSP sidelined or ignored the views of other agencies, including the State Department, and the CIA, when they did not accord with its preconceived notions.[6] This was helped by the National Intelligence Estimate (NIE) of October 2002, which made a convincing case that Iraq represented a clear and present danger to the United States due to its WMDs and its attempts to restart its nuclear program.[7]

Thus, Rumsfeld and Cheney repeatedly claimed in late 2002 and early 2003 that Saddam had stockpiles of WMDs as well as links with Al Qaeda terrorists who could use them to attack cities in the United States. The most touted evidence was a report, which claimed that Muhammad Atta, the chief hijacker in the 9/11 attacks, had met Iraqi intelligence officials in Prague in early April 2001. This report was later discredited as Atta, according to the FBI, was at that time traveling in the United States, between Florida and Virginia.[8] Another widely touted piece of evidence was the purported attempt by Saddam to buy up to 500 tons of uranium oxide from Niger. The documents were later proven to be faked and had been peddled to Italian diplomats by entrepreneurial African diplomats. Indeed, when the evidence was turned over by the Bush administration to the International Atomic Energy Agency (IAEA), it took the agency just two hours, using the Google search engine on the Internet, to find that the documents were faked, as the minister who purportedly signed it had been out of office for ten years.[9] The third piece of evidence was that Saddam had imported aluminum tubes that were purportedly used to make enriched uranium. But the State Department, after consulting U.S. nuclear experts, concluded that the tubes were of a wrong specification and were, in fact, meant for multiple-rocket launching systems. This was corroborated by UN weapons inspectors.[10] Much of this disinformation, it turned out, originated from anti-Saddam political figures in exile in the West who had worked hard over the years to unite the Iraqi political opposition and had every reason to convince the United States to topple Saddam.[11]

Thus, President Bush designated Iraq, Iran, and North Korea as the "Axis of Evil" in his State of the Union address on January 28, 2002. He also laid out the rationale for invading Iraq, stating that "year after year, Saddam Hussein has gone to great lengths, spent enormous sums, taken great risks, to build and keep weapons of mass destruction."[12] After its dramatic success in Afghanistan, the United States was now determined to attack Iraq, charging that it had hidden WMDs, had repeatedly flouted its commitments not to deploy nuclear weapons, and failed to allow for open UN weapons inspections. It also charged that Iraq had links with Al Qaeda and had been covertly supporting it. But it is clear that Al Qaeda most certainly had little if any contact with Saddam Hussein, given that Al Qaeda's primary target is not the United States but apostate and oppressive Arab regimes such as those in Iraq. Saddam also had little incentive to provide any deadly weapons to a terrorist group that would most certainly use them on his regime since it is dedicated to overthrowing his secular national government and replacing it with an Islamic one dedicated to imposing *sharia* or Islamic laws as interpreted by the radical Islamists. Indeed, the 911 Commission that was established after 9/11 investigated this issue and concluded that no collaborative relationship between Saddam and Al Qaeda existed.[13]

Instead, the Bush administration concentrated on the issue of WMDs, which Iraq allegedly developed in defiance of its commitments to the United Nations. The United States challenged the United Nations to act against Iraq for its "decade of defiance." However, the United States could not present any convincing evidence except for a long list of Iraq's infringement and noncompliance with UN resolutions since 1991.[14] Other members of the Bush government justified invasion on the grounds of the evil nature of Saddam's regime, which was compared to Hitler's.[15]

In the United States itself, various leading conservative and realist-oriented scholars voiced concerns over the seeming inevitability of war. For instance, in a widely circulate paper, John Mearsheimer and Stephen Walt both opposed invading Iraq. They argued that history had demonstrated that Saddam in fact could be contained and that war was not necessary. Mearsheimer and Walt explained how Saddam went to war against Iran in 1980 and occupied Kuwait in 1990 because Iraq itself was vulnerable, and because he had good reason to believe his targets were weak. In both cases, his goal was to rectify Iraq's strategic dilemmas; in 1980, for instance, he faced open provocation by the new post-Shah revolutionary Shiite regime in Iran for Iraqi Shiites to topple his government. Saddam was thus no warmonger bent on destabilizing and dominating the neighborhood.

Saddam also did not use chemical or biological weapons in the Gulf War of 1991 although he had them at the time, for fear of U.S. nuclear retaliation. This meant that he could in fact be deterred. Even if he did flout his commitments to the United Nations after the Gulf War, he would not have wanted to court nuclear annihilation by threatening to use them on the United States. Given the poor state of the Iraqi armed forces compared to during the First Gulf War, Iraq was also not in a position to attack Kuwait again, and therefore did not constitute a threat to the Gulf states. Despite many months of searching, no evidence could be found to support the contention that Saddam had ever clandestinely transferred any WMD to Al Qaeda. Indeed, Saddam himself had demonstrated repeatedly that his own survival was of paramount importance, which meant that deterrence and containment would work, and preventive war was unnecessary. Mearsheimer and Walt therefore concluded that "the historical record shows that the United States can contain Iraq effectively—even if Saddam has nuclear weapons—just as it contained the Soviet Union during the Cold War. And that conclusion carries an obvious implication: there is no good reason to attack Iraq at this time."[16]

Republican realists, as distinct from academic realists, also came to the same conclusion. Writing in the *Wall Street Journal*, Brent Scowcroft, who had served at national security adviser to Bush senior during his presidency, warned that invading Iraq would "destroy the war on terrorism." Scowcroft stated that there was little evidence Saddam was linked to terrorism or to the 9/11 attacks. He also predicted that invading Iraq would lead to the long-term military occupation of the country.[17]

These criticisms pointed to an obvious flaw in Bush's decision to attack Iraq. Saddam Hussein did not constitute a clear and present danger to United States, or to regional or international security. While he might have to be contained, Saddam was certainly not an immediate priority in the global war against Al Qaeda. Given that Saddam did not pose a conventional threat to its neighbors such as Kuwait, the fact that he did not evidently possess WMDs (since none were subsequently found, the obvious conclusion being that he had indeed destroyed them), that he could have been deterred or contained even if he had such weapons, and that he had no incentive to assist Al Qaeda, how would invading Iraq and replacing his regime with one more amenable to the United States contribute to the GWOT?

Indeed, by early 2003, through the implementation of a thorough UN inspections regime, the United States had already ensured that any serious WMD threat from Iraq would be minimized. Thus, the proper course of action at this point that would best serve the U.S. national interest was not to have invaded Iraq but instead conserved resources to focus attention on Al Qaeda and perhaps other countries that were demonstrably far more committed and advanced in the acquisition of WMDs, including nuclear weapons, such as Iran and North Korea. Indeed, with the United States subsequently bogged down in Iraq, it could not focus enough attention on North Korea, which did in fact carry out a nuclear test in 2006.

Other problems should have been obvious. For instance, it should have been anticipated that the invasion and occupation of Iraq could very well turn out to be a complicated and long drawn-out affair, involving a long period of occupation and a massive problem of reconstructing a fractured country, as Scowcroft had warned. However, it seemed that instead of planning for such probable contingencies, the decision to go to war appeared based on the assumption of the best, most optimistic outcome. Moreover, it should also have been anticipated that such a war would be hugely alienating to the Muslim world as it would be seen to be unjust given the lack of any open provocation by Saddam. More seriously, it would contribute to a dramatic increase in terrorism by providing Al Qaeda and other radical groups with new recruits to their cause. It would also empower radical Islamists in a number of Muslim countries. Voicing the collective dismay of pro-U.S. regimes throughout the Middle East, Egypt's president, Hosni Mubarak, thus warned that "not one Arab leader will be able to control the angry outburst of the masses," and that there would be a hundred Osama bin Ladens if the United States proceeded to attack Iraq.[18]

Given the paucity of hard evidence against Iraq, the international community, including allies of the United States, was not impressed with U.S. entreaties for the United Nations to authorize the use of force. On September 12, 2002, President Bush brought his case against Iraq to the UN General Assembly and challenged the United Nations to take action against Baghdad. Bush also stated that while the United States would work with the UN Security Council for the necessary resolutions, it would act alone if the United Nations failed to cooperate.[19] This threat was reaffirmed a month later when the U.S. Congress gave President Bush the authority to use force against Iraq without getting prior approval from the United Nations.[20] After intense U.S. pressure and lobbying, the United Nations adopted Resolution 1441 on November 7, 2002, which found Iraq to be in "material breach" of prior resolutions. The United Nations set up a new inspections regime and warned of "serious consequences" if Iraq failed to disarm.[21] On January 27, 2003, however, the head of the IAEA, Mohamad El Baradei, declared that his agency could find no evidence of an ongoing Iraqi nuclear weapons program.[22]

But Colin Powell, the U.S. Secretary of State, returned to the United Nations on February 5, 2003 and accused Iraq of hiding its WMDs. This was contradicted by UN weapons inspectors, who reported to the UN Security Council on February 14 that they had not discovered any WMDs. In the end, the Security Council could not agree on the authorization of force, given the opposition of three of the permanent members, viz. France, Russia, and China. President Bush responded by concluding that the United Nations' failure to act had caused it to "fade into history as an ineffective, irrelevant debating society."[23]

There was also worldwide opposition to any attack on Iraq. In a declaration on February 22, 2003 signed in Kuala Lumpur in Malaysia, 114 developing states of the Non-Aligned Movement opposed the use of force against Iraq.[24] In the absence of any direct provocation from Iraq, or indeed any evidence that Iraq had threatened the security of the United States or its allies in any way, there was a general worldwide consensus that there was no justification for war in self-defense as provided for under Article 51 of the UN Charter.

The U.S. Offensive

On March 20, 2003, the U.S.-led offensive began. The First Gulf War of 1990 was authorized, and therefore legitimized, by the United Nations and was aimed at recovering Kuwait, which had suffered attack and invasion from Iraq. This time, however, there was little international support, the United States being mainly supported by British troops. International condemnation was swift, with Russian President Vladimir Putin describing military action as completely unjustified.[25] China pointed out that the attack had violated the UN Charter. French president Jacques Chirac expressed regret that the action was launched without the explicit approval of the United Nations.[26] Leaders in Muslim countries such as Malaysia and Indonesia also questioned the legality of going to war without the backing of the Security Council.[27] Demonstrations broke out in many parts of the world, including in Britain, Australia, and the United States itself, as well as in countries allied to the United States, such as Japan and South Korea.[28]

The U.S. strategy relied heavily on the lessons learnt from Operation Enduring Freedom in Afghanistan, and also on the previous Gulf War in 1990. Compared to the earlier conflict in 1990, there was now much greater reliance on precision-guided munitions, aided by vast improvements in electronic sensors and information technology that enabled U.S. battlefield commanders to increase battlespace awareness regardless of the time of day and weather conditions. This, together with effective air–ground coordination of attacks, had the effect of increasing both the tempo and intensity of the battle, while at the same time expanding the geographical scope of the battlefield. The ability to find and attack Iraqi targets with great accuracy also meant that the number of troops required, at least for the conventional phase of the operations, could be reduced. Faced with this overwhelming military juggernaut, most Iraqi troops chose to flee, their decision greatly aided by revulsion at Saddam's regime and the loss of morale, which had already pervaded Iraqi military ranks since the catastrophic defeat at the hands of the coalition in the Gulf War of 1990.

The U.S. strategy was dubbed "Shock and Awe" for the intensity, precision, and speed of its offensive. Ground forces invaded from Kuwait, with British forces concentrating on taking Basra, while U.S. forces moved toward Baghdad in two main pushes—the Marines from the southeast and the Third Infantry from the southwest. Fierce resistance was encountered in Nasiriya and several other towns but by April 3, U.S. forces had reached Baghdad. The capital fell on April 9, after which the focus of the war moved to northern Iraq. There, U.S.-backed Kurdish forces quickly took control of Kirkuk and Mosul. Finally, the key town of Tikrit, Saddam's hometown, fell to U.S. forces on April 14.[29]

The United States had achieved a stunning battlefield victory unparalleled in speed and decisiveness. While there were inevitable comparisons with seminal military events such as Nazi Germany's blitzkrieg through France in 1940, there are in fact no real historical parallels, given the unprecedented rate of advance and fighting power relative to the number of troops. Compared to 560,000 U.S. and allied troops in the First Gulf War, which lasted 48 days and resulted in 365 casualties, the Second Gulf War saw the United States and Britain deploy about 100,000 troops and achieve victory in 26 days (up to the fall of Baghdad) at a cost of 160 casualties.[30] This appeared to vindicate Rumsfeld, who had argued that the maturity of the military–technological revolution (dubbed the "Revolution in Military Affairs" [RMA]) meant that a much smaller force was required, rather than the hundreds of thousands of troops that might have been required.

The swift and decisive victory strengthened the hand of the neoconservatives in the Bush administration who had contended that the new strategy would work, and that the objective of building a friendly Iraq devoid of WMDs, and one which could become a beacon of democracy for the rest of the Middle East, was proceeding apace. Immediately after the collapse of Baghdad, the United States announced that an Office of Reconstruction and Humanitarian Assistance (ORHA), under retired General Jay Garner, would run Iraq. Essentially, Iraq would initially be under U.S. military rule and would then transit to an interim Iraqi administration and finally elections that would lead to a representative government as well as the adoption of a constitution.[31] The assumption was that Iraqis would welcome the invasion with open arms, would be able to take over after elections were organized, and U.S. troops could then be withdrawn. Moreover, it was expected to be a relatively inexpensive war, with Iraq's oil wealth expected to largely pay for the whole enterprise.

Unexpected Challenges in Iraq

The United States, however, was immediately confronted with a number of significant and complex problems which it had failed to plan for. The most serious was the fact that there was no readymade government-in-exile or political opposition that could take over in Iraq. Instead, there were a number of competing exiled politicians with little support inside Iraq, including the U.S. favorite to take over, Ahmed Chalabi, who led the Iraqi National Congress. Within Iraq, Saddam's authoritarian regime meant that no real political alternatives were present. Moreover, Iraq had complex tribal politics and divisions, between and within the three major groups, namely the Sunnis, Shiites, and the minority Kurdish in the north. Post-Saddam, nation-building in Iraq would be lengthy and problematic, given ethnic and religious divisions, the lack of a democratic tradition, weak or nonexistent institutions, and an infrastructure in shambles.

The United States completely underestimated the complex challenges involved in rebuilding a shattered country, including restoring basic services, rebuilding the infrastructure, establishing institutions, building a new government, restarting oil production, and achieving political consensus over the future direction of the country in the face of tribal, ethnic, and religious divisions. Indeed, it was soon clear that the United States had failed to effectively plan the so-called Phase 4 of the invasion, which was how to stabilize the country after the first three phases of a military operation, namely, preparation for combat, initial operations, and combat. According to Isaiah Wilson, the official U.S. Army historian for the invasion of Iraq in 2003, while there were plans for Iraq, none of them operationalized the problem beyond regime collapse. The U.S. military thus lost the initiative just three months into the occupation.[32]

The swift descent of Iraq into chaos, insurgency, and civil war was shocking as it was to some degree predictable, with perhaps the benefit of hindsight, given the arrogance, complacency, and incompetence with which the United States had approached postconflict Iraq. As Peter Galbraith recounted, American–Iraqi experts who met President Bush two months before he had ordered the invasion had to explain to the President what the Sunni–Shiite divide in Iraq was all about.[33] Subsequently, a number of key strategic errors early in the occupation led to the spread of the insurgency. Not only was there an inadequate plan for recovery and reconstruction, the U.S. military failed to stamp its authority over the entire country due to the sheer lack of military personnel in Iraq. There were just 141,000 U.S. troops in Iraq in late 2004.[34] This number has not varied considerably, with troop strength at 153,000 in May 2006.[35] This comparatively small force could not stop the widespread looting following the end of the conflict. The failure to secure the country after the war cost the United States precious credibility and support in Iraq. More seriously, the resulting security vacuum was quickly filled by militias belonging to different groups, as well as a motley array of anti-U.S. insurgents, consisting of Al Qaeda-linked *jihadists*, Iraqi Sunni nationalists, ex-Ba'ath Party loyalists, and Shiite militias belonging to radical factions. The borders were also left open, as the United States did not have sufficient troops to seal them. This enabled insurgent *jihadists* to move freely from Syria, and also enabled Iran to supply Shiite factions in the south with arms.

The arrival of Paul Bremmer as head of the Coalition Provisional Authority (CPA) to replace Jay Garner in May 2003 marked a crucial turning point. A civilian, Bremmer had little prior experience on Iraq or indeed in nation-building. He promised a tough approach to the daunting problems he faced: cracking down on crime and rebuilding the Iraqi police force, weeding out pro-Saddam elements from the government, restoring basic services such as electricity and water, and repairing the oil infrastructure.[36] Bremmer immediately implemented decisions which had serious strategic implications. Bremmer ordered a thorough program of de-Ba'athification, under which members of the Ba'ath Party under Saddam Hussein would be dismissed from government, denied their pensions, and if necessary, investigated for crimes. This not only created alienation among those who had lost power and now a means of livelihood, but resulted in the collapse of basic services as the machinery of government ground to a halt.

More seriously, the decision to dissolve the Iraqi armed forces and the Ministry of the Interior, which commanded the police and security services, left hundreds of thousands of security personnel without jobs and pay.[37] Not only did this create a vast pool of alienated people who became susceptible to joining insurgent groups, it also deprived the country of any effective security. Given the small number of U.S. and allied forces on the ground in Iraq, local Iraqi forces were essential to provide the necessary security for reconstruction to begin.

Moreover, the armed forces and the police were key national institutions in a country that had deep sectarian differences. Dissolving them meant taking away the glue that could hold the country together. The Saddam regime had relied on these, as well as the Ba'ath Party apparatus, to maintain control over a fractious state that the British had cobbled together in the 1920s when it forced the Kurds, Shiites, and Sunnis living in Mesopotamia to live under the state of Iraq. Without these admittedly dictatorial institutions of power, the glue that held Iraq together disappeared and led to its swift unraveling. In sum, these crucial decisions led to the collapse of the Iraqi state as the institutions of government fell apart. More seriously, the decisions were perceived by Iraqis that their country was being treated as a defeated state under direct U.S. occupation, with Bremmer taking on the role akin to that of Douglas MacArthur in postwar Japan. With so many disaffected but trained men in the streets in a country awash with weapons, the demobilization of the party and the armed services was an open invitation to join an armed nationalist uprising against the invader.

Throughout 2003, as the anti-U.S. insurgency began to take shape, the U.S. military conducted counterinsurgency raids, detaining many thousands of Iraqis, many of whom were subsequently found to be innocent, often after many months of incarceration under shocking conditions. These raids, and the harshness with which the detainees were treated, contributed to the anger and resistance against the U.S. occupation. Prisoners were crammed into inadequate facilities such as the prison at Abu Ghraib, where inhumane conditions, the use of torture, and the humiliation of inmates were later revealed.[38] The story and the pictures of the Abu Ghraib scandal were widely circulated throughout the world and did much to fuel Iraqi resentment against the United States. It also inflamed opinion across the Muslim world.

The problem was the way the United States was treating the newly conquered populace, in the manner of a defeated and occupied country. Hashim Ahmed has cited the missteps and boorish behavior, which became key factors in driving the insurgency. As Hashim commented, "US personnel trample on tribal honor and customs when searching private homes and individuals, and detain suspects for months without providing information or access to detainees...US standard operating procedures in response to ambushes and attacks have caused the deaths of innocent bystanders, infuriating the populace."[39]

Moreover, there was also an external element involved, as both Syria and Iran feared a pro-U.S. regime in Baghdad, which would allow the United States to maintain bases in Iraq that could threaten both of them. Thus, their logical response has been to tacitly support anti-U.S. insurgents to ensure that the United States remained bogged down in Iraq.[40]

By 2004, the insurgency was in full swing. This was a mostly Sunni Arab uprising, as they had dominated the country under Saddam Hussein despite being a minority comprising about 20% of the total population of 27 million, and were now the biggest losers under a U.S.-occupied Iraq. Indeed, the United States backed not just the Kurds, who strongly supported the United States in the war in order to secure their eventual goal of independence, but also the Shiites, who comprise around 60% of the population. Although the majority of early attacks were in the so-called Sunni triangle bounded by Baghdad in the east, Ramadi in the west, and Tikrit in the north, where the majority of Sunnis live, the insurgency soon progressed beyond this area as attacks took place in other parts of the country.

Apart from Iraqi nationalists and ex-Ba'athists, the driving force of the insurgency has been radical Islamists. The alienation and suffering led to a number of Iraqis responding to the call to *jihad* by radical Islamist groups, the largest and best organized of which is the Jama'at al-Tawhid wal-Jihad (JTJ) or Monotheism and Holy Struggle Movement. It subsequently pledged its allegiance to Al Qaeda and became known as "Al Qaeda in Iraq" (AQI). Soon, the Sunni revolt targeted Shiite collaborators of the United States, becoming as much a fight to prevent Shiite domination (as well as eventual Iranian domination, given the close ties that the major Shiite parties have with neighboring Iran) as a war against the Christian invader.

Al Qaeda in Iraq

The JTJ was initially established in Germany in the 1990s as an anti-Jewish militant cell by Abu Musab Al-Zarqawi, a Jordanian who fought the Soviets as a *mujahideen* volunteer in Afghanistan in the 1980s. He then returned to a Taliban-run Afghanistan, where his organization was based in Herat. After the U.S.-led attack on Afghanistan in late 2001, he went to Iraq, where he reportedly established links with the radical Ansar al-Islam in Kurdish-held northern Iraq. Following the U.S. invasion of Iraq in 2003, he developed his organization into a network of local and foreign *mujahideen* fighters resisting U.S. and coalition forces. The JTJ has used suicide car and truck bombings against foreign troops, Iraqi government security personnel and installations, and civilians working for humanitarian organizations. It has been blamed for some of the most deadly attacks in Iraq, including the assassination of the top Shiite religious leader Ayatollah al-Hakim, a suicide boat attack on oil pumping stations on the coast, the assassination of the president of the Iraqi Governing Council, many deadly bomb attacks on Iraqi security personnel and installations, and the beheading of a number of kidnapped foreigners, whose gruesome murders were videotaped for distribution. Many bombings have targeted Shiites, whom Abu Musab saw as collaborators and not true Muslims.[41] In turn, this prompted revenge killings of Sunnis by Shiites, resulting in a rapid and vicious descent into sectarian violence.

The most serious and devastating attacks carried out by Al-Zarqawi's group were the coordinated suicide attacks against Shiite worshippers celebrating the Ashoura ceremony in Karbala and Baghdad in March 2004. At Karbala, several tens of thousands of pilgrims had gathered around the Iman Hussein shrine, one of holiest in the Shiite faith. A suicide bomber walked into the crowd and detonated a bomb. This was followed by grenade and other bomb explosions in the area around the shrine. Simultaneously, a suicide attack at the Al-Kadhimiya mosque in Baghdad killed many worshippers. In all, 271 people were killed and a further 393 injured.[42] The United States blamed Al-Qaeda and its local affiliate, the JTJ for the attacks, which were aimed at sowing Sunni–Shiite animosities to provoke civil strife that would complicate U.S.-led plans to return Iraq to normalcy. The Iraqi judge investigating the attacks concluded that it was financed from abroad, and probably carried out by Al-Qaeda. Al-Qaeda itself issued a denial of responsibility, blaming instead "American crusaders" for the deadly attacks.[43]

Soon after the attacks though, Al Zarqawi formally pledged his allegiance to Al Qaeda in October 2004. JTJ now became known as Tanzim Qaidat al-Jihad fi Bilad al-Rafidayn (literally, "the Al Qaeda Organization for Jihad in the Land of Two Rivers" or simply as "Al Qaeda in Iraq").[44] Thereafter, it became the focal point of radical Islamist violence in Iraq. It established a strong presence in cities such as Samarra and Fallujah. U.S.-led coalition forces retook Samarra in September 2004. Fallujah was attacked by U.S.-led forces in April 2004 and more successfully again in November 2004. However, almost daily deadly attacks continued to take place after that. Recognizing the serious threat that Abu Musa posed to the United States in Iraq, the U.S. government placed a $25 million bounty on Al-Zarqawi, the same sum as for Osama bin Laden. The financial incentive appeared to have worked, as Al-Zarqawi was apparently betrayed and killed in an attack in 2006.[45] But AQI remained dangerous, continuing to carry out numerous attacks and bombings despite the death of its charismatic leader.

Thus, from its small beginnings, AQI quickly developed into a major terrorist and insurgent force. Although the bulk of fighters are local Sunnis, foreign volunteer *mujahideen,* particularly from Saudi Arabia, joined the war. Just as Afghanistan in the 1980s was the cauldron from which Al-Qaeda developed, Iraq after the U.S.-led intervention become the breeding ground for a new generation of terrorists. The *mujahideen* in Iraq, pitted against the most technologically advanced armed forces in the world, have honed superb urban terrorist skills, such as in improvised explosive devices (IEDs), sniper attacks, truck bombs, sabotage, assassination, and kidnapping. Once the foreign *mujahideen* return home to the Middle East, Asia, and Europe, they could pose a serious security threat to their own governments and societies. More seriously, they could reconstitute a post-Al Qaeda network that would replace the Al Qaeda that had emerged from the chaos of Afghanistan in the 1980s. This new post-Al Qaeda network would have been trained in the battlefields of Iraq, honed its skills against the best military force in the world, and would have learnt from Al Qaeda's mistakes. The long-term consequences of the Iraq conflict could therefore be the emergence of an even more deadly global terrorist network.

The Search for Strategy

The number of U.S. troops killed since the start of the Iraq war reached 3,968 by February 2008 (before the surge took place), with over 29,000 wounded, indicating the severity of the insurgency and the intensity of fighting.[46] Indeed, the bulk of casualties were sustained after the supposed establishment of a legitimate Iraqi government following elections at the end of January 2005. In the face of the obvious, initial denials gradually gave way to the acknowledgment that a new strategy was needed for Iraq. In December 2005, President Bush thus presented the "National Strategy for Victory in Iraq" stating that the U.S. strategy for winning the war would rest on training Iraqi security forces, helping Iraq establish a democracy, and targeting economic development and rebuilding efforts in areas that had been cleared of insurgents.[47] In effect however, this was a continuation of the policy of siding with two groups, the Shiites and the Kurdish, against the Sunnis.

Continued casualties prompted U.S. Congress to appoint a ten-member bipartisan panel in March 2006 known as the Iraq Study Group (or Baker–Hamilton Commission, after the cochairmen Jim Baker and Lee Hamilton), to assess strategy on Iraq. In December 2006, the Baker–Hamilton report, officially titled *The Iraq Study Group Report: The Way Forward—A New Approach,* was released.[48]

The panel report recommended that the United States threaten to reduce economic and military aid to the government in Baghdad unless it met a series of benchmarks for security and development, in an effort to provide the necessary incentives for a unified and effective government in place of the fractured political leadership in Iraq. Significantly, it advocated that "the United States must make it clear to the Iraqi government that the United States could carry out its plans, including planned redeployments, even if Iraq does not implement its planned changes." This is because "America's other security needs and the future of our military cannot be made hostage to the actions or inactions of the Iraqi government."[49] The report also suggested the engagement of Iraq's neighbors, Syria and Iran, to help end the fighting. It also recommended that funds and troops for Iraq should be reduced, with U.S. combat troops withdrawn by 2008. On the other hand, economic and military support for operations in Afghanistan against the Taliban and Al Qaeda should be increased.[50] The Baker–Hamilton report was thus basically a plan and justification for a phased but fairly rapid withdrawal from Iraq based on the expectation that the Iraqis themselves could be ready to take over by 2008 and that Iraq's neighbors would act constructively to facilitate the U.S. withdrawal.

Predictably, the report drew mixed reactions, with critics of the Bush administration's strategy on Iraq feeling somewhat vindicated. But the key to its implementation was acceptance by the Iraqis themselves. However, some recommendations of the report, such as the strengthening of the central government's authority, including over oil, was anathema to the pro–U.S. Kurdish, who rejected it. The benchmarks requiring the Shiites to accommodate the Sunnis also resulted in the Shiites rejecting it. Within the United States, neoconservatives called it a document for surrender. In response, the neoconservative American Enterprise Institute released a rival document in January 2007 by Frederick Kagan entitled *Choosing Victory: A Plan for Success in Iraq,* which argued instead that "victory" in Iraq was vital to America's security and that defeat would lead to regional conflict, humanitarian catastrophe, and increased global terrorism. Kagan's report thus advocated instead a "substantial and sustained" troop surge in Iraq.[51]

In January 2007, President Bush appeared to accept this latter option of a troop surge rather than any radical departure in policy that would lead to early withdrawal when he announced a new strategy in Iraq. Bush proclaimed that the consequences of failure would be dire: radical Islamic extremists would grow in strength and gain new recruits; they would be in a better position to topple moderate governments, create chaos in the region, and use oil revenues to fund their ambitions; Iran would be emboldened in its pursuit of nuclear weapons; and finally, "our enemies would have a safe haven from which to plan and launch attacks on the American people."[52] Under the new plan, the United States would double the number of U.S. combat troops in Baghdad and patrol alongside Iraqi forces inside the city, rather than conduct operations from bases outside the city. The plan was to have sufficient Iraqi and U.S. security personnel to secure places after the militants had been cleared out. The Iraqi government would also be set a series of benchmarks including taking control of all provinces by the end of 2007 and passing legislation that would share oil revenue among all of the country's ethnic groups. Bush also vowed to crack down hard on the flow of support from Syria and Iran, thus rejecting the Baker–Hamilton proposal that both countries should be engaged diplomatically. However, although he made no mention of ultimate withdrawal, Bush also made clear that the U.S. commitment was not open-ended. It also appeared that Bush had now transferred the onus for victory against the insurgency to the Iraqi government of Prime Minister Nouri Maliki.

To lead the new strategy, Bush selected General David Petraeus, who had led the 101st Airborne Brigade in the initial offensive in Iraq in 2003 and then commanded an area south of Mosul where his emphasis on nonmilitary measures such as reconstruction projects are said to have contributed to relative peace in the area until he left, even as the rest of the country became affected by the insurgency.[53] Petraeus, an intellectual general with a PhD from Princeton, selected an elite team of intellectual officers with PhDs to work with him in Iraq, including the now famous Lt. Col. David Kilcullen of the Australian Army, whose idea of "disaggregation" is later explored at length in this book. The surge took place between February and June 2007, with some 30,000 fresh troops arriving to increase the number of U.S. troops to a record 168,000 by September 2007.[54]

In that month, Petraeus testified before the U.S. Congress what the extra troops had made possible. He stated that the United States had "employed counterinsurgency practices that underscore the importance of units living among the people they are securing," such as the establishment of many joint security stations and patrol bases manned by Coalition and Iraqi forces throughout Iraq.[55] However, Petraeus also noted the significant and fortuitous political developments on the ground that helped greatly. He informed Congress that:

> The most significant development in the past six months…has been the increasing emergence of tribes and local citizens rejecting Al Qaeda and other extremists. This has…been most visible in Anbar Province. A year ago the province was assessed as 'lost' politically. Today, it is a model of what happens when local leaders and citizens decide to oppose Al Qaeda and reject its Taliban-like ideology.[56]

He testified that insurgent attacks and sectarian violence had declined, and that by middle of 2008, 30,000 U.S. troops could be withdrawn.

However, he acknowledged that the situation in Iraq remained "difficult."[57] He also briefed Congress on the task ahead, making reference to the comprehensive approach that also included diplomacy, international cooperation, and information warfare, which he had earlier shared with the Pentagon, entitled "Security While Transitioning: From Leading to Partnering to Overwatch." According to Petraeus:

> This approach seeks to build on the security improvements our troopers and our Iraqi counterparts have fought so hard to achieve in recent months. It reflects recognition of the importance of securing the population and the imperative of transitioning responsibilities to Iraqi institutions and Iraqi forces as quickly as possible, but without rushing to failure... it highlights the importance of regional and global diplomatic approaches... in recognition of the fact that this war is not only being fought on the ground in Iraq but also in cyberspace, it also notes the need to contest the enemy's growing use of that important medium to spread extremism.[58]

Iraqi Prime Minister Maliki confirmed in September 2007 that violence dropped by 75% in Baghdad and Anbar province since the surge.[59] The relative peace that returned to Baghdad as well as developments in Anbar province has indeed been startling. But it was not the surge that was primarily responsible. The improvement in the security environment can be attributed in large part to other developments on the ground in Iraq. They include the fact that the Mehdi Army, controlled by the Shia extremist cleric Muqtada Sadr, was ordered by Sadr himself to cease from military action including reprisals against Sunnis. A more significant factor was the open revolt of tribal leaders against Al Qaeda. In a surprising and totally unexpected development, Sunni tribes that had collaborated with AQI in support of the anti-U.S. insurgency switched sides and instead joined the local militias supported by the Baghdad government and the United States.[60] The Sunni nationalist insurgent groups were alienated by the AQI's arrogance, brutality, flouting of tribal customs, and determination to impose a Taliban-type austerity on local communities.[61] Despite the common misperception that the insurgents were all Sunni extremists in one form or another, the fact is that the opposition comprised diverse groups whose interests do not often coincide. The Sunni tribal split with AQI illustrated the clash of radical Islam, with its uncompromising, fundamentalist outlook, and the reality of well-established tribal traditions and relationships based on customary practices, which are pre-Islamic and differ from Islam. The Sunni tribes have deep roots in rural Iraq while AQI has been led by foreigners, such as Saudis, Egyptians, and Chechens who are often either ignorant of local customs or are dismissive of them.

As David Kilcullen explained in his blog in *Small Wars Journal*, one of Al Qaeda's standard tactics in establishing itself in local communities has been to marry its leaders to women of prominent tribal chiefs. But in Iraqi rural society, the practice has been to marry within the tribe. The direct spark for the revolt against AQI stemmed from the brutal murder of a sheikh when he refused to give the daughters of his tribe to them in marriage. His death created a revenge obligation on the part of his tribe, which then turned on AQI. AQI tried to crush the revolt through force, which in turn sparked a full-scale tribal revolt. However, there were also more fundamental economic grievances, such as AQI's interference with local businesses centered around import–export, smuggling, and construction. Thus, tribesmen told Kilcullen that AQI "had it coming."[62]

However, it is also undeniable that a key factor has been the much more pragmatic and flexible approach on the part of the U.S. military under General Petraeus. Its willingness to work with nationalist insurgents who had been attacking U.S. and Iraqi government troops enabled the unexpected defection to take place. This was achieved by providing economic incentives to join regional associations as well as neighborhood guard units. Led by a charismatic and influential tribal chief, Sheikh Abdul Sattar, the so-called Anbar Awakening movement saw some 80,000 join government-sponsored militias (known as "Concerned Local Citizens") by the end of 2007.[63] These tribal militias have encouraged mass defections from AQI and ejected it from swaths of western and northern Iraq, including much of Baghdad.[64] In the end, the surge worked because the more sophisticated and flexible strategy that Petraeus employed in Iraq coincided with unexpectedly favorable political developments on the ground. The fact that the surge "worked" however, became political capital in Washington, with the Bush administration and neoconservatives feeling vindicated with the apparent efficacy of greater military force.

Nonetheless, there were criticisms by some members of Congress over the failure of the surge to promote reconciliation between Sunnis and Shiites, and the fact that Petraeus appeared to be planning to maintain a fairly high troop presence for a number of years.[65] Indeed, in a subsequent testimony in April 2008, Petraeus, in admitting again that despite progress the situation was "fragile and reversible," pointedly also refused to set a timetable for withdrawal. Instead, he recommended a process of evaluation and assessment regarding troop levels.[66] Reports to Congress by other agencies were also pessimistic; for instance, one released by the Government Accountability Office in September 2007 stated that of the 18 benchmarks mandated by Congress in May 2007, Iraq had failed to meet 11 of them, noting that "the number of Iraqi security forces capable of conducting independent operations has declined, and militias remain active."[67]

Despite the success in Anbar, Petraeus himself noted that "Anbar is unique and the model it provides cannot be replicated everywhere in Iraq."[68] Indeed, Sheikh Abdul Sattar, the leader of the Anbar Awakening, was assassinated in September 2007 in a car bomb attack, potentially dealing a blow to the Sunni resistance to Al Qaeda given the fractious nature of the tribes involved.[69] More seriously, without a political settlement between Sunnis and Shiites, permanent peace is not likely to return, given that the current peace between both groups is entirely dependent on the U.S. presence, which will be drawn down at some stage given the occupation's deep unpopularity in the United States itself. With Sunnis now openly supported by the United States, the stage is set for a more violent and widespread conflagration should sectarian conflict resume. Indeed, the Sunnis have not defected to the U.S. side solely out of anti-AQI sentiments. They remain deeply suspicious of the United States and have done so to be in a better position to defend their interests after a U.S. drawdown of its military presence. The Sunnis do not trust the Shiites, whom they believe are proxies of Iran. In turn, however, the Shiites are also deeply suspicious of the Sunni Awakening movement, as the Sunni accommodation thus far has not been with the Shiites but with the United States. The Shiites have every reason to fear that the United States is now supporting a group that would represent a potential threat to the authority of the Shiite-dominated government in Baghdad. In fact, if there is no lasting consensus on a power-sharing formula, it is probable that the Sunnis would take up arms again.

In addition, while AQI faced a serious setback with the tribal revolt, which has sapped its strength through mass defections and the loss of sanctuaries, it is far from finished. Its fluid structure and its ideological appeal in the context of a political, social, and economic crisis means that it will continue to attract young, alienated Sunnis. The security situation in Iraq has improved, with about 9,000 civilians killed in 2008 compared to 25,000 in 2007, and U.S. military casualties reduced to about 300 in 2008 compared to 900 in 2007.[70] However, there remains a great deal of violence, and AQI has continued with bomb and other terrorist attacks in Iraq, including targeting the leaders of Sunni groups now working with U.S. forces.[71] In January 2009, for instance, 23 people were killed and 110 wounded in a suicide bombing of a meeting of Sunni tribal leaders in Yusufiya, just outside Baghdad.[72]

More seriously, according to a testimony by Mike McConnell, the Director of National Intelligence, to a U.S. Senate hearing in February 2007, while the flow of foreign militants into Iraq had slowed during the final months of 2007, there is evidence that AQI could shift its focus to carrying out attacks outside of Iraq.[73] This could happen as the opportunities for carrying out terrorist attacks in Iraq diminished, pushing AQI to plan attacks outside the country. A precedent was already established when Al-Zarqawi carried out suicide bombings in Amman, in Jordan, in November 2005, targeting Westerners.[74] This followed an earlier, audacious plan to use chemical weapons to attack the intelligence headquarters in Amman in 2004.[75] The fear that AQI could at some stage evolve into a post-Al Qaeda network attacking targets outside Iraq, including possibly the United States itself, is based on its interest in WMDs including chemical weapons and its radical pan-Islamist ideology, which is not restricted to Iraq itself.[76]

Despite the relative calm and stability accompanying the U.S. troop surge, violence in fact increased in northern Iraq as a result of Turkey's incursion in pursuit of elements of the Kurdistan Workers' Party (PKK), which has been waging a war for an independent Kurdistan free from Turkish control. The PKK's incessant guerrilla and terrorist attacks in Turkey resulted in Turkey's parliament authorizing the armed forces to carry out military action against the PKK in northern Iraq in October 2007. On the other hand, the PKK, frustrated by the increasingly inward-looking policies of the Iraqi Kurds, hoped to provoke Turkey's intervention in northern Iraq and thus widen the Kurdish conflict in Turkey into a general war that might bolster its objective of a Greater Kurdistan. Turkey carried out attacks in northern Iraq, including air strikes in December 2007, with the help of intelligence supplied by the United States. The United States also opened up Iraqi airspace for Turkish military operations against the PKK, which had been designated by the United States as a terrorist organization.[77] Turkey also undertook a week-long ground offensive in February 2008, in which it targeted PKK bases in the Zap Valley that was used by the rebels for cross-border attacks. Turkey reluctantly ended its offensive after the United States pressured it to withdraw out of concern over a broader regional conflict and in view of the strong protests of the Iraqi government. The Turkish military claimed success, citing 240 rebels killed and the fact that the attack demonstrated that northern Iraq could not be a safe haven for the PKK.[78] However, the fact that the attack took place at all, with initial U.S. permission and intelligence assistance, demonstrated to the Iraqi Kurds, hitherto the strongest allies of the United States thus far, that the United States cannot be trusted as an ally, and that the Iraqi Kurds must ultimately look after their own interests.

The Shiite Power Struggle

Another serious threat to stability in Iraq has been the open struggle for power among Shiites. Soon after the Sunni tribal revolt and the U.S. troop surge, which led to greater calm throughout Iraq, the Maliki government took the decision to disarm the Mehdi Army led by Moqtada Sadr. This led to a spiral in violence as clashes took place between government troops and the Mehdi Army.

The Mehdi Army is a Shiite militia that sprang from the Sadrist movement, widely regarded as the only real mass movement in Iraq. The movement consists of a number of Shiite charities and was created by the respected Shiite cleric, Ayatollah Mohammed Sadeq Al-Sadr, who was killed by Saddam Hussein in 1999. Following the U.S. attack on Iraq in 2003 and the collapse of the Saddam regime, Moqtada Al Sadr, son of the late cleric, established the Mehdi Army, initially consisting of a few thousand fighters. The name "Mehdi" is taken after a revered figure in Shiite history. In the chaos that followed the U.S. attack, the Mehdi Army emerged to patrol the streets in poor sections of Baghdad, distributing food in an area renamed Sadr City. It attracted thousands of poor urban Shiites who have failed to see any benefits from the end of the Saddam regime. By December 2006, the Mehdi Army was estimated to have about 60,000 members. Because of the widespread availability of weapons such as assault rifles and rocket-propelled grenades, due to the failure of the United States to secure them after the fall of Saddam's regime, the Mehdi Army is also well-equipped to wage urban warfare. Its members have also infiltrated the government, the armed forces, and the administration, and have been widely linked to sectarian attacks on Sunni Muslims. The United States has accused Iran of arming, training, and funding the Mehdi Army, which would not be surprising.[79] Iran sees the chaos as the perfect opportunity, through unsatisfied Shiites, to expand its influence in Iraq and the Middle East.

While Moqtada is considered young and inexperienced, especially when compared to the much older clerics who dominate the Shiite community in Iraq, he has established a committed following among young, poor, and disaffected Shiites. As he lacks a proper religious education, he claims authority solely on the basis of lineage. This does not sit well with the other Shiite clerics in Iraq and his relationship with them has been tense. Despite his lack of religious credentials, Muqtada believes in clerical rule, a position at odds with the dominant Shiite religious authority, the moderate Grand Ayatollah Ali Al-Sistani. There have been deadly clashes between the Mehdi Army and the rival Badr Corps led by Ayatollah Sayyid Mohamed Baqir Al-Hakim. Moqtada has been accused of being responsible for some of the deadly assassinations of major Shiite religious leaders, such as the August 2003 car bomb that killed Al-Hakim, although his followers have blamed the attacks on Sunni insurgents. The Badr Corps in turn have dominated the government and security services in Baghdad and the southern provinces through its parent organization, the Islamic Supreme Council of Iraq (ISCI), led by Shiite cleric Abdul Aziz Al-Hakim, son of the late Ayatollah Hakim alleged murdered by Moqtada's group. Yet, the Mehdi Army is estimated to control half of Baghdad and some 80% of Shia-dominated areas.[80]

Moqtada has given fiery speeches denouncing the foreign occupation, and led an uprising against U.S.-led forces in Najaf in 2004 following the closure of his newspaper, Al Hawza, on charges of inciting violence. An Iraqi judge also issued a warrant for his arrest for the murder of a leading Shiite cleric, Imam Abdul Majid Al-Khoei. The result was much fighting between the Mehdi Army and U.S.-led forces in Najaf, Basra, and Sadr City in April 2004. Following the intervention of Grand Ayatollah Ali Al-Sistani in August 2004, Moqtada agreed to disband his militia but this did not happen although the confrontation petered out. While Moqtada did not participate in the elections in early 2005, his followers constitute a powerful bloc within the United Iraqi Alliance of Shiite groups loosely led by Al-Sistani and he remains perceived as a champion of the Shiite poor in Iraq. After the elections in Iraq in 2005, however, his followers have used intimidation tactics to enforce Muslim laws or the *sharia* amongst Shiites in Iraq.[81]

The Mehdi Army largely observed a six-month ceasefire called by Moqtada in August 2007, thus contributing to much less violence and greater stability in late 2007 and early 2008. This was however shattered by the Maliki government's offensive against the Mehdi Army in Basra in March 2008. Maliki's justification was that the central government had to bring security to Basra, Iraq's main port and oil-exporting center. He vowed "no retreat, no talks, no negotiations," and personally oversaw military operations in Basra. The real reason for the military offensive, however, may have been the provincial elections in October 2008, with the ISCI, a key player in the government, hoping to improve its position ahead of the elections, in view of apprehension that the Mehdi Army would make substantial gains due to widespread disenchantment with the performance of ISCI. Although Maliki himself is not from the ISCI but the Al Da'wah party, he allied himself with ISCI in order to deal with the increasingly powerful Mehdi Army. However, 28,000 government troops were unable to dislodge the Mehdi Army, despite air support from the United States. The Mehdi Army stood its ground and fought off attacks with mortars and rocket-propelled grenades. The fighting soon spread to other areas of Iraq, including Baghdad, threatening to turn into a full-scale intra-Shiite civil war. The fighting also opened up a greater role for Iran, which stepped in to mediate between the two sides. On March 30, 2008, after 359 people had been killed on both sides, a ceasefire was brokered by Iran, which has close ties with both ISCI and the Mehdi Army.[82]

Thus, from having little influence in Iraq under the firm hand of Saddam Hussein, Iran has now emerged as a key player, positioning itself with the objective of securing a Shiite-dominated government in Iraq, however fractious, that would be able to counter the Sunnis and the Kurdish after a U.S. withdrawal. The biggest loser in the long-term politics of Iraq will be the United States, while the biggest gainer will be Iran, which after all is in close geographical propinquity as a next-door neighbor. The fall of the Saddam regime and the subsequent empowerment of Shiites in Iraq have left the Middle East vulnerable to Iran, which is now in a position to exert greater influence that could destabilize a region of great strategic importance to the United States.

It is thus clear that there have been serious implications arising from the invasion of Iraq, apparently unanticipated when the United States made the fateful decision in 2003 to attack it. These include the possible failure of the state in Iraq and a long civil conflict, which would sap U.S. strength and resources, draw in neighboring states, and destabilize the entire region. The removal of the Saddam regime has increased Iran's influence through the empowerment of the Shiites in Iraq, with unpredictable geopolitical consequences given Iran's regional ambitions. The United States has also faced a nationalist Sunni insurgency that, coupled with radical Islamists in AQI, has cost the lives of 4,236 U.S. troops by the end of January 2009.[83] The long-term prognosis for Iraq remains pessimistic. As a recent International Crisis Group report commented, "Iraq will remain a deeply fragile state as long as the main players fail to overcome their differences and reach agreement on the distribution of power, territory and resources, and as long as the US fails to reach an understanding with neighbors both worried about Iraq's instability and willing to fuel it if necessary to protect their interests."[84]

More seriously, from a country under Saddam Hussein where Al Qaeda could not survive, it has now a substantial radical following in the country. Meanwhile, the Muslim world's outrage at U.S. actions in Iraq has greatly helped the cause of radical Islam. This has been inimical to the wider GWOT, as demonstrated in the globalized Islamist insurgency that has broken out since 9/11. Given the enormous expenditure of men and material on the part of the United States in attacking Iraq, these outcomes not only represent a very poor return but also suggest that monumental strategic mistakes had been made.

CHAPTER FOUR

The Iraq Conundrum and Its Implications

Misdiagnosis of the Problem

The decision to invade Iraq had clearly not been thought through carefully. The story of how Iraq became conflated with the Global War on Terror (GWOT) begins with the flawed diagnosis of the events of 9/11 and the nature of the global terrorist threat. Just days after the seminal 9/11 terrorist attacks, President Bush, addressing a joint session of Congress and the American people, gave his diagnosis of the threat that America faced. Bush rhetorically asked the question "why do they hate us?" According to Bush:

> They hate what we see right here in this chamber—a democratically elected government. Their leaders are self-appointed. They hate our freedoms—our freedom of religion, our freedom of speech, our freedom to vote and assemble and disagree with each other.[1]

This statement encapsulates the misdiagnosis and subsequent flawed strategy that led directly to the chaos of Iraq. The question of motivation for terrorism is a complex one and cannot be reduced to a simplified bipolarity, namely, those who hate democracy and are prepared to destroy it, and those who value democracy. If, in fact, it is a question of hating the West and its values so much as to want to completely destroy it, then the GWOT can be seen as a form of civilizational conflict between radical Islamists and the West. The only way to counter this uncompromising, existential threat would be to use kinetic military force to find and arrest or kill the enemy. But this flawed diagnosis led to a flawed strategy and ultimately to the conundrum in Iraq.

While many Muslims around the world deplore violence, they also see Osama bin Laden as a true champion of the suffering Muslim communities in places such as Chechnya, Palestine, and Kashmir. Yet, Muslims do not hate democracy. According to a Pew survey report in June 2003, the overwhelming majority of Muslims believe that Western-style democracy can work in their countries, and most Muslims place a high value on freedom of expression, freedom of the press, multiparty systems, and equal treatment under the law.[2] Why then do a minority of Muslims fall prey to radical Islamist ideology that seeks to impose a strict version of the *sharia* or Muslim laws, are prepared to use violence to achieve those ends, and sees the West, especially the United States, as its mortal enemy?

Jason Burke has succinctly observed that:

> The root causes of modern militancy are the myriad reasons for the grievances that are the first step on the road to terrorism. It is not a question of absolute deprivation but of how deprivation is perceived. Yet, social and economic problems, though the link to terrorism is indirect, are critical as a pre-condition. Such problems are growing more, not less, widespread and profound throughout the Islamic world.[3]

The question of the root causes of Muslim alienation is not the subject of this book, suffice to say that some studies have highlighted the salience of fundamental causes such as political repression, poverty, economic disparities, and environmental degradation that underlie Muslim alienation and rebellion around the world. There has been a strong sense of alienation among many Muslims in the Middle East, Central Asia, and Southeast Asia, stemming from local political, economic, and social grievances, a sense of relative deprivation, deep socioeconomic disparities, the presence of discrimination and prejudice, mismanagement and corruption by authorities, and the ignorance and insensitivity of central governments to local concerns. All these have resulted in a problem of legitimacy for the states concerned, even though many of them are strongly Muslim in character.[4] Other studies have found that there are no common causes of terrorism, such as religion or poverty. Instead, the cause of terrorism is a complex mix, in which political reasons seem to weigh greater than economic ones.[5]

As Jason Burke correctly observed, for those who feel angry and disempowered, radical Islam provides an answer. In an age of globalization, however, the message of radical Islam is easy to pick up:

> This legitimizing discourse, the critical element that converts an angry young man into a human bomb, is now everywhere. You will hear it in a mosque, on the Internet, from your friends, in a newspaper. You don't have to travel to Afghanistan to complete the radicalization process; you can do it from your front room, in an Islamic centre, in a park.[6]

Advanced communication technologies in an age of globalization have helped to facilitate the spread of radical ideology—and indeed any type of millenarian or apocalyptic ideology in this postmodern age. It creates a virtual world where these ideologies take root and grow, affecting the real world through its ability to self-radicalize individuals, link up cells as well as develop terrorist ideas and plans. It facilitates the development of a worldwide network of *jihadists*. The phenomenon of self-radicalization means that even without the direct recruitment efforts of radical groups, individuals could still be enticed to join militant terrorist groups.

Al Qaeda has understood and cleverly exploited the opportunities of a more interlinked global world. According to Bruce Hoffman, Al Qaeda "stubbornly adheres to its fundamental strategy and objectives—continuing to inspire the broader radical *jihadist* movement."[7] As a result, despite the worldwide security operations that have resulted in the killing or capture of the bulk of Al Qaeda's operatives and leaders, it has adapted so well that the threat from it today in fact comes from its radical ideology, not its organization. According to Hoffman, Al Qaeda today can be conceptualized as comprising four distinct but not mutually exclusive dimensions. There is Al Qaeda Central, which comprises remnants of the pre-9/11 Al Qaeda organization. Then, there are the Al Qaeda Affiliates and Associates, which comprise those who have benefited from funding, training, and provision of arms from Al Qaeda. Thirdly, there are the Al Qaeda Locals, who have been involved in *jihadist* campaigns in places such as Algeria, Chechnya, the Balkans, Afghanistan, and more recently in Iraq, may have received some training at an Al Qaeda facility, and are receptive to the Al Qaeda brand of radical pan–Islamist ideology. Finally, there is the Al Qaeda Network of homegrown radicals all over the world who have no direct connection with Al Qaeda but who have been influenced by radical propaganda and are prepared to join in the cause as well as carry out terrorist attacks.[8] In other words, the threat from Al Qaeda has evolved from the pre-9/11 organization to a broad-based ideological threat underpinning what might be described as a global insurgency involving local militants who have few if any operational ties with Al Qaeda but who subscribe to its brand of militant violence.

What are Al Qaeda's aims? According to Daniel Byman, Al Qaeda's grievances are in fact quite clear. Its grievances include the U.S. military presence in the Arabian peninsula after the First Gulf War, which is seen as blasphemous and an attempt to subjugate Islam; a bias toward Israel, which is ultimately aimed at the Muslim world; the subordination of the Muslim world; the creation of a hegemonic U.S.-dominated international system that is unfavorable to Muslims; and a willingness to inflict Muslim deaths in struggles around the world. What is significant about these grievances is that they are largely political. In fact, Osama bin Laden's grievances are fundamentally focused on power—who possesses it, why it is used and how it has been abused, to the detriment of Islam.[9] Through his religious edit (or *fatwa*) and declaration of war on the United States in 1996, Osama bin Laden has sought to confront the "far enemy," viz. the United States, which he charged to be at the head of the "Zionist–Crusaders alliance." He saw the U.S. military presence in the Arabian peninsula as blasphemous and he faulted the United States for its support for the corrupt, apostate regimes in the Muslim world, particularly the one in Saudi Arabia. Without U.S. support, he believed, these regimes, which were oppressing the Muslim world, would be overthrown, leading to the establishment of a pan-Islamic caliphate that would restore justice and end oppression.[10]

Thus, despite the religious context, the aims of Al Qaeda appear to be rooted in political issues and socioeconomic grievances. Its modus operandi is the waging of global *jihad*, one which has increasingly resembled a broad-based global insurgency. It follows that Bush's diagnosis, upon which his administration's response had been based, is flawed. Not only that, a response focusing mainly on the application of kinetic military force, which the United States undoubtedly possesses in abundance, cannot adequately deal with a global insurgency that is rooted in the deep-seated alienation that many Muslims feel. The nature of the fight is in fact not a military battle of wills but a battle of ideas and legitimacy. It is a problem that cannot be redressed solely through the prism of a narrowly defined, hard security approach that only focuses on a "kill or capture" policy, on the erroneous assumption that if Al Qaeda leaders, operatives, and supporters are killed, captured, or cowed into submission, the GWOT would be won.

Thus, Gareth Evans of the International Crisis Group correctly concluded that:

> We are dealing with a complex, multi-dimensional phenomenon, which demands a complex, multi-layered response. Good policy sometimes require not simplification but complexification...the struggle against violent extremism can be won, but it is going to be neither quick nor easy, and it is going to require a lot more thought and application and persistence, a lot more balanced approach, and a lot more attention to underlying causes and currents as distinct from surface manifestations.[11]

An effective counterterrorism approach therefore requires a "complex, multi-layered response." In other words, a comprehensive approach at the global, regional, and local levels is needed, not the unilateral, unidimensional military-oriented approach pursued by the Bush administration.

The Conflation of Threats

The story of how the GWOT became conflated or merged with other issues, such as Iraq, which had little or no bearing on the global terrorist threat, is one which tells of a failure of analysis, a lack of clarity over the nature of the threat, and a failure to prioritize goals and objectives. In the months following 9/11, Bush was to declare a global war against terror, which appeared at first to focus on Al Qaeda, the perpetuators of 9/11. Then it expanded to include Al Qaeda's state sponsor, the Taliban regime, which ruled Afghanistan. It also expanded to all manner of extremist groups particularly those linked to Al Qaeda or which subscribed to its radical ideology. All this was more or less accepted by allies of the United States, given that citizens of many countries had been among those who perished in 9/11, and given the threat posed by radical Islamists, particularly to pro-U.S. regimes in the Middle East. Thus, Operation Enduring Freedom in Afghanistan, which took place soon after the events of 9/11, had the support of many U.S. allies. Despite unhappiness among many Muslims, its actions there had broad international legitimacy since Al Qaeda had training camps in Afghanistan under the sponsorship and protection of the Taliban regime.

The Bush administration, however, soon began to expand its objectives. Flush with its swift removal of the Taliban regime in late 2001, the United States now set its sights on three "rogue states" that had nothing to do with Al Qaeda and were unrelated to the GWOT. In January 2002, President Bush designated Iraq, Iran, and North Korea as the "Axis of Evil." He also charged that Saddam Hussein had hidden weapons of mass destruction and had flouted commitments not to deploy them.[12] The United States also charged that Iraq had links with Al Qaeda.[13]

How the GWOT came to result in the U.S. invasion and occupation of Iraq, despite the fact that it did not have weapons of mass destruction nor links with Al Qaeda can be explained by several factors, which collectively explain the catastrophic collapse in both leadership and strategy in Washington. First, the neoconservative worldview became dominant in the brave new post-9/11 world. As Francis Fukuyama explained, the central question after the end of the cold war was how to define the national interests that would underpin the foreign policy of the new global hegemon, viz. the United States.[14] One perspective that became increasingly influential is best exemplified by Charles Krauthammer's seminal article, "The Unipolar Moment," in *Foreign Affairs* (Winter 1990–91).[15] This was later expanded in another article in *The National Interest* in its winter issue of 2002–3, in which he argued that the unipolar moment had become the unipolar era for the United States.[16] In February 2004, Krauthammer's speech at the American Enterprise Institute asserted and defended the neoconservative worldview that guided the Bush administration.[17]

Describing his prescription for a post-cold war and post-9/11 foreign policy as "democratic realism," Krauthammer proposed this axiom: that the United States will support democracy everywhere, but it will commit blood and treasure only in places where there is a strategic necessity, that is, places central to the larger war against the existential enemy, the one that poses a global mortal threat to freedom. He thus argued, in the context of the GWOT, that the U.S. attacks on Afghanistan and Iraq were justified. According to Krauthammer, "establishing civilized, decent, non-belligerent, pro-Western polities in Afghanistan and Iraq and ultimately their key neighbors would, like the flipping of Germany and Japan in the 1940s, change the strategic balance in the fight against Arab–Islamic radicalism."[18] Krauthammer was also critical of multilateralism, which he felt was designed to restrain the Great Powers. Why should a benign hegemon such as the United States be subject to any restraint?[19] Instead, Krauthammer argued that the United States should be guided by its own independent judgment both about its own interests and about the global interest.[20] He thus advocated a doctrine of preemption against openly hostile states pursuing weapons of mass destruction, which he felt was an improvement on classical deterrence strategy. Classical deterrence strategy promised retaliation should the enemy attack first, but that would be too late. Preemption, on the other hand, would deter the acquisition of weapons of mass destruction in the first place. According to Krauthammer, "whether or not Iraq had large stockpiles of weapons of mass destruction, the very fact that the United States overthrew a hostile regime that repeatedly refused to come clean on its weapons has had precisely this deterrent effect...we are safer today."[21] Thus, the United States should no longer patiently wait for multilateral diplomacy and sanctions to work. Instead, it should now use its massive military capabilities, preemptively if necessary, to confront states that sponsored terrorism, with the goal of undermining and overthrowing their regimes, and then imposing democracy.[22] In sum, therefore, the neoconservative doctrine of democratic realism is a form of "muscular Wilsonianism," minus international institutions, which seeks to use U.S. military power to support U.S. security interests and democracy simultaneously. As Fukuyama was to later lament, Iraq has proved that such a strategy is utterly unrealistic in its overestimation of U.S. power and its ability to control events around the world.[23]

Nonetheless, the new doctrine fitted well with the growing unilateral impulse in the United States, which must be seen in the context of its growing technological and military power, coupled with a growing sense that encumbrances of alliances, international norms and laws, and of the United Nations, should not prevent the United States from pursuing its national security interests. Well before 9/11, there was already increasing skepticism over whether nonproliferation regimes would work. There was a general feeling that the United States faced new threats of such a dire nature, such as terrorists using weapons of mass destruction, that it must escape the constraints of the multilateral structures it helped to build after World War II, if it was to effectively deal with the new security challenges. After all, since the United States possessed massive military capabilities at its disposal, why not use it to defend U.S. security interests more aggressively and proactively?

Indeed, underpinning the growing confidence in the U.S. post–cold war military capabilities has been its ability to apply overwhelming force throughout the world using precision-guided, stand-off weapons systems, its superb surveillance capabilities, which has made possible battlespace awareness while denying it to the enemy, and its ability to fight in an expanded battlespace in all conditions day and night. This overwhelming conventional military capability has come about through a fundamental military transformation dubbed the Revolution in Military Affairs (RMA), a process that has been going on since the end of the Vietnam War. This process has been driven by the search to make military power a usable political instrument once more in the face of public sensitivity to collateral damage and the need to win quick, decisive wars. The new approach appeared vindicated in the First Gulf War and later in the U.S. attack on Afghanistan after 9/11. The new capability has not come cheaply, with the U.S. military budget equal to the combined budgets of the next twelve largest military powers. Thus, Michael Mandelbaum, who described the United States as a "hyper-power," observed in 2002, albeit before the United States was humbled by the insurgencies in Iraq and Afghanistan, that "the central feature of the world at the outset of the twenty-first century is the enormous power of the United States."[24]

The impact of 9/11 has thus been to heighten the sense that the United States should use its enormous power and technology to meet the emerging security challenges from both rogue states and terrorists, unilaterally if need be, without the encumbrances of less courageous allies, which after all want to only protect their own narrow national interests. Indeed, a major factor that explains the blunder into an unnecessary war in Iraq is the huge psychological impact of 9/11. It was the first time since the Japanese attack on Pearl Harbor in 1941 that the United States had been directly attacked. The shock of the iconic twin towers of the World Trade Center being hit by hijacked passenger planes, their spectacular collapse in front of television cameras, and the deaths of almost 3,000 people forcefully and dramatically brought home the danger that terrorists and rogue states posed to the United States. It triggered a sense of alarm over what would have happened had the terrorists used weapons of mass destruction, and led to a search for how the tremendous power and resources of the United States could be utilized to deal with the new dangers.

The events of 9/11 provided the perfect opportunity for the neoconservatives to push their agenda for change in Iraq. Paul Wolfowitz, Donald Rumsfeld, and Dick Cheney became key figures within the Bush administration in pursuing this new doctrine of preemption, in which they believed that the application of U.S. power would result in a reformed, democratic post-Saddam Iraq, which would in turn lead the way to democracy in the Middle East. This would result in a strategic victory over radical Islam and at the same time pave the way for a lasting peace in the Middle East, since it is an accepted axiom that democracies do not go to war with each other.[25] Mearsheimer and Walt have argued that an unstated objective was also the desire to make Israel more secure, a result of pressure from the pro-Israel lobby, which they contend was a critical factor, though they have probably overstated their case as it was only one of a number of factors.[26]

Thus, within days of the events of 9/11, the Bush administration adopted a radical new strategy: no longer was the United States going to patiently wait for multilateral diplomacy and sanctions to work, it would now use its massive capabilities to forcefully confront *all* states that sponsored terrorism, with the goal of undermining, overthrowing them, and then imposing democracy.[27] This led to the "Axis of Evil" designation on Iraq, Iran, and North Korea, as the three states allegedly had weapons of mass destruction and were supposed to be covertly supporting anti-U.S. terrorist groups. However, the problem with this was that the three were most certainly not part of an "Axis" in the way that Nazi Germany, Japan, and Italy were part of a loose fascist Axis during World War II. Moreover, the three states in question were unrelated to Al Qaeda and had no linkages with it. Iraq too had neither links with Al Qaeda nor did it possess weapons of mass destruction. Indeed, in 2006, the U.S. Senate, quoting a Central Intelligence Agency (CIA) report in 2005, acknowledged that there was no evidence of formal links between Saddam Hussein and Al Qaeda.[28] Despite searching all over Iraq after the U.S. invasion, U.S. forces could also find no evidence that Iraq had weapons of mass destruction.

This astonishing conflation of Iraq and the GWOT was helped by faulty intelligence and a collective group-think mentality that helped justify the invasion of Iraq. For instance, the National Intelligence Estimate (NIE) in October 2002 made a convincing case that Iraq represented a clear and present danger to the United States due to its weapons of mass destruction and its attempts to restart its nuclear program.[29] Thus, Defense Secretary Donald Rumsfeld and Vice-President Dick Cheney repeatedly claimed in late 2002 and early 2003 that Saddam had stockpiles of weapons of mass destruction as well as links with Al Qaeda terrorists who could use them to attack U.S. cities. Deputy Defense Secretary Paul Wolfowitz's speech on January 23, 2003 justified invading Iraq on grounds of the alleged link between Iraq and the war on terror. According to him, "the weapons of mass destruction and the terrorist networks with which Iraq is in league are not two distinct threats...they are part of the same threat...depriving Iraq of its chemical and biological weapon of mass destruction, and dismantling its nuclear weapons development program, is crucial to victory in the war against terrorism."[30]

Thus, the impact of 9/11 had been tremendous. It led to a fundamental change in the way the United States felt its huge military capabilities should be used, as well as what the proper objectives of its foreign policy should be. Dealing with Al Qaeda and global terrorism, containing the problem of weapons of mass destruction, spreading democracy around the world, defeating radical Islam, targeting "rogue" states, and regime change in Iraq all became conflated.

The Implications of Iraq for the GWOT

The U.S. attack began on March 20, 2003. By 9 April, Baghdad had fallen. In contrast to the First Gulf War, which was duly authorized by the United Nations and was a more or less collective undertaking although the brunt of the fighting was undertaken by the United States, Britain, and France, the attack on Iraq in 2003 was swiftly condemned by much of the world.[31] While Bush boasted of a grand coalition of the willing, the reality was that the United States stood very much alone, with the active participation only of Great Britain.

A motley group of states did send troops and other support personnel but they stayed away from the actual fighting, and withdrew as soon as they could. Some states, such as South Korea, Japan, and other U.S. allies, sent troops virtually out of duress in order to demonstrate support for the alliance relationship with the United States, given the Bush administration's dictum that "either you are with us, or you are with the terrorists."[32] So fearful was the government of Japan to any casualty, given widespread domestic opposition to both the U.S. invasion of Iraq and Japan's abetment of this by committing forces, that Japanese troops had to be protected from harm by U.S., British, and Netherland troops. Japanese troops, 1,100 in number deployed in Samawa in January 2004, began their withdrawal in June 2006.[33] Other states, such as Poland and Mongolia, sent troops as well, despite not facing any radical Islamist terrorist threat of their own. However, they saw a real opportunity to ingratiate themselves with a superpower that would be a useful ally against the real security referents for these countries: Russia in the case of Poland, and Russia and China in the case of Mongolia. Thus, Iraq suffered the curios ignominy of Mongol troops, albeit a small company of 173 soldiers, patrolling its streets. The last time this had happened was Genghis Khan's invasion in 1258, when his Mongol army captured and destroyed Baghdad.[34]

The manner in which the United States initially treated Iraqis, virtually as the newly conquered populace of a defeated and occupied country, the failure to secure the country, the failure to carry out meaningful reconstruction, and the destruction of key Iraqi state institutions such as the disastrous decision to disband the Iraqi security services including the armed forces, led directly to a burgeoning anti-U.S. insurgency. The insurgents belonged to different groups, consisting of Al Qaeda-linked *jihadists*, Iraqi Sunni nationalists, ex-Ba'ath Party loyalists, and Shiite militia belonging to radical factions. The United States soon became bogged down in Iraq as a result of the outbreak of the insurgency.

Although complex and in many ways nationalistic in nature, the insurgency increasingly drew *jihadists* from around the world and strengthened the Islamist elements in Iraq. Indeed, the main local *jihadist* organization, the Jama'at al-Tawhid wal-Jihad (JTJ) led by Abu Musa Al-Zarqawi, allied itself to Al Qaeda and joined its global *jihad* by formally changing its name to Al Qaeda in Iraq (AQI) in 2004. The impact of the U.S. invasion and occupation of Iraq for the GWOT has thus been to create both the conditions and the opportunities for Al Qaeda to recruit both locally and globally to fight in the perceived U.S.-led war against Islam. Just as Afghanistan attracted *mujahideen* from all over the world to fight against the godless Soviet communists who had invaded it, Iraq attracted *mujahideen* to volunteer to fight in the defense of Islam. Just as Osama bin Laden's Maktab Al-Khidamat (Afghan Services Office), the predecessor to Al Qaeda, recruited and trained many for what they perceived as the ultimately heroic and successful war against Soviet forces, AQI attracted a motley crew of Syrians, Saudis, Egyptians, Yemenis, Sudanese, and other radicalized Muslims from all over the world to serve in Iraq.[35]

The greatest beneficiary of the U.S. invasion of Iraq has been Al Qaeda. At one fell swoop, the United States had helped Al Qaeda get rid of one of the key targets of its *jihad*—Saddam's hated regime. Saddam's regime was the very kind of despotic and apostate regime that Al Qaeda has been dedicated to undermining and overthrowing throughout the Muslim world.

More significantly, the U.S. attack and invasion of Iraq was an unexpected strategic bonus for Al Qaeda. For an organization that had been hunted all over the world since 9/11, the Iraq conflict provided an unexpected boost to its recruitment and its radical propaganda. Al Qaeda's claim of a Western crusade against Islam appeared justified by the U.S. attack on Iraq and the subsequent suffering of many Iraqis. The images shown on Al Qaeda videos and Al Jazeera television of the victims of the Iraq conflict, including the unavoidable civilian collateral deaths, shocked and enraged Muslim audiences all over the world. Instead of being seen to have helped topple a hated dictator, freed the Iraqi people from oppression and dealt a blow to terrorism, the United States appeared to Muslim audiences to have made false accusations against a Muslim country, bombed it into submission, armed one side against the other to encourage a civil war, and then allowed its people to suffer the consequences. Although it is true many did not like Saddam Hussein's despotic and arbitrary regime, the U.S. cure appeared far worse, given the evident chaos, violence, and massive civilian casualties that accompanied the aftermath of the U.S. invasion. The number of civilian casualties in Iraq since the U.S. invasion in 2003 has been a matter of dispute as the U.S. military has not kept count of civilian casualties. The independent British research group, the Iraq Body Count, estimated about 50,000 dead up until late 2006, but a joint U.S.–Iraqi team of epidemiologists, utilizing cluster sampling methods normally used to estimate mortality in famines and after natural disasters, arrived at an estimate in October 2006 of 655,000 who have died as a consequence of the invasion.[36]

The astonishing level of violence and the large numbers of civilian deaths since the U.S. invasion in 2003 put Osama bin Laden in a position where he could benefit strategically through the appeal of his radical message. In a videotape aired by Al Jazeera in April 2006, Osama made an argument that resonated with many Muslims, when he asserted that the West was carrying out a war against Islam, making reference to the destruction of the infrastructure and the tragedy that befell Muslims in Iraq. Describing it as a "malicious crusade against Muslims" (ignoring the fact that many Shiites had died as a result of a vicious bombing campaign against them by AQI), bin Laden linked events in Iraq to the global *jihad* by arguing that Iraq has become a key battlefield between "the Crusaders" and Islam:

> The epicenter of these (Crusader) wars is Baghdad, the seat of the *khalifate* rule. They keep reiterating that success in Baghdad will be success for the US...failure in Iraq the failure of the US. Their defeat in Iraq will mean defeat in all their wars, a beginning to the receding of their Zionist–Crusader tide against us. Your *mujahideen* sons and brothers in Iraq have taught the US a hard lesson...they

are steadfast and patient and keep killing and wounding enemy soldiers every day.[37]

Thus, an Iraq that was safe from Al Qaeda and had few if any Al Qaeda operatives there under the draconian eye of Saddam Hussein soon became mired in a deadly civil war that has also attracted non-Iraqi *jihadists* from all over the world. The conflation of Iraq with Al Qaeda had resulted in a self-fulfilling prophecy.

The consequences for the broader GWOT have been highly negative. Thus, Daniel Byman lamented that "Iraq is becoming a new field of *jihad*, a place where radicals come to meet, train, fight and forge bonds that last when they leave Iraq for the West or for other countries in the region." According to Byman:

> The (Iraq) war served a Darwinian function for *jihadist* fighters. Those who survived ended up better trained, more committed, and otherwise more formidable than they had been when they began. Otherwise they would have perished. Unfortunately, the skills the *jihadists* picked up in Iraq are readily transferable to other theatres.[38]

Byman lists sniper tactics, experience in urban warfare, improved ability to avoid enemy intelligence, the use of human-portable surface-to-air missiles, improvised explosive devices (IEDs), and the ethos of suicide bombing.[39] Thus, the consequences of the invasion and conflict in Iraq will be felt for years to come, with implications that will resonate well beyond its borders.

More seriously, Iraq has helped Al Qaeda and its radical associates worldwide to overcome the unprecedented security operations directed against it. According to Al Qaeda's deputy leader, Ayman Al-Zawahiri, "we thank God for appeasing us with the dilemmas in Iraq and Afghanistan. The Americans are facing a delicate situation in both countries. If they withdraw they will lose everything and if they stay, they will continue to bleed to death."[40] Indeed, U.S. actions in Iraq have not only become an important rallying call and powerful propaganda tool, they are a distraction for the United States and have also afforded Al Qaeda the breathing space it needed to survive the U.S.-led counterterrorism onslaught. As Murad Batal Al-Shishani concluded, "American-occupied Iraq is both the catalyst and incubator for the birth and evolution of the third generation of *Salafi-jihadists*... without the Iraqi theatre, the entire Al Qaeda-inspired global *jihad* movement would be faced with critical ideological and recruitment problems."[41] Indeed, without the invasion of Iraq, Al Qaeda might not have survived the worldwide security onslaught and might well have been eradicated.

Instead, despite losing the bulk of its leaders and operatives, Iraq has played a major role in helping to convince others to join Al Qaeda's global *jihad*. The rallying call issued by Al Qaeda to defend Islam, which it portrays as being under attack, has been heard by radical Islamists all over the world, many of whom have proclaimed themselves to be members of Al Qaeda. There is now, for instance, Al Qaeda in Iraq, Al Qaeda in Europe, Al Qaeda in Saudi Arabia, Al Qaeda in the Malay Archipelago, Al Qaeda in North Africa, and so on. Severe tactical losses after 9/11 have thus been translated into strategic victories. The actions of the United States have unwittingly helped Al Qaeda's strategic objective, which was to act as a vanguard in order to spark the global *jihad* that would lead to the establishment of a new caliphate ruled strictly according to Muslim laws or the *sharia*. Thus, a British parliamentary committee in August 2003 concluded that the Iraq war has hampered the struggle against Al Qaeda by enhancing its appeal among Muslims in the Middle East and elsewhere.[42]

Not only has the Al Qaeda brand achieved prominence, with militant groups all over the world dedicating themselves to the Al Qaeda ideal and its objectives, but individuals are becoming self-radicalized through the Internet and by being exposed to radical Islamist literature and media. Thus, the phenomenon of the self-radicalized individual has emerged in recent years, epitomized by those who had little prior contact to Al Qaeda before 9/11 but who nevertheless have formed militant cells since then to carry out violent attacks such as the London train bombings in 2005. According to Marc Sageman, the Al Qaeda that we know today could be seen to have evolved in three phases: those who joined during the war against the Soviets in Afghanistan in the 1980s; those who trained in Al Qaeda camps in Afghanistan in the 1990s; and those who joined after 9/11 and the overthrow of the Taliban in Afghanistan as well as the U.S. invasion of Iraq. This third wave consists of many who have been recruited on the Internet, including second generation Muslim migrants in Europe and North America. Al Qaeda can therefore be seen today as a social movement that has spread far beyond the original organization.[43]

This rapid and startling transformation of Al Qaeda from an organization and fairly distinct network in 2001 into a global self-replicating hydra has laid the basis for a new challenge from Al Qaeda—that of a global insurgency that is posing a serious global security challenge. This global insurgency does not have any real central directing authority and indeed has none or very tenuous links with Al Qaeda itself, but consists mainly of local groups motivated by the same radical ideology, driven by causes such as the U.S.-led invasion of Iraq, and fired up by local political, economic, and social grievances.

The result is that the threat of global terrorism has not abated since 9/11. President Bush's triumphant boast on the deck of the aircraft carrier, the USS *Abraham Lincoln*, on May 1, 2003 in the aftermath of declaring victory in Iraq, that "we do not know the day of the final victory (over terrorism)...but we have seen the turning of the tide," has proven hollow with the many terrorist attacks that have taken place worldwide since then.[44] Although the United States itself has not suffered another terrorist attack, several plots were disrupted, and many deadly terrorist attacks mounted by militant Muslim groups have taken place in Bali, London, Moscow, Istanbul, Casablanca, Saudi Arabia, Pakistan, Philippines, and various other locations around the world. Despite massive efforts on the part of the United States, the GWOT has not gone well. This can be attributed to the series of disastrous strategic mistakes made by the Bush administration, especially in invading Iraq.

More serious is the long-term impact on the broader ideological war for the hearts and minds of Muslims around the world, whose support against radical ideology would be crucial in containing and finally defeating this global insurgency. U.S. actions in Iraq have caused a catastrophic fall in the standing of the United States in the eyes of the Muslim world. According to a Pew survey in 2003, "the bottom has fallen out of support for America in most of the Muslim world," with favorable ratings for the United States in the aftermath of the attack on Iraq falling from 61% to 15% in Indonesia, and from 71% to 38% among Muslims in Nigeria. Conversely, the standing of Osama bin Laden has been significantly enhanced, with half or more in the Palestine Authority, Indonesia, Jordan, Morocco, and Pakistan saying that they had confidence that he would "do the right thing regarding world affairs."[45]

The political impact of the war in Iraq is likely to linger for many years. At best, U.S. military action in Iraq was motivated by political and geostrategic considerations. Indeed, many non–Muslims, including U.S. allies in Europe, share this skepticism about U.S. motives. But among Muslims, it is shaping and hardening attitudes of Muslims all over the world about the United States and the West in general. In particular, the Muslim world is angry with the illegality of the U.S. actions and the conviction among many Muslims that the United States is really carrying out a crusade against Islam.

Iraq's Impact on the United States

The U.S. invasion and occupation of Iraq has been a costly affair in terms of lives and material. It thus had the consequence of sparking debilitating domestic rancor over the wisdom of the course of action pursued by the Bush administration. The aftermath of invading Iraq, with thousands of soldiers killed or wounded due to the insurgency as well as the failure to find evidence of Saddam's alleged weapons of mass destruction, focused attention on the reasons for having gone to war in the first place. The subsequent controversies over faulty intelligence and misrepresentation to justify war not only damaged the credibility of the U.S. government domestically but also led to the erosion of domestic trust in and support for the Bush administration.

After the war in Iraq formally concluded, no evidence of any weapon of mass destruction, nor the up to 20 Scud missiles that were supposed to have been used to deploy them, and the so-called mobile laboratories, have been found, despite extensive searching of the country by U.S. forces.[46] The Bush administration then argued that just because they have not been found did not mean they did not exist, as they could have been hidden or destroyed. However, even if they were not found, the Bush administration now argued that the war was justified as Iraq had not complied with UN resolutions to declare and destroy them. Rumsfeld thus testified before the Senate Armed Services Committee on July 9, 2003 that "the coalition did not act in Iraq because we had discovered dramatic new evidence of Iraq's pursuit of weapons of mass destruction...we acted because we saw the existing evidence through the prism of our experience on 9/11," thereby downplaying the issue of the evidence for weapons of mass destruction.[47] The Bush administration thus drew a distinction between programs and actual weapons, despite the fact that the U.S. public had supported war on the basis of an imminent threat from Saddam.[48]

Hans Blix, the chief UN weapons inspector, was thus highly critical of the United States for fabricating evidence against Iraq and of planning the war well in advance.[49] The political controversy reduced the legitimacy of U.S. actions in Iraq, damaged the credibility of the Bush administration, and has deleterious consequences on future

U.S. foreign and defense policies. If the United States needs to use preemption against threats as it feels it cannot afford to wait for radical terrorists or rogue states to possess weapons of mass destruction and thereby threaten or use them against the United States, then accurate intelligence and the ability to act objectively on such intelligence is essential. The war against terrorism also depends on the United States using its enormous power judiciously and employing it precisely to deal with real, not irrelevant, threats. Moreover, the controversy over faulty intelligence has eroded the public's trust in the intelligence with which the U.S. government uses to plan its war against terrorism.

In addition, U.S. casualties, which stood at 4,236 U.S. troops by the end of January 2009 has eroded domestic U.S. support for foreign adventures.[50] As Michael Glennon observed, "the danger after the second Persian Gulf War is not that the United States will use force when it should not, but that, chastened by the war's horror, the public's opposition, and the economy's gyrations, it will not use force when it should."[51] One thinks of Iran and North Korea, both of which have much better documented efforts at developing weapons of mass destruction, and which are more likely to sell or pass them on to terrorist groups. Chastened by Iraq, with political capital squandered on an irrelevant conflict, can the United States effectively deal with both?

Implications of Iraq for the International System

The First Gulf War of 1990 was authorized, and therefore legitimized, by the United Nations and was aimed at recovering Kuwait, which had suffered attack and invasion from Iraq. In 2003, however, there was little international support, the United States being supported mainly by British troops. International condemnation was swift. China pointed out, quite rightly, that the attack had violated the UN Charter, as Iraq did not constitute a threat and the United States thus could not claim self-defense under Article 51. French president Jacques Chirac expressed regret that the action was launched without the explicit approval of the United Nations.[52] Demonstrations broke out in many parts of the world, including in countries closely allied to the United States, such as Britain, Australia, Japan, and South Korea.[53]

The U.S. attack on Iraq has led to the erosion of the close alliance relationship it had since 1945 with a number of countries around the world. Public perceptions of the United States took a massive dive. According to a Pew survey, U.S. favorability ratings plummeted among allies such as France, Germany, Britain, Italy, and Spain. Six months after the United States attacked Iraq, its ratings in Britain, a key ally, declined from 75% to 48%.[54] Support for Western Europe taking a more independent approach to security and diplomatic affairs also rose significantly.[55] Another Pew survey in 2004, a year after the attack on Iraq, showed that discontent with the United States and its policies intensified rather than diminished. Opinion of the United States in France and Germany remained strongly negative, while British views became more critical. According to the Pew survey report:

> Perceptions of American unilateralism remain widespread in European and Muslim nations, and the war in Iraq has undermined America's credibility abroad. Doubts about the motives behind the US-led war on terrorism abound, and a growing percentage of Europeans want foreign policy and security arrangements independent from the United States. Across Europe, there is considerable support for the European Union to become as powerful as the United States.[56]

The negative perceptions of the United States were not unexpected, given that the United States had acted unilaterally without the concurrence and support of its key allies, and worse, had clearly violated international law in launching a preemptive attack on Iraq. The Europeans and indeed, much of the rest of the world, were skeptical about the evidence that the United States presented regarding the threat of terrorism and from weapons of mass destruction that Iraq allegedly posed, and felt that not only was the threat fabricated to justify an attack, but the United States had became distracted from the threat from global terrorism posed by the Al Qaeda network. The U.S. attack on Iraq in 2003 therefore can be said to have contributed significantly to the fracturing of the Atlantic alliance.

In addition, the United States, in acting unilaterally, also appeared to be abandoning the international system centered on multilateralism, alliances, and the United Nations that it had helped establish and nurture since the end of World War II. This unilateralist streak had already been evident in U.S. policies since the Clinton presidency. Prior to 9/11, the United States had abandoned arms control and nonproliferation regimes such as the landmines treaty, a treaty to limit small arms, the Anti-Ballistic Missile treaty, and the Biological Weapons Convention, and also refused to ratify multilateral environmental protection treaties, such as the Kyoto Protocol. The United States has since also refused to join the International Criminal Court and has in fact gone about undermining it through bilateral agreements with various states to exempt the United States from its jurisdiction. This apparent abandonment of the post-1945 international system that the United States had helped to construct has led to great uncertainty. Unilateralism has endangered the post-1945 international system, which has underpinned a general global stability for much of the postwar era, by undermining the norms, regimes, and institutions established to maintain the stability of the system. Indeed, the demise of the United Nations' predecessor, the League of Nations, was due to Great Powers, including the United States, failing to support it. This led to global instability as states resorted to unilateral approaches in pursuit of their national interests, with disastrous consequences as it ultimately led to the outbreak of the World War II.

Similarly, the present post–cold war international system, particularly after 9/11, has been in a state of flux, forcing smaller states to focus on building bilateral alliances with Great Powers and increasing the probability of interstate wars. The United Nations and the international system have been so seriously undermined that Secretary-General Kofi Anan lamented in September 2003 that the United Nations was facing "a fork in the road." The reason, according to Kofi Anan in a clear reference to the United States, was the resort to unilateralism, which represented a fundamental challenge to the principles upon which, however imperfectly, world peace and stability had rested, that is, in dealing with threats to the peace through containment and deterrence, by a system based on collective security and the UN Charter. As Kofi Annan stated, this could set precedents that would lead to a proliferation of the unilateral and lawless use of force, with or without justification. Thus, Annan concluded, "this may be a moment no less decisive than 1945 itself, when the United Nations was founded." He thus asked "whether it is possible to continue on the basis agreed then (after 1945), or whether radical changes are needed."[57]

The attack on Iraq was also meant to demonstrate U.S. strength and resolve against "rogue" states that supported terrorism, leading to greater security. But the lessons of Iraq for global terrorists and rogue states might not be what the United States expected. While U.S. Undersecretary of State John Bolton observed that "a number of regimes will draw the appropriate lesson from Iraq that the pursuit of weapons of mass destruction is not in their national interest," the opposite seemed to be the case.[58] Indeed, North Korea believed that the lesson of Iraq is that it can only defend itself from the United States by developing a nuclear deterrent. Not surprisingly, this led to its nuclear test in 2006, a development that the United States, bogged down in Iraq, was unable to prevent. Despite its denials, Iran also appears to be developing nuclear weapons of its own, with concerns being expressed by the UN watchdog, the International Atomic Energy Agency.[59] The lesson that Iraq taught North Korea and Iran was clear: both have to develop nuclear weapons in order to deter a U.S. attack on them, given that the Bush administration had openly named them, together with Iraq, as part of the "Axis of Evil."

Implications for Regional Security

The U.S. attack on Iraq also altered the geopolitics of the Middle East. Under Saddam Hussein, there was a relatively stable regional balance of power between the putative regional power, Iran, and the rest of the Muslim world. Despite the fact that Shiites in Iraq are in the majority, Saddam Hussein exploited Shiite divisions and also used a mixture of bribery and outright force to maintain minority Sunni control of the country. In the north, the restive Kurdish were also kept in check with open brutality, though the Kurdish were able to assert autonomy following the First Gulf War due to the establishment of a "no fly zone" in northern Iraq, which was enforced by the U.S. Air Force.

The U.S. invasion in 2003 however, overthrew the Saddam regime and unraveled the intricate system that kept Iraq stable and prevented external players such as Iran from interfering in its internal politics. The subsequent blunders in Iraq, which led to the outbreak of the anti-U.S. insurgency and the emergence of open civil conflict between the Sunnis and Shiites, and amongst various Shiite factions, demonstrated the poverty of U.S. knowledge of the complex tribal and ethnic nature of Iraqi politics. The United States, in destabilizing Iraq, thus opened the way for a variety of foreign players to increase their influence in Iraq. This included Al Qaeda, which brought in foreign *mujahideen* fighters, and Turkey, which through its incursion in early 2008 demonstrated its determination of preventing northern Iraq from being used as a safe haven for its own Kurdish rebels.

A chief beneficiary of the U.S. invasion of Iraq and the overthrow of the Saddam regime has been Iran. The United States failed to appreciate the wider geopolitical ramifications of its removal of the Ba'athist regime in Iraq, and appeared to have abandoned the previous policy of preventing radical Khomeni-inspired Shiite influence in Iraq, one that might go on to destabilize Saudi Arabia and other oil-rich states in the Persian Gulf, where significant numbers of Shiites reside. This was the reason why the United States had supported Iraq during the Iraq–Iran war from 1980 to 1988. Indeed, under the Reagan administration, the United States did nothing to stop Iraq from developing weapons of mass destruction, including chemical weapons such as nerve gas, which Iraq deployed on the battlefield during that conflict. The CIA also shared battlefield intelligence with Iraq.[60] Indeed, in the absence of U.S. forces, the Shiites in Iraq would eventually come under the influence of Iran. This would not only give Iran control over the vast oil wealth of the country but would also enable it to become the dominant power in the Persian Gulf. Such a scenario would be inimical to U.S. interests, given the hostility between the United States and Iran following the Iranian Revolution in 1978.

Thus, sound geopolitical calculations mean that the United States, in fact, needs a stable Iraq free from possible Iranian influence. This is not likely to happen as the U.S. invasion has resulted in a Shiite resurgence in Iraq. This resurgence is epitomized by the fact that the three key political players today have close ties with Iran. One of the largest Shiite groups is the Islamic Revolution in Iraq (SCIRI), which was based in Tehran before the U.S. invasion. Indeed, its armed wing, the Badr Corps, allegedly received money and weapons from Iran. SCIRI gained in popularity through its provision of social services to Shiites in Iraq, much like Hezbollah in Lebanon, and was thus able to build a power base in southern Iraq. Today, SCIRI is known as the Supreme Islamic Iraqi Council (ISCI) and is part of the government in Baghdad. The current prime minister, Nouri Maliki, is from the Al Da'wah party, which like SCIRI had opposed the Saddam regime and received the support of Iran. Both parties have pragmatically worked closely with the United States given the need for U.S. forces to help them consolidate power, but they remain close to Iran. In March 2008, President Mahmoud Ahmadinejad of Iran paid a landmark trip to Baghdad, where he was warmly received by Prime Minister Maliki despite the fact that the United States had accused Iran of arming Shiite militias in the south that had attacked U.S. and British troops.[61]

However, a rival Shiite powerbase emerged in post-Saddam Iraq in the form of the Mehdi Army led by Moqtada Al-Sadr, which draws its support from poor Shiites in Iraq. The United States has alleged that Iran has supplied Moqtada with weapons, which have been used against U.S. troops to deadly effect, such as explosively formed penetrators (EFPs) that can penetrate armor.[62] After the Baghdad government decided to attack the Mehdi Army in early 2008 in an attempt to disarm it, its senior commanders reportedly took refuge in Iran.[63] On March 30, 2008, after 359 people had been killed on both sides, a ceasefire was brokered by Iran.[64]

It is thus clear that Iran will be a key player in Iraq after the eventual departure of U.S. forces, given its geographical propinquity as a next-door neighbor as well as its close ties with all the major Shiite groups in Iraq. This represents a most unsatisfactory outcome for the United States and its allies in the Middle East, as Iraq provides Iran with much greater opportunities to expand its influence in the region. Thus, apart from Al Qaeda, Iran has been the other major beneficiary of the U.S. invasion of Iraq. The U.S. invasion has irretrievably altered the geopolitics of the Middle East, one that has more or less existed since the end of World War II. Despite outward efforts to remain together, the unitary state of Iraq has, to all intents and purposes, ended no matter how hard the United States tries to patch it back together. This is because the Kurds are determined to have their own state in the north, and the Sunni Arabs do not want to be ruled by Shiites, whom they perceive as agents of Iran and the United States. Iran has emerged as a key winner, set to dominate a post-U.S.-occupied Iraq and further afield. It is a situation that the Reagan administration in the 1980s and the subsequent administration of Bush (Sr.) that the United States had wanted to avoid, which explained Reagan's support for Saddam during the Iran–Iraq war and the halting of the U.S.-led advance in the First Gulf War in 1990–91, which preserved Saddam's regime. Not surprisingly, the United States' Arab allies in the Middle East are bewildered by the carelessness and incompetence, which characterized U.S. strategy under the Bush administration. Sunni Muslim–led regimes in the Gulf region, including Saudi Arabia have been worried in the aftermath of the U.S. invasion of Iraq about the possible spread of Shiite influence in the region, a fear that is not unfounded.[65]

The Loss of Legitimacy

More seriously, the United States has lost moral authority and legitimacy through several controversial decisions regarding the international laws of armed conflict. The first was sparked by the question of what to do with the large numbers of captured *mujahideen* and Taliban fighters in Afghanistan. On January 25, 2002, the then White House counsel Alberto R. Gonzales, in a memorandum to President Bush, stated that the president should declare the Taliban and Al Qaeda outside the coverage of the Geneva Conventions. Gonzales argued that the war on terrorism "renders obsolete Geneva's strict limitations on questioning of enemy prisoners." In other words, the use of torture would be justified.[66] President Bush thus stated that "Taliban detainees are unlawful combatants and, therefore, do not qualify as prisoners of war under Article 4 of Geneva...because Geneva does not apply to our conflict with Al Qaeda, Al Qaeda detainees also do not qualify as prisoners of war."[67] This, however, violated a key principle of international law, in that although they might be unlawful combatants, they should have received humane treatment consistent with the provisions of the Geneva Conventions. The Bush administration's stand was partially reversed in July 2007 after much criticism, when President Bush signed an executive order requiring the CIA to comply with prohibitions against "cruel, inhuman or degrading treatment" as set down in Article 3 of the Geneva Conventions.[68]

However, this still did not explicitly reverse the use of torture. Following the infamous Gonzales memorandum, a report prepared by a legal team in the U.S. Defense Department declared in March 2003 that President Bush was not bound by either an international treaty prohibiting torture or by a Federal antitorture law, as he had the authority as commander in chief to approve any technique needed to protect the nation's security.[69] This was followed up by a memorandum from the Secretary of Defense Donald Rumsfeld, which outlined 24 permitted interrogation techniques, some of which required the explicit approval of the Secretary of Defense.[70]

These controversial legal opinions and decisions thus explain the practice of "extraordinary rendition" that was practiced by the CIA. Under "extraordinary rendition," foreign terrorist suspects have been transferred to detention and interrogation in countries where U.S. and international legal safeguards do not apply. Suspects are detained and interrogated by U.S. personnel at U.S.-run detention facilities at these overseas locations, or are handed over to friendly allies for interrogation, under which they would usually be tortured.[71] According to a former CIA agent, Robert Baer, "If you want a serious interrogation, you send a prisoner to Jordan. If you want them to be tortured, you send them to Syria. If you want someone to disappear—never to see them again—you send them to Egypt." In late May 2005, the *Washington Post* revealed that the CIA established its own secret facilities in Eastern Europe, Thailand, Afghanistan, and at Guantanamo Bay.[72]

The *Newsweek* expose in May 2004 of the abuses, involving torture, sexual abuse, and humiliation at the U.S.-run Abu Ghraib prison in Baghdad shocked the U.S. public and outraged international opinion.[73] The lax moral standards accompanying the contentious legal opinions justifying the suspension of international law and the use of torture under the Bush administration inevitably led to the Abu Ghraib scandal. The publication of a series of photographs taken by soldiers at the prison revealed shocking abuses meted out to the prisoners.[74] Further investigations revealed in fact that most of the victims were not even terrorists but common criminals charged for offenses ranging from theft to rape. Thus, *Newsweek* concluded that "the Abu Ghraib torturers were just having a good, if sadistic, time."[75] This indicated a shocking laxity in military discipline, and a breakdown in the strict ethical standards, which ought to have governed the behavior of U.S. troops. In Iraq and in the Muslim world, the Abu Ghraib scandal epitomized the loss of moral direction of the Bush administration.[76]

U.S. unilateralism in favor of a military-oriented approach and the loss of its moral legitimacy have seriously eroded an important strategic strength that the United States had possessed, viz. its soft power. An important lesson that must be learnt after the failures in Iraq is that despite its overwhelming military power, the United States cannot have its own way everywhere and must instead make full use of multilateral alliances and institutions to legitimize and more effectively deal with transnational security threats that it cannot, in the long run, manage effectively on its own. In order to obtain the cooperation of others, it has also to learn to use soft power to persuade its allies and the Muslim world of its moral legitimacy in the war against global terrorism. That the United States had managed to squander its own legitimacy in such a short space of time has been breathtaking, especially given the worldwide sympathy and support it commanded immediately following the events of 9/11. Instead of the United States, it is Al Qaeda that is today seen, at least in significant sections of the Muslim world, as being morally legitimate, although many Muslims do not share its radical ideology, a stunning strategic triumph for it and an equally astonishing reversal for the United States, with deleterious consequences in the long run in the GWOT. Acutely embarrassed by the stain of Guantanamo, Abu Ghraib, renditions, and torture, as well as aware of the need to reclaim moral legitimacy, the true source of the U.S. power, one of President Obama's first acts upon his inauguration in January 2009 has been to sign executive orders outlawing the use of torture and ordering the detention centre at Guantanamo Bay to close within a year. According to President Obama, the United States would continue to fight terrorism but it would maintain "our values and our ideals."[77] This marked a major turnaround in U.S. counterterrorism policy but the damage from the many serious strategic mistakes of the Bush administration, to U.S. alliances, the international system and to U.S. soft power, would take much longer to repair.

In the final analysis, the Bush administration's decision to attack Iraq has been a major and catastrophic mistake. It has led to more uncertainty and less security in the international system, damaged U.S. alliances, altered Middle Eastern geopolitics, eroded the soft power of the United States, compromised the battle against Al Qaeda–inspired global terrorism, and finally, has turned out to be catastrophic for the unfortunate people of Iraq.

Most seriously, unilateral action in Iraq has severely damaged the international system and undermined the progress of international norms and international law. If the world's most powerful state, and hitherto the strongest supporter of the international system chose to flout the very system it supported, why should others not do the same in pursuit of their national interests? In retrospect, the question that must be asked is: Was Iraq worth the price of undermining the international system that has by and large preserved a measure of peace and stability since 1945? Was Iraq even necessary in the global war against terror? Worse, had the United States not been distracted by an unnecessary and ultimately debilitating war in Iraq, Al Qaeda would not have been able to survive and regroup in northwest Pakistan. More seriously, Al Qaeda today flourishes as a global insurgency, with its leaders and ideology, aided largely by U.S. mistakes such as attacking Iraq, and the commitment of serious human rights abuses epitomized by Abu Ghraib, able to reach out to a global Muslim audience it could not appeal to prior to those seminal events on 9/11.

The question that Joseph Nye posed is thus indeed appropriate— Will this generation of U.S. leaders fail what Henry Kissinger has called its historic test: to use preponderant U.S. power to achieve an international consensus behind widely accepted norms that will protect American values in a more uncertain future?[78] This appears to be the challenge—an enormous one—that the Bush administration has bequeathed President Obama.

CHAPTER FIVE

The Continuing Threat and Why the United States Failed

Assessing the Terrorist Threat

In a National Intelligence Estimate published in July 2007, U.S. intelligence assessed that Al Qaeda's central leadership has been able, since 2005, to regenerate the core capabilities needed to conduct attacks on the U.S. homeland. This was reiterated in the Annual Threat Assessment presented to the U.S. Congress in February 2008. According to the assessment, there had been progress in thwarting terrorist plots in Europe and the Middle East, and Al Qaeda in Iraq (AQI) had suffered major setbacks. Nonetheless, the assessment asserted that "Al Qaeda and its terrorist affiliates continue to pose significant threats to the United States at home and abroad, and Al Qaeda's central leadership based in the border area of Pakistan is its most dangerous component." According to the assessment, Al Qaeda has been able to retain a safe haven in the tribal areas of Pakistan bordering Afghanistan, which has provided it with many of the same advantages it had when it had bases in Afghanistan under the Taliban. Thus, Pakistan's Federally Administered Tribal Areas (FATAs) now serve as a staging area to support attacks in Afghanistan as well as a location for the training of new terrorist operatives for attacks in Pakistan, the Middle East, Asia, Europe, and the United States. An emerging concern is the influx of Western recruits, which will make it easier for Al Qaeda to plan future attacks on the West.[1]

The same assessment reported that while Al Qaeda had lost many senior operational planners over the years, its adaptable decision-making process and depth of skilled operatives have enabled it to replenish its

..nks. Al Qaeda's modus operandi has also changed. Osama bin Laden and his deputy, Ayman Al-Zawahiri, no longer run the organization on a day-to-day basis but continue to provide strategic leadership, inspiration, and unity. The threat from various Al Qaeda affiliates, associated groups, and networks all over the world has instead grown.[2] This assessment appears to endorse the arguments put forward by Bruce Hoffman in his testimony to U.S. Congress in February 2006, in which he observed that Al Qaeda had now decentralized into an amorphous network, with its worldwide affiliates now at the forefront of terrorist attacks.[3]

The intelligence assessment revealed two alarming aspects in the evolving threat of global terrorism. The first is growing concern over the potential emergence of new post-Al Qaeda networks growing out of Iraq, just as Al Qaeda itself emerged from the Afghanistan of the 1980s. AQI, it is feared, may leverage on its external networks, including those in Europe, to support external operations. The assessment thus expressed concern that as the U.S.-inflicted significant damage to it in Iraq, it might shift resources to mounting more attacks outside of Iraq, including possibly in the U.S. homeland.[4] Indeed, precedents of external attacks already exist, such as those planned or carried out by its then leader, Abu Musab Al-Zarqawi, in Jordan. In 2004, he plotted an audacious plan to use chemical weapons to attack the intelligence headquarters in Amman in 2004.[5] In November 2005, coordinated suicide bombings planned by AQI in Amman targeted Western hotels, killing 59 people.[6] Al-Zarqawi's prominence in Iraq and also links with radical Islamist networks and cells in the Middle East and Europe made him the de facto operations commander of Al Qaeda, to which he had pledged allegiance, until his own death in 2006. However, the *mujahideen* and radical Islamist network centered on Iraq that he helped to build have not been defeated and may instead have the potential to pose a serious terrorism threat beyond Iraq itself.

The second alarming aspect is evidence of the emergence of "homegrown" extremists inspired by militant ideology but without receiving any operational direction from Al Qaeda. According to the assessment:

> The spread of radical Salafi Internet sites that provide religious justification for attacks, increasingly aggressive and violent anti-Western rhetoric and actions by local groups, and growing numbers of radical, self-generating cells in Western countries that identify with violent Salafi objectives, all suggest growth of a radical and violent segment among the West's Muslim populations.[7]

Indeed, analysts have warned of a third radical Islamist terrorist wave, enabled by the Internet. According to Marc Sageman, this third wave has sprung up organically, linking virtually with other networks through cyberspace. The Internet has provided opportunities for young, bored Muslims to self-radicalize after reading or watching Islamist propaganda, and to link up with other like-minded individuals or groups. After studying the cases of 500 known terrorists, Sageman also concluded, interestingly, that no single characteristic explains why someone became a terrorist. However, in the majority of cases he examined, there was a shared relationship, indicating the importance of social bonds. Indeed, he noticed that small groups of *jihadists* usually organized as a group of trusted friends or relations, and have not been the result of direct Al Qaeda recruitment.[8]

There is already evidence that self-radicalized local militants are emerging as a threat. In 2006, seven homegrown would-be terrorists were charged over a plot to destroy the Sears Tower in Chicago as well as the FBI building in North Miami Beach.[9] In 2007, five men from a homegrown cell were charged with conspiring to attack U.S. soldiers with grenades and assault rifles at Fort Dix in New Jersey.[10] In 2006, two self-radicalized local Muslims who had planned to attack targets in Washington such as the World Bank and the Pentagon were detained.[11] The New York Police Department also released a report in August 2007, citing ten recent plots that were developed by homegrown militants with little or no support from Al Qaeda.[12] Although such terrorist plots have not been well-organized, and indeed have been amateurish, they point to the future trajectory of the amorphous global terrorist challenge that is being enabled by the Internet.

Predictions of the future trajectory of the terrorist threat are necessarily speculative and fraught with uncertainty. But forecasters, reflecting the apprehensions of many analysts, have come to some interesting possibilities. According to Marvin J. Cetron, for instance, terrorist ranks are growing worldwide. He notes the negative impact of the Iraq conflict, with militants fanning out across the globe after fighting there, threatening both the West and its allies, especially Saudi Arabia. He predicts, less convincingly, that the terrorists will eventually obtain weapons of mass destruction (instead, it is more likely that attacks, at least in the short-term, will follow the more conventional path of using explosives and suicide bombers, albeit with greater innovation to achieve mass casualties, such as in 9/11). Finally, he asserts that terrorists will rise to power in government. Cetron presents a list of states at risk, such as Sudan, Syria, Pakistan, Afghanistan, states of the former Soviet Union, and the Gulf States. He argues though that the state most at risk is Saudi Arabia, where it is plausible that an Islamist revolution led or inspired by Osama bin Laden could take over Riyadh, with dire consequences for the U.S. economy and U.S. national security, given the United States' deep dependence on oil imported from the Middle East.[13] Such predictions might sound alarmist, but it must be remembered that it was the failure of imagination that had prevented the United States from taking Al Qaeda seriously before 9/11. From the events of 9/11, despite many setbacks, Al Qaeda's challenge through its ideological appeal has been remarkably broad, strategic. and long-term in nature.

Explaining U.S. Failures

The broad radical Islamist challenge as it has evolved can be contrasted with the very mixed counterterrorism performance of one of its key targets, the United States. While the United States demonstrated its superb military prowess in making short work of the regimes in both Afghanistan and Iraq, it soon found itself mired in an insurgency in Iraq and facing a resurgent Taliban in Afghanistan. Globally, the threat of Al Qaeda–inspired terrorism has grown exponentially despite Al Qaeda's loss of many commanders and operatives since 9/11. This suggests that while the United States might have won a number of tactical battles, it has suffered severe strategic reverses. It has failed to galvanize a global alliance and build a consensus on a strategy to counter the challenge of global terrorism. The failure of the United States to do so can be attributed to the alienation of its own allies through its controversial actions such as the invasion of Iraq, the loss of its legitimacy in the international arena through its unilateral approach, and the dissipation of its soft power through policies and actions, which many deem to be illegitimate. More seriously, it has destroyed its own standing in the Muslim world, where the true center of gravity in the global war on terror lies, sending some into the extremist fold. In stumbling into Iraq, it has lost over 4,000 dead and 30,000 wounded by January 2009, stretched the U.S. armed forces to a breaking point, and would, according to one estimate, have squandered some $3 trillion in war costs, a staggering price for the poor payout, namely, a civil conflict in Iraq, an unnecessary war that has helped the radical Islamist cause and an Iraq that would probably end up in the orbit of Iran.[14]

In explaining the U.S. failures in the global war on terror, including its disastrous stumble into Iraq, Francis Fukuyama is well-qualified to make a judgment. In 1989, he wrote the celebrated article, "The End of History," in which he lauded the "total exhaustion of viable systematic alternatives to Western liberalism" as a result of the defeat of communism and the end of the cold war. This, he believed, would herald a new age marked by democracy and the spread of liberal ideals.[15] In 2007, however, he acknowledged that he had not anticipated that "US behavior and misjudgments would make anti-Americanism a chief fault-line of global politics."[16]

Fukuyama listed four key mistakes made by the Bush administration. The first has been the doctrine of preemption, which was broadened to include Iraq and other "rogue states." The cost of such a purely military approach was too high to be realistic, even for a superpower like the United States. The second miscalculation was failing to anticipate the global reaction to the U.S. exercise of its post–cold war hegemonic power. The third mistake was to overestimate the effectiveness of conventional military power in dealing with weak states and transnational terrorist networks, epitomized by the U.S. failure to bring stability to Iraq after occupying it. Finally, the Bush administration's use of power "lacks not only a compelling strategy or doctrine, but also simple competence." Fukuyama concluded however, that the fault, in the final analysis, did not lie with the mistakes made by the Bush administration but with an international system without checks and balances that tempted a hegemon to use its power with less and less restraint.[17]

Thus, the strategic failures and mistakes that have characterized the global war on terror and which led to the invasion of Iraq and its aftermath can be attributed to a number of factors, such as the failure in the decision-making process, ineffective intelligence, incompetence, and a dysfunctional international system. However, Fukuyama missed asking the real question: What are the fundamental causes behind these failures?

There are two key causes of the U.S. failures. The first is the American "way of war," in other words, the way the United States has used its vast military power to secure its interests. Recent literature has suggested that it is the perception of military power by the United States and how it is to be utilized that shaped the kinetic, military-oriented response to the events of 9/11. Seen in this prism, the U.S. response makes sense. The second is the failure of grand strategy and more broadly of strategic leadership. The masterful use of grand strategy by the United States can be seen in its successfully defeating Germany and Japan in World War II, and subsequently having the foresight to implement a grand strategic plan to contain communism. This began with the simultaneous planning to win the peace while World War II was still on. Thus, as soon as the Axis powers capitulated, the United States put into place its far-sighted plans to rebuild Germany and Japan, a Marshal Plan to prevent a communist takeover in Europe, and rebuilding international institutions and alliances around the world. This grand strategy led ultimately to the demise of communism in the Soviet bloc and the end of the cold war. However, no similar grand strategy had characterized the Bush administration's approach. Instead, there has been a lack of strategic foresight and clarity.

The American Way of War

The U.S. invasion of Iraq and the subsequent conflict has, in the words of Isaiah Wilson, the official U.S. Army historian of the Iraq war in 2003, "become the poster-child of America's failures at winning the peace in its war-fights abroad."[18] According to Wilson, "Iraq evidences America's failure to effectively pre-empt, and after initiating a war, restore the peace. 9/11 shows America's failure at identifying a looming threat and taking measures to prevent it."[19]

This U.S. failure can be attributed to what is called the American "way of war." The seminal work on this subject appeared long before the Iraq debacle, in the form of Russell F. Weigley's work in 1973.[20] Weigley argued, in a study of strategy and policy that developed in the United States from the War of Independence, that there has emerged a uniquely American Way of War. From the Civil War onwards, the United States had adopted a strategy of annihilation when it came to fighting wars, a consequence of the growth of U.S. industrial and military power. Such a strategy of annihilation was similar to the Clausewitzian ideal of the destruction of an enemy's armed forces and the complete over-throw of the enemy.[21] As Echevarria commented much later in 2004, the American concept of war "rarely extended beyond the winning of battles and campaigns to the gritty work of turning military victory into strategic success." Consequently, the American approach to war has been more a way of battle than an actual way of war. Thus, Echevarria asserted that "the American way of battle has not yet matured into a way of war."[22] Echevarria conceded that this is not really unique to the United States, and that the U.S. approach is similar to the overall Western approach to warfare. According to Echevarria, the European approach is best typified by the Prussian approach under Moltke, who although acknowledged the initial importance of the logic of war, insisted that its grammar took precedence during the actual fighting. In other words, once the war started, it was a question of winning the battles, which would accomplish most, if not all, of one's objectives. Thus, while politics brought war into being, war existed as a violent alternative to politics, rather than its logical extension. It is this perspective of war, rather than Clausewitz's view of policy and war as a logical continuum, that sums up the Western way of warfare.[23] This contrasts, for instance, with other forms of warfare, such as the revolutionary warfare advocated by Mao Tse-tung, in which the politics–war nexus is much closer and where indeed, political objectives always take precedence over the military instrument.

The United States has had considerable experience in fighting insurgencies, for instance, in the Philippines at the turn of the twentieth century and more recently, in places such as Bosnia, Kosovo, and Somalia. Overall, however, the U.S. performance in nonconventional warfare has been poor. The Vietnam War ought to have taught the United States useful lessons in dealing with insurgences, but the U.S. military's efforts to expunge the memory of the disastrous Vietnam campaign prevented it from learning what actually went wrong.[24] Instead, the military leadership drew the wrong conclusions from Vietnam, arguing, as U.S. General William Depuy did, that Vietnam had been an aberration in the historical trend of warfare and that the future would lie in armored warfare and the combined arms divisions in the fighting of large conventional wars.[25] Some even argued that it was the failure to fight conventionally that led to defeat in Vietnam.[26]

Instead of learning how to fight insurgencies, the United States came to the conclusion that it should avoid insurgent–type conflicts and only fight large conventional wars in which the U.S. technological superiority and massive firepower would ensure decisive victory. This curious way of learning from one's previous mistakes can in many ways be attributed to the prevailing "big war" culture within the U.S. military, one that has been supported by the vested interests of the military industrial complex and the bureaucratic interests of the Defense Department. The U.S. military hoped to refight World War II–type conventional battles in which the lethality of new military technology would help it overwhelm and decisively annihilate any conventional state opponent.

The post-Vietnam strategy is embodied in the so-called Weinberger Doctrine, which was announced in 1984 by Secretary of Defense Caspar Weinberger and later reiterated as the Powell Doctrine under General Colin Powell when he was chairman of the Joint Chiefs of Staff (JCS). The doctrine basically stated the conditions that must exist before the United States would commit forces into battle: the United States would not commit troops into battle without support from Congress and the people; it must have clearly defined political and military objectives should it choose to do so; it would use force in an overwhelming manner to achieve victory; the United States would only use force in defense of its vital interests or those of its allies; and, the use of force should be a last resort.[27] Thus, instead of learning to fight a full spectrum of conflicts, the United States decided to limit its involvement only to situations where it could prevail through the use of overwhelming conventional military power. This, however, was also a practical response to the post-Vietnam aversion to casualties, whether it was one's own or the inevitable civilian collateral damage that one's adversary might suffer.

However, the constraints which limited the use of force as an instrument of the state were to be gradually lifted throughout the 1980s as a result of a process of technological transformation known as the Revolution in Military Affairs (RMA). The RMA in the United States began with the concept of the "systems of systems" developed by Admiral William Owens. Such a new way of warfare would be made possible through a revolution in surveillance and electronic capabilities that can dispense with the age-old problem of the "fog of war," by providing superb battlefield awareness, thus enabling one to locate the opponent as well as to know the disposition of one's own forces in real time. Together with precision strike capabilities and an integrated systems approach to ensure seamless harmony among all the different parts of the vast U.S. military, this will enable devastating precision attacks over long distances, thereby reducing time and space as constraints. The opponent within an expanded battlespace could thus be attacked simultaneously and continuously. As Krepinevich noted, "the new structure of warfare integrates and synchronizes redundant, multiservice war-fighting systems in simultaneous attacks on the enemy throughout his entire depth and in the space above him as well."[28]

The RMA promised to restore the use of force as a viable and even preferred instrument of choice in the pursuit of political objectives. The allure of precision attack that could shorten wars, ensure decisive victory, and yet minimize both collateral damage to civilians and to one's own armed forces, promised quick, decisive wars in the face of the public aversion to casualties or prolonged conflict. The Gulf War of 1990–91 appeared to prove the efficacy of the emerging RMA, as the world was treated to an astonishing display of U.S. might and precision involving the use of precision-guided munitions, such as air-to-ground missiles and Tomahawk cruise missiles launched from ships anchored from afar. When the ground offensive began after weeks of massive air strikes, it was almost an anticlimax as Iraqi units disintegrated or simply fled. Fears of being bogged down in a long conflict with Iraq's armed forces, at the time one of the world's largest, did not eventuate as the U.S.-led coalition easily defeated Saddam's shell-shocked forces and restored the status quo when Iraqi troops were forced from Kuwait.

To proponents of air power, it appeared to validate the technology, operational concepts and doctrine that would revolutionize the U.S. approach to fighting wars, and thus support their contention that future wars could be won by air power alone. Thus, Lawrence Freedman noted that it was the Gulf War that had launched the RMA. However, he also observed that in the post–cold war era, without the threat of a nuclear exchange and a very strong superpower opponent, military planners had the luxury of preparing for a war as they would like to have fought, and were thus able to show what could be done in the Gulf War of 1990–91. Although this appeared to validate a particular line of technological and doctrinal development, Freedman warned presciently that "whether or not this presaged a revolution in military affairs depended on whether future patterns of conflict would offer similar opportunities."[29] In other words, would the military solution being constructed fit the shape of future security threats?

What was revealing was the officially commissioned study of the role of air power in the Gulf War, entitled *The Gulf Air War Survey*. While the survey documented the successes of airpower, both principal authors, Eliot Cohen and Thomas Keaney, also pointed out a number of deficiencies, such as the failure to find and destroy any of Saddam's Scud missiles. They also cautioned that many aspects of the air campaign employed tried and tested methods, such as the use of precision munitions and the tactical suppression of enemy air defenses. Cohen and Keaney were at pains to point out that a real RMA required not just technology but also organizational changes and doctrinal development, thereby needing a great deal of time and effort to put into effect.[30] The Survey thus hinted strongly at the need to be realistic in assessing whether air power had really come of age and if a true revolution had occurred as a result of the Gulf War.

However, whatever caution that was urged by objective analysis was soon dispensed with. To the neoconservatives who came to dominate the Bush administration from 2000, military transformation promised to underpin the aggressive preemptive approach that they were promoting. Thus, Secretary of Defense Donald Rumsfeld was an enthusiastic proponent of the New American Way of War from the outset. He set up a special office within the Defense Department to pursue the vision of military transformation, known as the Office of Force Transformation (OFT). This was done to fulfill the mandate laid down by President Bush himself, who declared, when he became Commander-in-Chief, that "we must build forces that draw upon the revolutionary advances in the technology of war that will allow us to keep the peace by redefining war on our terms." Bush declared that he was "committed to building a future force that is defined less by size and more by mobility and swiftness, one that is easier to deploy and sustain, one that relies more heavily on stealth, precision weaponry and information technologies."[31]

In 2002, after the initial stunning U.S. success in removing the Taliban regime in Afghanistan, Donald Rumsfeld wrote a celebratory piece in *Foreign Affairs*, in which he extolled the marriage of RMA-type precision strike capabilities with the use of special forces and local allies on the ground to rout the Taliban. In describing the key battle of Mazar-i-Sharif that set into motion the Taliban collapse, Rumsfeld lauded how "that day, on the plains of Afghanistan, the nineteenth century met the twenty-first century and defeated a dangerous and determined adversary—a remarkable achievement."[32] Within a month of the 9/11 terrorist attacks, the United States had carried out air strikes on Taliban and Al Qaeda bases in Afghanistan, using heavy bombers such as the B1 Lancer, B2 Spirit, and B52 Stratofortress, carrier-based fighter-bombers such as the F-18 Hornet, and cruise missiles launched from naval vessels. This was followed by a ground offensive, which consisted of U.S. Special Forces and the opposition Northern Alliance which had been battling the Taliban, backed by U.S. air power. Mullah Mohammed Omar, the leader of the Taliban, and the senior Al Qaeda leadership including Osama bin Laden, fled across the border to shelter among sympathetic Pashtun tribes in northwestern Pakistan, a lawless zone which the central government in Pakistan has never managed to control.

Rumsfeld believed that the U.S. experiences on 9/11 and in the subsequent campaign in Afghanistan had reinforced the need to move the U.S. defense posture in the direction of military transformation. He thus outlined the six transformational goals that the Defense Department should focus on: protect the U.S. homeland and bases overseas; project and sustain power in distant theaters; deny sanctuary to enemies of the United States; protect information networks from attack; use information technology to help U.S. forces fight jointly; and finally, to maintain unhindered access to space and to protect U.S. space capabilities from enemy attack.[33] He also reiterated that the United States would fight wars unilaterally if need be, on the grounds that wars "should not be fought by committee." Rumsfeld asserted that "defending the

United States requires prevention and sometimes pre-emption...the best—and, in some cases, the only—defense is a good offence."[34]

The new approach however, was problematic for a number of reasons. The transformational goals appeared to emphasize the blunt kinetic instrument of military force with little appreciation of how it functioned within the context of a broader and more holistic strategic approach that could achieve concrete political objectives. The kinetic, military-oriented approach indicated a lack of clarity as to how the United States should respond to the emerging threat of global terrorism. The new U.S. approach of the unilateral use of force that Rumsfeld proclaimed also did not make sense, given the multilateral and political approaches that must be taken in dealing with a complex historical social phenomenon such as global terrorism. Moreover, how would Al Qaeda be able to carry out an attack on U.S. space capabilities? The reference here to enemy attacks to such capabilities would only make sense if it meant peer state competitors to U.S. dominance, for instance, a rising China. Finally, preemption would be problematic if the military instrument was to be used without regard to international laws and norms for a variety of purposes designed to advance the U.S. national interest, as it would erode the global legitimacy of the United States, the very ingredient that gave the United States such global political power and influence since 1945.

Nonetheless, any doubts were quickly dismissed in the aftermath of the U.S. attack on Iraq. In March 2003, the United States invaded Iraq, to the chorus of international condemnation, including from its own European and Muslim allies.[35] The lead-up to the invasion was also preceded by unprecedented conflict between the U.S. Army and the neoconservative political leadership. Led by General Eric Shinseki, the Army Chief of Staff, the U.S. Army had been alarmed at the cutbacks to troop levels in favor of the greater use of technology, particularly expensive air and naval platforms. Shinseki was also concerned over the very optimistic assumptions that the Bush administration had adopted in the lead-up to invading Iraq. The Bush administration assumed that a transformed U.S. military, using overwhelming airpower and an economy of ground forces, would easily overpower Iraq. It also assumed that the aftermath would see local Iraqis welcoming the U.S. attack and occupation, while Iraq's massive oil resources would pay for the reconstruction of the country.

Given his own experience in Vietnam and Bosnia, Shinseki doubted if it could be done on the cheap and with few troops on the ground, as he realized that the complicated ethnic situation in Iraq would require far greater numbers of troops to dominate the ground than Rumsfeld felt necessary. Thus, while the Defense Department felt that about 100,000 troops would be required, Shinseki, in his now much-quoted answer to a question during his testimony before the Senate Armed Services Committee in February 2003, stated that "several hundred thousand troops" would be needed, particularly to restore and maintain a stable, safe, and secure environment for the population after the fighting had ended. This was rejected by Deputy Defence Secretary, Paul Wolfowitz, who described the general's view as "wildly off the mark," arguing that there was no history of ethnic strife in Iraq unlike in Bosnia or Kosovo, that Iraqis would welcome a U.S.-led liberation force, and that the nations that opposed war with Iraq would likely sign up to help rebuild it.[36]

Shinseki was unceremoniously retired after that and replaced by more amenable army leadership. According to journalist Thomas Ricks, at his retirement ceremony on June 11, 2003, Rumsfeld and other top civilian leaders did not turn up. Wolfowitz apparently asked to come but did not get an invitation.[37] The poor relations between the U.S. Army and the civilian leadership on the eve of a major war was extraordinary but it did demonstrate the contempt with which many in the U.S. military leadership felt toward the neoconservative civilians whose prescriptions they felt were ill-informed and unrealistic. Indeed, Shinseki spoke obliquely about the difference between command and effective leadership in his retirement speech. After that, according to Thomas Ricks, Shinseki disappeared from public view, like "a samurai ashamed of the behavior of his shogun."[38] Shinseki was to return, almost triumphantly, in 2009 to take charge of Veteran Affairs in the new Obama administration, an appointment which seemed aimed at alleviating the U.S. Army grievance over the treatment of its top commander by the previous Bush administration.

The U.S. strategy in Iraq in 2003 was dubbed "Shock and Awe" for the intensity, accuracy and speed of its offensive. The United States achieved a stunning victory unparalleled in speed and decisiveness. Compared to 560,000 U.S. and allied troops in the First Gulf War which lasted 48 days and cost 365 casualties, the Second Gulf War saw the United States and Britain deploy about 100,000 troops and achieve victory in 26 days (up to the fall of Baghdad) at a cost of 160 casualties.[39]

The stunning victory, which appeared to vindicate the proponents of the RMA, led to early celebratory views. Thus, Max Boot coined the phrase "The New American Way of War" in which he proclaimed that: "spurred by the dramatic advances in information technology, the US military has adopted a new style of warfare that eschews the bloody slogging matches of old... this approach was put on display in the recent invasion of Iraq, and its implications for the future of American war fighting are profound."[40] He concluded, as a result of the low casualties, that "the victory in Iraq shows that the military is making impressive progress toward making the American way of war both more effective and more humane."[41]

Subsequent problems in Afghanistan and Iraq, however, proved that the initial conventional successes have been illusory. Stunning battle-field successes have not translated into meeting political objectives, that is, stable, relatively democratic countries firmly within the U.S. impe-rial orbit. In Afghanistan, the failure to decisively rout the Taliban and the successful flight of both Taliban and Al Qaeda senior commanders, including Osama bin Laden, have returned to haunt the country. The fall of the Taliban regime failed to unite the country, instead bringing into power a disparate coalition of warlords, which has limited the authority of the national government in Kabul headed by Hamid Karzai.

The Taliban and Al Qaeda fled across the porous border into the lawless northwestern provinces of Pakistan, where they have found a secure base from which to regroup, recruit, train, and plan attacks against coalition forces in Afghanistan. Despite strong criticism voiced by a number of governments with the United States over its invasion of Iraq in 2003, NATO and non-NATO, commitment in Afghanistan numbered 35,500 from 37 countries in May 2007.[42] Yet this has not been enough because of the resurgence of the Taliban and the fact that some NATO countries refuse to allow their troops to get into harm's way, leaving the real fighting to U.S., British and Canadian troops. By January 2009, 1,055 international troops, including 637 U.S., 142 British and 107 Canadian soldiers, had been killed.[43]

This was, however, nothing compared to the level of violence that accompanied the anti-U.S. insurgency and sectarian conflict in Iraq, which broke out after the U.S. invasion in 2003. By 2004, the insurgency was in full swing, consisting of a motley group of Iraqi nationalists, ex-Baarthists, and Al Qaeda-linked radical Islamists. To this was added the complication of the anti-U.S. militia forces of the radical Shiite cleric, Moqtada al-Sadr, the Mehdi Army, which has clashed with U.S. and British forces as well as with the forces controlled by the Iraqi govern-ment in Baghdad. By the end of January 2009, the total number of U.S. casualties stood at 4,236 U.S. troops, with about 30,000 wounded.[44]

Instead of demonstrating the superiority of U.S. military power, Afghanistan and Iraq have instead validated the prescient observation of Steven Metz, who pointed out in 2001, on the eve of 9/11, that the

RMA would not work against terrorists and insurgents. Metz pointed out that because nonstate enemies can focus and specialize, they pose extraordinary challenges for advanced states. According to Metz:

> The current RMA...is focused almost entirely on power projection against Soviet-style opponents relying on conventional armor-heavy, combined arms operations. The perfect enemy for the current RMA is a regional power like Iraq or North Korea with a rigid, centralized decision-making system and armed forces based on limited-range, easy-to-detect weapons platforms...much less attention is devoted to the development of revolutionary capabilities to counter non-state enemies.[45]

Thus, despite enormous sacrifices in humanpower and material, all that the United States has managed to do since 9/11 has been to demonstrate the weakness of its RMA-capable armed forces to asymmetric challenges, such as terrorism and insurgent wars mounted by nonstate challengers. The continued vulnerability in both the Iraq and Afghanistan theaters of the much vaunted U.S. armed forces to very basic weaponry, such as improvised explosive devices (IEDs), rocket-propelled grenade (RPG) launchers, and mortars, as well as to basic insurgent and terrorist tactics, such as suicide bombings, ambushes, assassinations, and sniper attacks, point to the failings of the current RMA, which appears fatally fixated on conventional warfare. The attacks mounted by AQI in Iraq, and by the resurgent Taliban in Afghanistan, point to the failure to achieve a decisive victory over such nonstate challengers, and hint at the obvious—that this would be a long war of attrition with possibly no decisive outcome, where the key to getting the upper hand would be political rather than military.

The Afghanistan and Iraq experiences should thus be sobering for those advocating military transformation. This is not to say that continued military development in terms of doctrine, organization, and technology is not worthwhile as there remain state challengers to security. However, it is important to recognize the limits of the current RMA. Indeed, the promise of almost bloodless, decisive warfare conducted on the cheap cannot be fulfilled. If anything, Afghanistan and Iraq suggest that there is much greater continuity than change in the nature of warfare. These theaters reiterate the fundamental, historical characteristics of war, which is destructive and violent, and reminds us of the continued need for political will, good strategy, and the preparedness to take casualties. In Clausewitzian terms, war is not a sterile scientific exercise but is subject to subjectivities such as emotion, chance, and politics. Thus, despite technological changes, which can only alter the grammar of war, the essential underlying logic and character of war remains constant—it tends to violence and can be unpredictable.[46]

The difficulties encountered by the United States and its allies in Iraq and Afghanistan have also pointed the way for potential Western adversaries to obviate the Western and U.S. advantage in superior conventional military firepower—by fighting asymmetrically. As Jeffrey Record observed, "future enemies will fight us asymmetrically—in ways that do not test out strengths, because we cannot prevent the global diffusion of our technology."[47] This could take a number of forms, such as the use of insurgency, terrorism, and niche warfare capabilities such as antitank missiles and IEDs in urban environments where the superior capabilities of conventional military forces are nullified, as Hezbollah demonstrated in its success in inflicting damage on Israel's much vaunted armored forces during Israel's attack on Lebanon in 2006. At sea, asymmetric techniques were hinted at when U.S. warships found themselves surrounded by small Iranian speedboats in an incident in the Persian Gulf in early 2008.[48] Indeed, one viable way to overwhelm large U.S. task forces would be to use swarm tactics at sea, utilizing small craft or massed cruise missiles. More significantly, the U.S. invasion of Iraq had been meant to preempt the development of weapons of mass destruction and to dissuade others from attempting to do so. But the lesson that Iran and North Korea, the other two putative U.S. targets in the Bush's "Axis of Evil" designation, learnt was simply that they had to acquire nuclear weapons in order to deter a U.S. attack. North Korea thus tested a nuclear device in 2006, while the United States, bogged down in Iraq and Afghanistan, could only look on in impotence.

Failure of Grand Strategy

As Steven Metz observed, "the US military was configured to break the will of conventional opponents through rapid decisive operations, not to break the will of an irregular opponent through protracted psychological and political actions."[49] After his own service in Iraq, British General Nigel Aylwin-Foster gave a much-read critical assessment of the performance of the U.S. military. According to him, "the US Army has developed over time a singular focus on conventional warfare, of a particularly swift and violent style, which left it ill-suited to the kind of operation it encountered as soon as conventional war-fighting ceased to be the primary focus."[50] The general concluded that the planned U.S. Army Transformation needed to focus less on generating war-fighting capability and much more on the development of a workforce that is genuinely adaptive to changes in purpose, as opposed to merely adapting to be even better at conventional war-fighting.[51]

These observations indicate the disconnect between policy and the military instrument. They point to the failure to observe a fundamental, tested dictum of Clausewitz, that is, that war is a continuation of politics by other means, not its replacement.[52] More significantly, these observations point to what some analysts have argued is the fundamental cause of U.S. failures—the lack of grand strategy, which in turn is a function of competent leadership. This explains the pyrrhic nature of the U.S. battlefield successes, as tactical battlefield success in Iraq and Afghanistan have not translated into strategic gains in the Global War on Terror (GWOT).

Instead, U.S. actions since 9/11 have had a number of negative consequences. U.S. unilateralism has destabilized the international system of norms, institutions, and laws, which however deficient offered the best hope of building the international consensus and legitimacy needed to counter the global radical Islamist terrorist challenge. U.S. actions in Iraq have also altered the regional geopolitical landscape, with uncertain consequences for the future security of the Middle East and for the United States itself. Moreover, the military-oriented, kinetic approach pursued thus far in the GWOT has failed to deal with the fundamental causes of Muslim alienation and has instead helped in the terrorist cause championed by Osama bin Laden.

Viewed from the perspective of counterterrorism, the U.S. approach has been ineffective. According to American historian Thomas Mockaitis, the term "counterterrorism" itself has come to signify a comprehensive approach to dealing with the problem of terrorism, in what in conventional war would be called grand strategy. The problem, however, is that "a truly comprehensive and effective counter-terrorism strategy has yet to be devised."[53] According to Mockaitis, grand strategy would entail addressing the causes of discontent upon which extremism feeds as well as a "hearts and minds" campaign. Drawing from the lessons of successful counterinsurgency in theatres such as Malaya in the 1950s, Mockaitis argued that a hearts and minds approach can help separate the moderates from the extremists, the first step in getting vital intelligence on terrorist whereabouts and intentions. However, such a campaign must be based on two considerations: "avoiding any action likely to drive moderates and extremists together, and taking positive steps to separate moderates from extremists."[54] As part of this grand strategy, the United States also needed an enlightened foreign policy in order to build a consensus on counterterrorism. However, in surveying the unsophisticated, military-oriented, and short-term approach of the U.S. response under the Bush administration, Mockaitis concluded that "enlightened foreign policy is...far harder to develop, deploy and sustain than an armored division."[55]

The unilateral, military-oriented strategy employed by the United States under the Bush administration had undermined efforts to build a global consensus on the strategy that must be employed to defeat Al Qaeda and its ideology. David Omand therefore concluded that "the absence of international agreement on a long-term and comprehensive counter-terrorist strategy is an increasing weakness in our collective efforts to match a developing threat."[56] This weakness may well be redressed under the new Obama administration that took power in January 2009 but building international consensus over counter-terrorism strategy will be a long and difficult road requiring much patience and diplomacy, especially given the need to repair the neglect and damage inflicted by the previous Bush administration.

Options in Iraq and Strategy in the War on Terror

One of the first steps in regaining the legitimacy that the United States and its Muslim allies need in order to regain the initiative from radical Islamists in the war for hearts and minds is a resolution to the Iraq conundrum. But this is where the serious dilemmas lie. The only way to contain and ultimately defeat the insurgency, and maintain order in a fragile environment, is to stay for many years and commit sufficient troops to doing so. But already costing half a trillion U.S. dollars and the lives of over 4,000 U.S. military personnel, the U.S. public does not support a long and expensive occupation of the country, particularly given the deep recession sparked by the subprime housing loan crisis in the United States in late 2008.

Precipitous withdrawal, however, will play into the hands of Al Qaeda and radical *jihadists* who will proclaim victory and embolden them to challenge various Arab governments throughout the Middle East, leading to greater instability. More seriously, leaving behind a precarious state with weak institutions with the potential of a deadly civil war breaking out will provide the same conditions that enable terrorist training, recruitment, and organization to flourish, eventually paving the way for more deadly terrorist attacks in the West.

It will also leave the Shiites in charge, opening the door to a massive increase in Iran's influence as well as control over Iraq's vital oil resources, and increasing its ability to destabilize the entire Persian Gulf. Thus, at issue here is how to extricate the United States from Iraq whilst somehow preventing an Iranian takeover. In fact, such a scenario is actually probable should the United States withdraw entirely, given the pro–Iranian orientation of all the major Shiite parties currently dominating the government in Baghdad. This would pose a serious threat to the stability of the Persian Gulf as Iran would be in a position to challenge the Sunni-dominated Gulf states and Saudi Arabia, particularly given their large Shiite populations. In turn, this would directly affect U.S. economic and security interests, given the deep dependence of the U.S. economy on oil. The hard fact is that energy, security, and the Middle East are deeply intertwined given the U.S. dependence on imported oil from the Middle East, and the importance of oil as a driver of the U.S. economy, which in turn underpins U.S. global power.[57] Despite the new Obama administration's stated determination to develop alternative sources of energy that would reduce the U.S. dependence on imported oil, energy independence is in reality a long way off, which means that the United States will remain hostage to political developments in the Middle East for the foreseeable future.

On the other hand, it could also be argued, withdrawal would reduce civil conflict as the main protagonist, the United States, which caused the civil conflict by siding and arming some groups against others, is no longer part of the equation. Despite potential civil war, according to this more optimistic scenario, war weariness will eventually force Sunnis, Shiites, and the Kurds to come to some sort of accommodation. Iranian influence would increase but Arab Shiites in Iraq do not necessarily welcome Iranian control. And shorn of U.S. occupiers, radical ideologues would lose the reason for their appeal. In fact, should they continue killing Shiites as they have done in the past, they would rapidly lose their legitimacy in the broader Muslim *umma* as well. But this scenario appears too optimistic, given the severity of the anti-U.S. insurgency and the high level of sectarian violence until the surge took place.

The whole Iraq debacle has serious consequences on the GWOT. A tough new generation of global *jihadists* who have honed their skills in Iraq against the world's best military force could emerge in time to challenge the rest of the Middle East and the West. There may well be more serious challenges to come from the radical Islamists. For instance, Pakistan is emerging as a key battleground on account of the growing challenge from radical Islamists and the presence of nuclear weapons.

The consequences of the ill-conceived U.S. invasion of Iraq have been profound, with major consequences not just for the GWOT but also on the U.S. body politic. The "Shock and Awe" that the world witnessed in 2001 and in 2003 when the United States attacked Afghanistan and Iraq, swiftly deposing both the Taliban and the Saddam regime, faded quickly in the light of the subsequent insurgency in Iraq and the continuing difficulties in Afghanistan as a result of the resurgence of the Taliban. Despite the acknowledgement by President Bush that the United States and the rest of the world is now engaged in "the long war" against global terrorism, the fact is that, just several years after the seminal events of 9/11, the United States appears to have been worn down psychologically by the war in Iraq and the long fight against radical Islam. As George Friedman ruefully observed, the United States has psychologically begun to tear itself apart over both Iraq and the war on terror.[58] This was reflected in the sometimes bitter partisan debate over the rights and wrongs of Iraq between the Democrats and Republicans in the run-up to the U.S. presidential elections in 2008.

Any emerging consensus among analysts of the mistakes and failures in Iraq and in the broader global war on terror do not disguise the deep unease over the future trajectory of the global terrorist and other asymmetric threats, including from nuclear-armed "rogue" states, and the ability, despite its vaunted military power and worldwide reach, of the United States in meeting these challenges. A new strategic direction thus awaited the outcome of the U.S. presidential elections at the end of 2008. A victory by the venerable Republican candidate, John McCain, would not have led to a fundamental revolution in strategy, although the slow evolution toward a more calibrated, comprehensive approach in meeting the challenge of global terrorism would have continued.

The victory by the Democrat candidate, Barack Obama, has been more interesting, as he has pledged to remove U.S. troops from Iraq. How this could be done without even more serious consequences for Middle East geopolitics, U.S. energy security, and the GWOT, however, remains to be seen.

CHAPTER SIX

The Evolution of U.S. Counterterrorism Strategy: From GWOT to COIN

The U.S. Strategy for Countering Terrorism

In March 2001, months before the 9/11 terrorist attacks, Bruce Hoffman presciently testified before the U.S. Congress on the need for a grand strategic approach to countering the evolving threat of terrorism. According to Hoffman, because terrorism has become more complex, amorphous, and transnational in nature, "the distinction between domestic and international terrorist threats is eroding." Hoffman expressed criticism of the law enforcement and criminal justice approach to countering terrorism, arguing that it is also an intelligence and national security issue. The law enforcement approach, according to Hoffman, was thus "problematical, if not dangerously myopic, and deprives the U.S. of a critical advantage in the struggle against terrorism."[1] He thus called for a "clear, comprehensive and coherent strategy," concluding that "without such a strategy, we risk embracing policies and pursuing solutions that may not only be dated, but may also have become irrelevant; we also lose sight of current and projected trends and patterns and thereby risk preparing to counter and respond to possibly illusory threats and challenges."[2]

Such a national strategy for combating terrorism was given priority following the seminal 9/11 terrorist attacks. The National Security Strategy released a year later in September 2002 declared that the objectives of the United States were to "champion aspirations for human dignity," strengthen alliances to defeat global terrorism, work with others to defuse regional conflicts, prevent states threatening the

United States with weapons of mass destruction (WMDs), transform national security institutions to meet the challenges of the twenty-first century, as well as the promotion of free markets and free trade, development, and democracy.[3] The strategy could not be said to be a coherent document, given the breathtakingly broad set of U.S. objectives that it sought to achieve.

In February 2003, President Bush unveiled the U.S. National Strategy for Combating Terrorism, the strategic guiding instrument for the Global War on Terror (GWOT). The 30-page document began with a quote from President Bush on November 6, 2001, in which the U.S. President vowed that "no group or nation should mistake America's intentions: we will not rest until terrorist groups of global reach have been found, have been stopped and have been defeated."[4] The language of the document was also couched in grand civilizational terms: "we will never forget what we are ultimately fighting for—our fundamental democratic values and way of life," which the terrorists are supposedly aiming at.[5]

The objective of the National Strategy for Combating Terrorism was to identify and defuse threats before they reached U.S. borders. A central goal is to "prevent terrorists from acquiring or manufacturing the weapons of mass destruction that would enable them to act on their worst ambitions."[6] The United States "will not hesitate to act alone . . . including acting pre-emptively against terrorists to prevent them from doing harm to our people and our country."[7] Thus, a proactive, preemptive approach was adopted. What was interesting was also its advocacy of a comprehensive approach, one that recognized that "we will not triumph solely or even primarily through military might." Instead, "we must fight terrorist networks, and all those who support their efforts to spread fear around the world, using every instrument of national power—diplomatic, economic, law enforcement, financial, information, intelligence, and military."[8] Unfortunately, what followed was a unidimensional approach based on the kinetic application of military power, not the comprehensive approach that was set out here.

The language of the new National Strategy for Combating Terrorism appeared to draw on the ideas of the advocates of the "new" terrorism, such as Bruce Hoffman, who argued that a new form of globalized, religious, millenarian terrorism had arisen since the 1990s, one that was different from the ethnopolitical terrorist groups that appeared after the end of World War II.[9] The document thus described how the new global environment has facilitated the rise of new, transnational terrorist networks such as Al Qaeda. Thus, Al Qaeda is described as "a multinational enterprise with operations in more than 60 countries," pays for its operations through criminal activities, and "use the advantage of technology to disperse leadership, training and logistics not just regionally but globally." Furthermore, such new terrorist groups have become less dependent on state sponsors and have increasingly become self-sufficient by exploiting the global environment to support their operations. Thus, the new terrorist threat that has emerged through globalization is "a flexible, transnational network structure, enabled by modern technology and characterized by loose interconnectivity both within and between groups."[10]

The understanding of Al Qaeda and what it represented, that is, a new form of global terrorism, also drew on the work of Rohan Gunaratna, whose seminal book *Inside Al Qaeda*, was the first in-depth study of Al Qaeda to appear after 9/11. Overnight, following the events of 9/11, Gunaratna achieved a prominent international media profile as his knowledge and advice was much sought after, particularly by governments. In his book, Gunaratna asserted that Al Qaeda was "an unprecedented transnational phenomenon," and that "Al Qaeda's organizational and operational infrastructure differs markedly from other guerrilla or terrorist groups."[11] According to Gunaratna:

> …no group resembling Al Qaeda has previously emerged. Al Qaeda has moved terrorism beyond the status of a technique of protest and resistance and turned it into a global instrument with which to compete with and challenge Western influence in the Muslim world. Al Qaeda is a worldwide movement capable of mobilising a new and hitherto unimagined global conflict.[12]

The National Strategy for Combating Terrorism thus declared, in the face of this existential threat, the intention of the United States and its partners to defeat terrorist organizations of global reach. The document also spoke of victory, which it acknowledged would occur not as a single defining moment but would instead consist of a world free from the fear of terrorist attacks.[13] In terms of specifics, the strategy advocated the 4Ds—defeating terrorist organizations, denying them sanctuary and state sponsorship, diminishing the underlying conditions that terrorists seek to exploit, such as poverty, deprivation, social disenfranchisement, and unresolved political and regional disputes, and finally, to defend U.S. citizens and interests at home and abroad.[14]

Consistent with the neoconservative agenda that became dominant in Washington after 9/11, the document also concluded with a strong pitch for democracy as the antidote to terrorism and hinted strongly at a broader objective of a U.S.-dominated world order:

> Ridding the world of terrorism is essential to a broader purpose. We strive to build an international order where more countries and peoples are integrated into a world consistent with the interests and values we share with our partners—values such as human dignity, rule of law, respect for individual liberties, open and free economies, and religious tolerance. We understand that a world in which these values are embraced as standards, not exceptions, will be the best antidote to the spread of terrorism.[15]

The National Strategy for Combating Terrorism thus reflected a mix of rational assessments and neoconservative prescriptions. The strategy received an update in September 2006, when President Bush released a new document.[16] Compared to the first document in 2003, the revised National Strategy appeared defensive and even ideological, written to justify the course of action that the Bush administration had undertaken but that had come under fierce criticism from even its own supporters and allies.

The revised National Strategy for Combating Terrorism claimed that the United States had "made substantial gains in degrading the Al Qaeda network," lauded the implementation of the controversial Patriot Act, and reiterated that the promotion of democracy is the best long-term answer to Al Qaeda's agenda, though it acknowledged that "the ongoing fight for freedom in Iraq has been twisted by terrorist propaganda as a rallying cry."[17] The objective of the updated document is to set the course "for winning the War on Terror."[18] This strategy included the long-term promotion of democracy, which the document held would be the antithesis to terrorism.[19] The revised national strategy thus conveniently neglected the fact that in democratic parliamentary elections in Palestine in January 2006, Hamas was elected to power; and that democratic elections for the Iraqi National Assembly in January 2005 have put pro-Iranian religious parties in control. This championing of democracy also sounded hollow to many outside the United States and reflected a failure to appreciate the enormous damage to the U.S. soft power, legitimacy, and credibility as a result of unilateral actions such as the use of torture, renditions, military tribunals, and abuses in Iraq and on Guantanamo Bay.

The short-term strategy consisted of four parts: the prevention of attacks by terrorist networks; denying WMDs to rogue states and terrorist allies who seek to use them; denying terrorists the support and sanctuary of rogue states; and denying terrorists control of any nation that they would use as a base and launchpad for terror attacks.[20] Significantly, the document appeared to adopt a more multilateral approach, in its emphasis on "strengthening coalitions and partnerships," recognizing that "since September 11, most of our important successes against Al Qaeda and other terrorist organisations have been made possible through effective partnerships." Thus, the United States would now "ensure that…international cooperation is an enduring feature of the long war we will fight." This multilateral approach is important as "ultimately, it will be essential for our partners to come together to facilitate appropriate international, regional and local solutions to the challenges of terrorism."[21]

Compared to the earlier document of 2003, the revised national strategy was less strategic and more tactical in orientation, as well as more defensive in the light of the many criticisms of the counterterrorism strategy of the GWOT under the Bush administration. However, the comprehensive approach that was acknowledged to be necessary in the first document appeared to have been downgraded at the very time that it should have been given greater prominence in the light of the many mistakes and problems as a result of the overreliance on the use of kinetic military force. Indeed, the revised national strategy failed to acknowledge the mistakes of the previous five years, reiterating instead the need for continued operations in Iraq. It also conflated "rogue states," WMD proliferation, and terrorist groups—one that led to the quagmire in Iraq and the failure to remain focused on the threat of global terrorism, justified an extralegal approach to countering terrorism even though this had severely eroded U.S. legitimacy and soft power to the detriment of the war on hearts and minds, and reiterated the neoconservative agenda of promoting democracy as the antidote to terrorism, even though democracy could well lead to *greater* terrorism. The latter objective has also proven problematic given the perception by the rest of the world that it was really all part of the neoconservative Project for the New American Century designed to help the United States establish hegemonic global control in the post–cold war era.[22]

Fostering Intellectual and Human Capital

One curious aspect of the revised National Strategy for Combating Terrorism of 2006 is its commitment to "foster intellectual and human capital." This stems from the realization that an expert community of counterterrorism professionals would be required for a "generational struggle" in the long war against terrorism. The document stated the commitment of the United States to "establish more systematic programs for the development and education of current professionals in counterterrorism-related fields." The United States would substantially expand training for personnel throughout the government as well as counterterrorism personnel in not only existing training programs in counterterrorism policies, planning, and strategies but also in religious philosophies, languages, and "appropriate area studies." In the context of the GWOT, this could only mean Islam, Arabic, and the Middle East although naturally it was not politic to actually name them in a national strategy document. Moreover, the United States would "support multidisciplinary studies throughout our educational system to build a knowledgeable pool of counter-terrorism recruits for the future." The document pledged to "expand US foreign language education beginning in early childhood and continuing throughout formal schooling and into the workforce." Finally, fostering intellectual and human capital would also entail reaching out to international partners in academic and nongovernmental forums to enhance knowledge about the counterterrorism challenges that the United States faces.[23]

This new and somewhat belated emphasis on fostering intellectual and human capital has come about as a result of continuing criticism over the lack of professional skills and knowledge necessary to better carry out the GWOT. This, however, can be traced to the lack of investment in the necessary academic resources since the end of the cold war. In his testimony before the U.S. Congress in February 2006, several months before the revised National Strategy for Countering Terrorism was enunciated, Bruce Hoffman pointed out that the United States was stymied by the protracted insurgency in Iraq and was failing to effectively counter radical Islam's effective use of propaganda and related information operations. Hoffman argued that although many reasons have been proffered for this state of affairs, from "the diversion of attention from bin Laden and Al-Zawahiri caused by Iraq to inchoate US public diplomacy efforts," the real cause of the current stasis in the GWOT "is at once as basic as it is prosaic: we still don't know, much less, understand the enemy." Hoffman stated that what has been missing has been a "thorough and systematic understanding" of the enemy, encompassing motivation, mindset, decision-making processes, command and control relationships, and ideological constructs.[24]

Hoffman argued that the key to U.S. success in the GWOT lies ultimately in the ability to counter Al Qaeda's ideological appeal. Effectiveness in doing so will undermine Al Qaeda's message and thus hinder its ability to attract recruits to replenish its ranks. However, to do so effectively required that the United States know the enemy well. It must understand the origins, motivations, and ideology of the radical Islamist movement. Without the investment in this knowledge, Hoffman pointed out, the United States would not be able to penetrate its cells, sow discord, and dissension to weaken it from within, and would fail to preempt and prevent terrorist operations. The United States would remain on the defensive, reacting to terrorism rather than proactively anticipating the enemy's modus operandi, recruitment, and targeting.[25]

This interesting observation regarding the ignorance of the enemy on the part of the United States as lying at the heart of the many strategic mistakes it has made since the 9/11 terrorist attacks also pointed to the fact that the United States needed a more rational decision-making process and strategy focused on defeating the enemy and based on deep empirical knowledge, not on presumptions about the enemy, or directed by an ideological, normative agenda, or indeed, be side-tracked by other objectives, such as maintaining U.S. global hegemony through the promotion of democracy.

This ignorance of the enemy was observed by the U.S. diplomat Peter Galbraith in his book *The End of Iraq: How American Incompetence Created a War Without End.* Galbraith cited a meeting between President Bush and three Iraqi Americans two months before the invasion of Iraq. As the three talked about the Sunni–Shiite divide, it soon became clear that the president did not know what this was. Thus, Galbraith concluded that decision-making in the Bush administration had been marked by a "culture of arrogance," one that did not believe there was any need to do any real homework.[26] After 9/11, it was also widely acknowledged that the U.S. armed forces and security agencies lacked the requisite language and area studies skills to effectively counter terrorism. U.S. military operations in Afghanistan thus faced some daunting challenges due to the lack of personnel who could speak the local Pashtun and other languages.[27] Similarly, the shortage of Arabic speakers has been acknowledged to have hampered U.S. operations in Iraq, the interrogations of terrorist suspects in U.S. custody and also in countering *jihadist* propaganda.[28]

More serious has been the dearth of intellectual capital. A study of the profile of research and university faculty members of the U.S. Middle East Studies Association (MESA) between 1990 and 2002 revealed that senior faculty who were retiring were not being replaced and that economics, sociology, and language were areas within Middle

East studies that were potentially endangered.[29] There was decreasing student interest and faculty positions were often impermanent and nontenured. Since 9/11, a number of initiatives have helped to increase research into the Middle East but the report noted that "given the need to make up for losses in the field and to respond to the need for experts, the amount of new funding is far from lavish." Indeed, the report also noted that heightened recognition of the importance of Middle East studies had occurred at a time when state budgets and private institution endowments are in straightened circumstances.[30]

There have also been strong criticisms that Middle East studies have been ideologically biased and anti-U.S., and that the research grant process has been flawed, with conservative scholars claiming that Middle East studies has become a "tendentious, ideologically-driven lefty academic enterprise" and "an intellectual failure."[31] Khalid Phares was more scathing, commenting that "even as the war with *jihadism* is raging in the real world...the bulk of (America's) students are being educated today by an elite that refuses to teach the real history and politics of the *jihadists*...unless an intellectual revolution takes place and academic reform follows, it is unlikely that the United States will produce the talents needed for the current and future conflict of ideas."[32]

However, although criticisms from right-wing scholars could themselves be biased, there has unfortunately been a lack of debate and diversity, caused in part by the decline of social science and area studies since the end of the cold war. Indeed, there has been a general worldwide drift in academic social sciences toward neo-Marxist postpositivism after the end of the cold war, which has been hostile to realist, positivist (i.e., empirical) scholarship, and is profoundly antistate in orientation. The rise of such approaches has not been unhealthy as it has helped to promote human security, as opposed to state security, at a time of globalization, with all its attendant challenges and possibilities. But the problem has been balance, perhaps rather inelegantly put by John Mearsheimer, who accused the "post–Cold War idealists" of attempting to impose hegemony over social science discourse; he thus challenged British universities to restore a balanced approach by hiring realists in the field of international relations once more.[33] In Australia, a similar criticism has been voiced by academics frustrated at the lack of research opportunities into terrorism from a more empirical, state–centric focus due to what they perceive to be the attitude of left-wing scholars apparently bent on reinforcing an antistate discourse. The research environment has thus been described as an "Alice in Wonderland world of peer-referenced journals read only by participants in this mutually reinforcing discourse."[34]

Waging Ideological War

The observation that the key to U.S. success in the GWOT lies ultimately in the ability to counter Al Qaeda's ideological appeal is a persuasive assessment of where the center of gravity in the war on terror lies.[35] Many analysts argue that this centre of gravity resides in the hearts and minds of the Muslim *umma* or worldwide Muslim community that Al Qaeda is trying to win over. Thus, Khalid Phares noted that "the *jihadists* have constructed an imaginary community (the *umma*) bound by fear of being aggressed by an imaginary, comprehensive plot executed by a historical enemy (the *kuffar*). But if Muslims from within that *umma* were to question the story and open the windows of that darkened cell built by the fundamentalists, the light would come in and shatter the *jihadists'* worldview." Khalid concluded therefore that the battle between radical Islamists and moderates within Islam is critical in this ideological war.[36] Jason Burke also argued that the ideological battle is the key, and that the only way to ensure a future without fear and uncertainty is by targeting the spread of radical ideology and thus halt the production line of new radical terrorists.[37]

Al Qaeda's message has been simple. According to the *fatwa* or religious edict declaring war on the United States issued by Osama bin Laden in 1996:

It should not be hidden from you that the people of Islam had suffered from aggression, iniquity and injustice imposed on them by the Zionist–Crusaders alliance and their collaborators; to the extent that the Muslim's blood became the cheapest and their wealth as loot in the hands of the enemies.[38]

According to bin Laden, therefore, "utmost effort should be made to prepare and instigate the *umma* against the enemy, the American–Israeli alliance occupying the country of the two Holy Places." Bin Laden went on to claim that many "sons of the land of the two Holy Places feel and strongly believe that fighting (*jihad*) against the *kuffar* (unbeliever) in every part of the world is absolutely essential."[39] In 2006, Osama bin Laden issued another message, in which he decried the invasion of Iraq as a "Zionist crusade against Muslims."[40] He argued that "*jihad* today is an imperative for every Muslim."[41] Further, according to bin Laden:

> The epicenter of these wars is Baghdad, the seat of the *khalifate* rule. They keep reiterating that success in Baghdad will be success for the US, failure in Iraq, the failure of the US. Their defeat in Iraq will mean defeat in all their wars and a beginning to the receding of their Zionist–Crusader tide against us.[42]

The goal of the radical Islamists is not merely the defense of Islam, which they argue is under attack, but ultimately a caliphate ruled by Muslim laws or the *sharia*. Only when this happens will it be possible to have peace and justice, and for Islam to reclaim the status it once had during the caliphate in Baghdad in the eight century AD. As Khalid Phares noted, *jihadism* in the radical Islamist interpretation is not just another ideology competing for the existing world order but is an ideology trying to destroy the current world order and replace it altogether.[43]

Yet despite its extreme views and espousal of violence, Al Qaeda's message has won support from some Muslims from around the world. Opinion polls in many Muslim countries show that Osama bin Laden is seen as a hero, although many Muslims do not share his radical ideological prescriptions.[44] According to Brynjar Lia, it is Al Qaeda's simple, populist message, built upon foreign occupation, religious desecration, and economic imperialism, that appeals to the masses of the alienated in Muslim countries. These are the reasons they would fight and causes they could die for, instead of any abstract notion of an Islamic utopian state, which Al Qaeda has consciously downplayed. Another reason for Al Qaeda's success has been its global, multinational approach, in which ethnicity and nationality are not barriers to membership. It is easy to join, as today, anyone who accepts its radical ideology can be a member.[45]

It has also exploited modern communications and the Internet very well, explaining its views and what one should do to implement the radical agenda. Through mosques, small group discussions, images on the Internet, CD ROMs, videos, Internet chat rooms, *jihadist* Web sites, testimonies of martyrs, training manuals, sermons by radical preachers, Al Qaeda's message of violence has reached millions of people. This stunning success in the information war is all the more perplexing given the U.S. advantage of being at the forefront of creating the information revolution and the domination of its global media and popular culture.

The rapid spread of radical ideology after 9/11 is evidence of the success of bin Laden's message. The world is today a far more radicalized place, helped by modern communications, and, according to Jason Burke, "Washington's incredible failure to stem the hemorrhaging of support and sympathy."[46] Put simply, bin Laden's message makes sense to millions. There are serious consequences of the U.S. failure to win the ideological war. As Burke points out, it is from these millions that the next wave of terrorists will come.[47] These mostly self-radicalized individuals will form networks with little connection to Al Qaeda the organization but would see *jihad* as a religious duty. How do you defend against individualized terrorism that could be so random, which has no prior record of involvement with violent groups, and that has no central organization or state support, and yet is fully committed to finding the necessary resources to carry out terrorist attacks?

The United States has been aware of the need to win this information war. However, it has not appreciated how important this is compared to the military and security efforts to preempt and defend against terrorism. Its focus under the Bush administration has been the kinetic application of military force and the use of hard security measures to stem the terrorist tide. Given the low priority in waging information warfare, its efforts have not surprisingly been half-hearted and even incompetent. For instance, after 9/11, the United States established a "Shared Values Initiative," a public diplomacy program to convince Muslims "not to hate us." The $15 million program, an initiative of Charlotte Beers, the then Undersecretary of State, included testimonial-style commercials featuring Muslim Americans enjoying freedom and prosperity in the United States.[48] But this advertising campaign fooled no one as disturbing images of Iraq, Abu Ghraib, and Guantanamo Bay told a different story to Muslim audiences. Overall, the United States has been extremely clumsy and ideological in its approach, believing in the superiority of its values such as democracy, liberalism, equal rights for women, individualism, materialism, sexual freedom, and the sanctity of the free market. But to societies, especially Muslim ones, that value spiritual values, community, and conservative sexual propriety, the promotion of globalized values based on U.S. social mores and norms seems patronizing and ethnocentric.

The undisguised support for controversial Israeli policies has also hampered the United States in its information war. For instance, the U.S. support for Israel's muddled and ultimately fruitless attack on Lebanon in 2006, one that resulted in strengthening the Hezbollah rather than weakening it, appeared to confirm to most Muslim audiences of the "Zionist–Crusader" alliance that is waging war on Muslims. This perception has made it hard, even dangerous, for the many moderate Muslims who are critical of radical ideology to speak out, as this would appear to be siding with the United States. The United States has therefore so far lost the war of hearts and minds.

This should not have been the case, as authoritative Gallup polls in 2008 indicate that a clear majority of Muslims themselves do not want to live under the kind of Taliban fundamentalist rule that Al Qaeda champions and thus do not subscribe to the radical vision espoused by Al Qaeda. Indeed 7% of Muslims worldwide supported the 9/11 terrorist attacks, but most of these gave political rather than religious reasons. More significant is the fact that the overwhelming majority, that is, 93%, did not support those attacks.[49] Many Muslim societies, instead of rejecting modernity and globalization, also desire to be Muslim as well as participate in development and embrace modernity. According to Gallup polls, a significant majority of Muslims prefer democracy (albeit based on aspects of the *sharia*) and reject both theocracy and an active role by religious teachers in public life.[50] Many Muslims, including radical Islamists themselves, disagree strongly with Al Qaeda's use of wanton violence to achieve its ends. Indeed, some Islamist movements believe they could achieve greater power and influence in Muslim countries through political mobilization and proselytizing, recognizing that the use of violence would alienate Muslims, resulting in their isolation. Thus, in 1997 and 2007, the largest and second largest armed Islamist movements in Egypt unilaterally gave up their armed struggle, and delegitimized the use of violence toward achieving their goals.[51] But the United States, because of its lack of intellectual capacity to understand, recognize, and exploit such differences in what seems a monolithic Islamist threat, has failed in the ideological battle for hearts and minds. Instead, bin Laden has convinced many Muslims not of the attractiveness of his own agenda but of the danger to Islam and of the existential evil represented by the United States and its allies, which all Muslims must oppose.

Alternatives to GWOT

The growing army of critics of the Bush administration's handling of the GWOT has included those who have suggested alternative courses of action that would more effectively meet the challenge posed by Al Qaeda and its ideology. The obvious line of criticism has been a general disagreement with the unilateral, military-oriented strategy adopted by the Bush administration, as opposed to a more broad-based strategy that is multilateral as well as comprehensive in approach, one that included political, economic, social, and psychological dimensions.

The unidimensional approach adopted by the Bush administration is not surprising given the historical American way of war, which has always favored the application of military force to achieve total victory over the enemy. The obvious antidote is to revive a Clausewitzian focus on the political ends, with military force treated as an instrument in achieving political objectives. This line of thought naturally leads to the prescription of comprehensive approaches to dealing with global terrorism.

Another focal point of criticism is the ideological approach of the Bush administration, which has been much criticized by realist-oriented experts on international relations and terrorism studies; witness, for instance, the realist versus neoconservative debate just before the start of the U.S. invasion of Iraq in 2003. John Mearsheimer and Steven Walt, in a widely circulated essay before the invasion, set out the realist critique of the neoconservative project. Mearsheimer and Walt were really posing a simple, if amoral question: What course of action would best serve U.S. national interests? They argued that Saddam Hussein was not an existential threat to U.S. interests in 2003 and that there was no good reason to attack him.[52] The point they wanted to make was that attacking Iraq would serve no good purpose as it would not advance U.S. interests and moreover would distract from the imperatives of the GWOT. The neoconservatives, however, rejected the amoral nature of the criticism, secure in what they felt was the far greater moral objectives in their course of action—the spread of democracy to the Muslim world.

The left-wing, neo-Marxist-dominated social science academic community also, predictably, harshly criticized U.S. counterterrorism measures since 9/11 as an attack on justice and an erosion of civil liberties. Some even went as far as to argue that the United States is itself a terrorist and rogue state.[53] Such views found enthusiastic audiences in universities, where amoral realism has been greeted with suspicion as being supportive of the state's interests, and therefore perceived to be inimical to the advancement of human security. Moreover, many of the "post Cold War idealists" see the state as *the* problem. However, the real impact on policy has come from realist-oriented scholars. Realist-oriented scholars (who have been treated with hostility as the adversary in a number of university campuses) could see the United States floundering and stumbling into an unnecessary war, without any clear grand strategy based on an objective assessment of the threat and what needed to be done about it. More importantly, the general tenor of their criticisms appeared right in the light of the Iraq imbroglio and the continued threat of global terrorism. They have thus been studied carefully by policy analysts and military thinkers within the government who have been searching for better alternatives to waging the GWOT. Indeed, these critics were able, for the most part, to explain the nature of the challenge, what was wrong with current strategy, and offered lessons from history and strategy that could improve counterterrorism strategy.

In 2003, Thomas Mockaitis and Paul Rich argued for a grand strategy in countering terrorism in their edited volume entitled *Grand Strategy in the War Against Terrorism*.[54] In exploring this subject, Mockaitis, a historian who has studied insurgencies, argued that the terrorist threat that the United States and its allies faced was, in fact, an insurgency, albeit an international one. The nature of the conflict, that is, a global insurgency, pointed the way to its resolution: a counterinsurgency campaign on a global scale.[55] This early work contains a number of important and influential ideas and therefore merits a closer analysis.

Like Mearsheimer and Walt, Mockaitis was an early critic of the U.S. decision to invade Iraq. Mockaitis issued this prescient warning:

> The Iraq War will, at best, have no effect on the war against terrorism; at worst, it could exacerbate an already bad situation... unilateralism could drive Arab moderates into the arms of the extremists. Iraq may yet implode in the wake of the American-led invasion, creating yet another failed state that has to be occupied and governed... war with Saddam has also had immediate implications for Iran, Syria, the Gulf States—in fact, the entire region. Under the circumstances, it is difficult to escape the conclusion that domestic political considerations and a desire to control Iraqi oil motivated the war.[56]

To counter the new global insurgency mounted by Al Qaeda, Mockaitis proposed a strategy based on "winning hearts and minds," one that had proven successful in the Malayan Emergency against communist guerrillas in the 1950s.[57] According to him, intelligence is the key to defeating insurgents. Obtaining accurate and timely intelligence, however, requires winning the trust of the general population. In order to win their trust, their legitimate grievances and needs must be addressed so that they will be won over and provide the crucial intelligence that would enable the terrorists to be targeted precisely. Mockaitis based his assessment on the argument that people support insurgencies out of a shared sense of wrong or frustration at not having their basic needs met. The global insurgency thus feeds on grievances widely felt in the Muslim world.[58]

Mockaitis, however, rejected the claims of the new terrorism analysts, such as Bruce Hoffman, who have argued that Al Qaeda represents a "new" form of terrorism. Although he acknowledges the differences between the current global insurgency and local insurgencies in the past, he argues that the differences are primary in scope and complexity, asserting that "despite the oft-repeated claims of pundits that a 'new terrorism' strides the globe, Al Qaeda operations resemble those of similar organisations over the last century."[59] Mockaitis called for a "comprehensive offensive strategy" to defeat Al Qaeda. Such a strategy must combine conventional and unconventional operations and the highly focused use of force so as not to alienate the general populace. This comprehensive strategy should comprise three prongs: a hearts and minds campaign, homeland security, as well as offensive military action.[60]

In later work in 2006–7, Mockaitis expanded on his earlier views through a more cogent criticism of the U.S. approach in the GWOT in the light of the invasion of Iraq. He argued that the United States had no coherent strategy beyond a disproportionate emphasis on state sponsors that could be eliminated by conventional military means.[61] If counterterrorism is to evolve beyond a series of tactical responses, it needs a realistic grand strategy. According to him, countering the global terrorist threat required a "balanced, long-term strategy that combats terrorist organizations while addressing the root causes of terrorism." He also pointed out that countering terrorism required legitimacy and unilateral U.S. actions undermined that legitimacy.[62] He urged the abandonment of the unhelpful concept of the GWOT since in international law, war has a precise definition and could not be readily applied to a gray area phenomenon like terrorism.[63] Instead, he argued for a shift toward law enforcement and covert operations, on the grounds that persistent, low-level pressure over time would be more effective than concentrated military force.[64]

Another useful addition to the debate came from Stephen Biddle, who argued that U.S. strategy should be based on containing rather than defeating terrorism, a line of thinking that Mockaitis has supported. According to Biddle, writing in 2004, the Bush administration had failed to clarify its aims in the GWOT. The key problem is this: should the United States insist on eradicating the terrorist threat (that is, "rollback"), or should it aim to contain the threat of terrorism within acceptable boundaries? Biddle warned of the enormous cost of "rollback" as compared to containment, which by definition, would tolerate greater terrorist violence as a semipermanent condition as the price of reducing the risk of near-term chaos in the effort to remake the Middle East politically.[65]

Mockaitis thus concluded in a recent book that:

> Whatever value it may have had in 2001, the GWOT has become a seriously flawed approach to opposing terrorism...the counterinsurgency (COIN) model, particularly as developed by the British over the last century, commends itself as a better model for addressing the terrorist threat. Although COIN and counterterrorism are not identical, they have a great deal in common. COIN requires a comprehensive strategy to address the economic, social and political causes of terrorist violence.[66]

Mockaitis raised a number of important points. An historian, he issued the important reminder that terrorism is a historical phenomenon, though he was by no means the first, with others such as David Rapoport having located modern terrorism within a historical context.[67] Despite its "new" features in a rapidly globalizing world, the traditional reasons for resorting to terrorism, that is, fundamental political, economic, and social causes, remain relevant. As an expert on insurgencies, he pointed out the essentially political, economic, and social basis underlying terrorism, even with those groups that championed an apocalyptic religious agenda. He brought back lessons of the British success in counterinsurgency in the Malayan Emergency, one of the few success stories in counterinsurgency, prompting a fresh look at the comprehensive strategy based partly on a successful hearts and minds campaign that was employed, in order to uncover its contemporary application. His characterization of the global terrorist threat as a global insurgency found resonance as the United States became bogged down in Iraq and faced a worldwide outbreak of terrorist attacks. Finally, the advocacy of a global counterinsurgency (global COIN, or GCOIN) strategy laid the foundation for further work in this area by others, most notably by David Kilcullen, whose work has become influential in U.S. counterterrorism and counterinsurgency strategy.

Whilst Mockaitis posed an alternative to the GWOT and to the assumptions of the new terrorism analysts such as Hoffman, others have examined the COIN concept and, in contrast, have found it wanting. In 2007, Steven Metz succinctly explained the lessons of Iraq: "the United States is adept at counterinsurgency support in a limited role but faces serious, even debilitating challenges when developing and implementing a comprehensive counterinsurgency strategy for a partner state."[68] Although the U.S. military had the conventional means to overpower rogue states, it has been totally ill-suited to the task of rebuilding and transforming societies. As Iraq demonstrated, the U.S. military was also unprepared for counterinsurgency, as its doctrine on counterinsurgency was outdated, being decades old and designed around cold war–style rural "People's War," where the United States would provide support to a threatened regime, a situation that was very different in Iraq.[69] As documented by Isaiah Wilson, the official U.S. Army historian for the invasion of 2003, the United States thus failed to develop a comprehensive plan for Phase Four of the campaign, which is the stabilization of Iraq and the handling over to civilian authorities.[70]

Metz thus concludes that traditional COIN strategies might not be the best response to insurgency. Departing from the historians such as Mockaitis, Metz points out that insurgency today has evolved into something different. "Iraqi model" insurgents, according to Metz, are more adept than their forebears in manipulating the psychological effects of violence. With the advent of the Internet, satellite television networks, and cheap digital video cameras, the audience for insurgent violence is immediate and extensive; contemporary insurgency is thus a form of "armed theatre." Moreover, few modern insurgencies rely on state sponsors, and are also potentially able to carry out terrorist attacks on the U.S. homeland.[71]

Metz thus argued that the whole concept of counterinsurgency has become obsolete and warned against reading too much into cold war counterinsurgency experiences and assuming that what worked against cold war insurgencies will work against contemporary ones.[72] In particular, he warned against attempting to draw too many lessons from the British and French counterinsurgency experiences in Malaya, Indochina, and Algeria, as these campaigns were focused on wars of imperial maintenance or nationalistic transition, not with modern-day communal conflicts where armed militias and organized crime play a part. Indeed, Metz felt the U.S. approach in response to Iraq and Afghanistan has been to derive new strategies from old conflicts, thus preparing to fight the last war.[73]

Metz thus departs from those who see counterinsurgency as another form of war that could be won by improved cold war–style counterinsurgency strategies. While Metz agrees that a comprehensive strategy, the hallmark of such cold war lessons, is needed, what is more important is the need to ensure political resolution as soon as possible and to avoid any protracted conflict. As modern-day insurgencies are complex affairs, they are also not amenable to a "one-size-fits-all" grand strategic approach.[74]

Metz also posed a more germane question: at the grand strategic level, does the United States want a security apparatus optimized for counterinsurgency? This would require profound changes, involving the creation of new organizations and stripping of some resources and functions from existing ones.[75] Should the United States choose to do so, it will have to invest heavily in change and cannot rely on old models and strategies in the face of changed circumstances. Metz, however, also makes the more pertinent point that since systematic reengineering is not something that the United States could do unilaterally nor rely on its military to achieve, it should not in fact get involved in counterinsurgency. If it has to in the most pressing of cases, it should only do so as part of "an equitable, legitimate and broad-based coalition," with the limited objective of relieving the suffering associated with violence.[76]

Metz thus recognized the limits of U.S. power and in a way reiterated the pre-RMA Powell Doctrine. He also rejected the grand strategic approach based on classical COIN to dealing with insurgencies that Mockaitis had advocated.

The Conflation of Terrorism and Insurgency

The interesting feature of the unfolding debate as documented in the brief survey thus far over what should replace the flawed GWOT is the conflation of terrorism and insurgency. Terrorism, according to the official U.S. Department of Defense's admittedly state-centric definition, is:

> The calculated use of unlawful violence or threat of unlawful violence to inculcate fear; intended to coerce or to intimidate governments or societies in the pursuit of goals that are generally political, religious, or ideological.[77]

The common understanding of terrorism has been informed by experiences with many such groups, such as political terrorism (e.g., Japanese Red Army, Baadar Meinhoff Gang) and ethnonationalist terrorism (e.g., the Irish Republican Army [IRA], the Basque Homeland and Liberty [ETA], Kurdistan Workers Party [PKK], Palestinian Liberation Organization [PLO]). Religious terrorism has also been a challenge and they include groups such as the Aum Supreme Truth.[78]

What characterizes terrorism is its focus on attacking civilians, and in some cases of extreme terrorist groups such as the Aum Supreme Truth, its apparently nonnegotiable goals. Terrorist groups may succeed in becoming a countergovernment. Others have succeeded in transforming themselves into political movements with sufficient legitimacy to win elections, for instance, in the case of Hamas. Despite the U.S. Department of Defense definition, terrorism can also be a tool of governments; state terrorism can be targeted, for instance, at ethnic minority groups. Alternatively, governments could support the use of terrorism, as Iran has done through its support of Hezbollah in Lebanon, and in the case of the United States, its support of the Contras in Nicaragua and the *mujahideen* in Afghanistan during the 1980s.

Insurgency, on the other hand, has been a term used interchangeably with guerrilla warfare. It has traditionally been violence aimed at establishing bases that are secure from the control of the central government and which would enable the establishment of what amounts to a countergovernment. Above all, insurgencies have a territorial and political agenda, even if the language is couched in religion. British Army doctrine defines insurgency as "an organized movement aimed at the overthrow of a constituted government through the use of subversion and armed conflict."[79]

In many cases, the distinction between insurgencies and terrorism is blurred because of the use by insurgents of terrorist tactics to further their aims.[80] Some groups formerly classified as terrorists, such as Hamas, PLO, and the IRA, in fact turned out to be quite capable of participating in the political process and proving some degree of popular legitimacy. Thus, insurgencies have negotiable political goals, territorial aspirations (and indeed may control both territory and population), and political organization. It also possesses some popular form of legitimacy, as in order to successfully control or aspire to control territory and population, it must have the support of significant elements of the population that it purportedly represents.

But the conflation of terrorism with insurgency became inevitable after global terrorism became conflated with the Iraq insurgency. The Iraq imbroglio, involving counterinsurgency operations to stem the armed opposition to the U.S. presence, inevitably became linked to the GWOT. The main *jihadist* group there responsible for many terrorist attacks in Iraq pledged allegiance to Al Qaeda and changed its name to "Al Qaeda in Iraq." Iraq also captured the imagination of those who want to defend an Islam under attack, just as Afghanistan did previously in the 1980s, and has become a central battlefield of the global *jihad*, attracting foreign *mujahideen* to fight in Iraq. Osama bin Laden himself acknowledged that the key to his global cosmic battle between Islam and the West would be decided in Baghdad, the seat of the caliphate at the height of Muslim glory a millennium ago, one which bin Laden would like to revive.

The logic on the U.S. side has been no less absurd, if the whole unnecessary Iraqi enterprise could be described as such. As Metz explained, the U.S. strategic logic (whether deliberate or by accident) was Napoleonic—draw the enemy into a decisive battle where it can be defeated. Iraq is therefore to be an epic and decisive battle in the GWOT.[81] Thus, President Bush stated in 2005 in his address to the U.S. people that "there is only one course of action against them: to defeat them abroad before they attack us at home," which would have been a rational preemptive strategy except that Iraq did not have anything to do with the global terrorist threat in 2003. But because Iraq had now become a self-fulfilling prophecy and involved in the global *jihad*, Bush thus argued that the sacrifice in Iraq was worth it because "it is vital to the future security of our country." What was more, Bush quoted bin Laden and agreed with the latter that "Iraq is a central front in the war on terror."[82]

The Anbar Awakening demonstrated that radical Islamist terrorists and ethnonationalist Sunni insurgents were not one and the same, and that their objectives in fact differed quite markedly. However, the fact remains that in U.S. strategy, terrorism has become conflated with insurgency, and there has been the blurring of lines between counterterrorism and counterinsurgency, as the discussion in this chapter shows. Thomas Mockaitis has called for a better strategy based on updating classical counterinsurgency strategy albeit applied on a global scale, whilst Metz doubts if *any* counterinsurgency strategy would work well at any level. Other advocates of a global counterinsurgency (GCOIN) strategy include Bruce Hoffman and David Kilcullen (whose ideas will be discussed in greater detail in the following chapter). Kilcullen has produced the best articulated GCOIN strategy to-date, one that has been influential in guiding U.S. evolution toward a new strategy to replace the discredited concept of the GWOT. However, as the Bush administration was not likely to substantially alter its strategy based on the GWOT, the full evolution of U.S. grand strategy to the concept of GCOIN could take place only after the U.S. presidential elections in 2008. This was won by the Democrat candidate, Barack Obama, who in fact retained Robert Gates as his Defense Secretary. This decision was not made out of political expediency aimed at winning over moderate Republicans. Gates, who had replaced Rumsfeld, had been developing a new, comprehensive approach to some acclaim, and it seems that President Obama has been eager to give him the chance to complete the job.

CHAPTER SEVEN

The Evolution of U.S. Counterterrorism Strategy: From COIN to Global Counterinsurgency

The state of affairs regarding U.S. grand strategy since 9/11 raises three key questions: Can lessons be drawn from classical counterinsurgency (COIN) that could be used in the Global War on Terror (GWOT)? Can insurgencies in places such as Iraq, Chechnya, Mindanao, Kashmir, Somalia, and Afghanistan be treated as part of this global insurgency? Should the global threat from Al Qaeda's violent *jihadist* ideology mean that it should be treated as a global insurgency, with the logical strategy to counter it being a strategy of global counterinsurgency (GCOIN)?

Lessons from Counterinsurgency

The advocacy of a comprehensive approach to counterterrorism based on classical COIN by Thomas Mockaitis and others as a replacement for the GWOT should come as no surprise. It was an inevitable line of thought, given the British experience in COIN campaigns, especially its celebrated success in defeating the communist insurgency during the Malayan Emergency in the 1950s. According to British Army doctrine, counterinsurgency (COIN) is defined as "those military, political, economic, psychological and civic actions taken by a government to defeat insurgency."[1] The British Army principles of COIN, as distilled through over 100 years of imperial policing, is a comprehensive approach, which emphasizes political objectives, such as the winning over of the hearts and minds of the population, rather than the kinetic application of overwhelming military power to defeat the adversary. This somewhat more economical approach was perhaps inevitable given that the British never really had the strength in numbers to be able to maintain a global empire.

The principles, as taught to British Army officers, are as follows: ensure political primacy and political aim; build coordinated government machinery (i.e., unity of effort); develop intelligence and information (without it, security forces conduct unfocused or random operations, and may alienate local and international populations); separate the insurgent from his support (a coordinated effort to win the psychological campaign for hearts and minds, linked to the need for the government to retain legitimacy, should be integral to this process); neutralize the insurgent (the aim should be to defeat the insurgent on his own ground using as much force as is necessary, but no more); and finally, plan for the long term (governments should make long-term plans to improve the economic and social life of its population thereby reducing or eliminating the political causes of the insurgency).[2] British COIN doctrine places great emphasis on restoring law and order, which in U.S. military parlance is "stabilization." According to the doyen of British COIN strategy, Sir Robert Thompson:

> An insurgent movement is a war for the people. It stands to reason that government measures must be directed to restoring government authority and law and order throughout the country so that control over the population can be regained and its support won...without a reasonably efficient government machine, no programme or projects, in the context of counter-insurgency, will produce the desired results.[3]

The British experience in Malaya that formed the basis of its COIN doctrine has been succinctly summarized by Richard Stubbs, who concluded that "the abandonment of a coercion and enforcement approach in favour of a hearts and minds approach paved the way for a relatively peaceful and prosperous aftermath to the fighting."[4]

British COIN lessons and U.S. mistakes in Iraq since the invasion in 2003 were closely studied by General David Petraeus, who helped oversee the substantial revision of the U.S. military's own COIN strategy. The revised Counterinsurgency Field Manual of December 2006 had inputs from a diverse group of people including some of the brightest officers in the U.S. armed forces. Petraeus is known as a scholar general, having topped the intensely competitive U.S. Army Command and General Staff

College class of 1983 and earned a PhD in international relations from Princeton.[5] As commander of the famed 101st Airborne, Petraeus took part in the invasion of Iraq in 2003 and was stationed in the northern city of Mosul, where his comprehensive approach, with its emphasis on restoring services and winning over hearts and minds has been credited with stabilizing that sector.[6] After he returned to head the U.S. Army Command and General Staff College in 2005, he oversaw the revision of the counterinsurgency manual and was then sent back to Iraq in early 2007 to command all U.S. troops there. Petraeus sought out and listened to the advice of some of the best-educated officers available, mostly with doctorates like himself. He also hired David Kilcullen, a lieutenant-colonel of the Australian Army with a PhD from the University of New South Wales, Australia, who was working for the U.S. State Department and is regarded today as a leading thinker on COIN and counterterrorism strategy.

The revised Counterinsurgency Field Manual that was released in December 2006 is 282 pages in length and is interesting in that it reads very much like a manual designed to explain the flaws in U.S. strategy in Iraq and how the United States should proceed to fix them. It begins by summarizing key lessons of past insurgencies: legitimacy is the main objective; unity of effort is essential; political factors are primary; counterinsurgents must understand the environment; intelligence drives operations; insurgents must be isolated from their cause and support; security under the rule of law is essential; counterinsurgents should prepare for a long-term commitment.[7] If this sounded like a list of the things the United States did *not* do when in invaded Iraq in 2003, consider Table 1.1 in the manual, which listed all the unsuccessful COIN practices which the United States *did* practice after it invaded Iraq. According to this table, unsuccessful COIN practices include the following: overemphasize killing and capturing the enemy rather than securing and engaging the populace; conduct large-scale operations as the norm; concentrate military forces in large bases for protection; focus special forces primarily on raiding; place low priority on assigning quality advisers to host-nation forces; build and train host-nation security forces in the U.S. military's image; ignore peacetime government processes, including legal procedures; and, allow open borders, airspace, and coastlines.[8]

Another point, which implicitly repudiates the view that the United States did not need a substantial ground presence in Iraq, is also found in the manual:

> ...maintaining security in an unstable environment requires vast resources...thus successful COIN operations often require a high

ratio of security forces to the protected population. For that reason, protracted COIN operations are hard to sustain. The effort requires a firm political will and substantial patience by the government, its people, and the countries providing support.[9]

Curiously, the manual also quoted from President John F. Kennedy regarding the need for serious homework before embarking on any foreign adventure, and more pertinently, on the limits of using military power alone to solve any problem:

> You (military professionals) must know something about strategy and tactics and...logistics, but also economics and politics and diplomacy and history. You must know everything you can know about military power, and you must also understand the limits of military power. You must understand that few of the important problems of our time have...been finally solved by military power alone.[10]

The language in the manual thus appeared to be implicitly critical of the neoconservatives who had ignored the Army's advice and then unceremoniously removed its commander, General Eric Shinseki in the lead-up to the invasion of Iraq. Indeed, Defense Secretary Donald Rumsfeld's approach has been exactly what the manual warned the United States should not to do: the expectation that the application of the United States' superior military force could solve problems abroad, and that military transformation had meant that this could be done with far fewer troops as well as quickly and on the cheap.

The solution to the many mistakes of the Bush Administration's strategy in Iraq is explained in detail in the manual. Primarily, the manual seeks to overturn this ingrained U.S. habit of emphasizing the application of kinetic military force as an easy solution. Instead, it emphases a comprehensive "hearts and minds" approach, asserting that "COIN is fought among the populace" and that "counterinsurgents take upon themselves responsibility for the people's well-being in all its manifestations," such as the provision of basic economic needs, essential services such as water, electricity and medical care, and the sustenance of key social and cultural institutions.[11]

The manual spends a great deal of effort in overturning the "American Way of War," by making the following useful points: sometimes, the more you protect your force, the less secure you may be, as ultimate success in COIN lies in protecting the populace, not the COIN force; sometimes, the more force is used, the less effective it is, due to the greater chance of collateral damage and mistakes; and, sometimes doing nothing is the best reaction, as the insurgents may be trying to provoke an overreaction. The manual also emphasizes the point that tactical success guaranteed nothing and that the prime objectives are political, not military:

> ...military actions by themselves cannot achieve success in COIN. Insurgents that never defeat counterinsurgents in combat may still achieve their strategic objectives. Tactical actions thus must be linked not only to strategic and operational military objectives but also to the host nation's essential political goals. Without those connections, lives and resources may be wasted for no real gain.[12]

The manual makes the following point about the use of military force, and the primacy of fighting the enemy's political strategy, in a way that has been alien to U.S. military culture and practice:

> The obvious military response is a counteroffensive to destroy the enemy's forces. This is rarely the best choice at company level. Only attack insurgents when they get in the way. Try not to be distracted or forced into a series of reactive moves by a desire to kill or capture them. Provoking combat usually plays into the enemy's hands by undermining the population's confidence. Instead, attack the enemy's strategy. If the insurgents are seeking to recapture a community's allegiance, co-opt that group against them. If they are trying to provoke a sectarian conflict, transition to peace enforcement operations.[13]

The manual is also at pains to point out, in particular, that "the decisive battle is for the people's minds."[14] Indeed, it states that:

> COIN is an extremely complex form of warfare. At its core, COIN is a struggle for the population's support. The protection, welfare, and support of the people are vital to success. Gaining and maintaining that support is a formidable challenge.[15]

Ultimately, the objective in winning the battle for hearts and minds is to establish "Home Nation institutions that can sustain government legitimacy."[16] Reading very much like a "How to Disengage from Iraq" strategy, the manual advocates a three-stage progression in COIN. The first is the initial stage, which is to "Stop The Bleeding," i.e., to protect the population, break the insurgents' initiative and momentum, and set the conditions for further engagement. The second is the middle stage, which the manual dubbed as "In-Patient Care—Recovery," in which the objective is achieving stability, through the development of relationships with Host Nation counterparts and with the local government. Finally, stage three is termed "Outpatient Care—Movement to Self-sufficiency," which is characterized by the expansion of stability operations across contested regions, ideally using Home Nation forces. The main goal for this stage is to transition responsibility for COIN operations to the Home Nation's leadership. Gradually, the Home Nation reduces the need for foreign assistance as it builds the systems needed to provide effective and stable government, and is thus able to provide security for its citizens, build up its legitimacy, and isolate the insurgents.[17]

Interestingly, the manual devoted about one highlighted page on the lessons of the Malayan Emergency, which appeared to mirror the problem with Iraqi forces. The manual noted approvingly the British strategy of reforming and retraining the entire Malaya Police Force, first by removing 10,000 corrupt and incompetent officers, and then by systematically training all levels, with the best sent to Britain for training. With better quality and disciplined security forces, better relations with the population resulted, leading to better intelligence. The British began to withdraw their forces as they progressively turned the war over to local security forces, who could conduct COIN without any drop in efficiency. Crucially, the manual noted that "the transformation required only 15 months."[18]

General David Petraeus was made commander of all U.S. forces in Iraq in early 2007, which gave him the opportunity to put the operational prescriptions of the Counterinsurgency Field Manual that he oversaw into practice in the field. However, the broader Iraqi strategy that was adopted was not his but that of the neoconservatives. As mentioned in Chapter 3, Frederick Kagan, in his piece entitled *Choosing Victory: A Plan for Success in Iraq*, argued that "victory" in Iraq was vital to America's security and that defeat would lead to regional conflict, humanitarian catastrophe, and increased global terrorism. Thus, Kagan advocated a "substantial and sustained" troop surge in Iraq.[19] This logic was accepted by President Bush, who chose General Petraeus to implement it. The surge took place between February and June 2007, with some 30,000 fresh troops arriving to take the number up to a record 168,000 U.S. troops by September 2007.[20]

Once on the ground, Petraeus lost no time in ensuring that COIN in Iraq followed the prescriptions of the newly revised Counterinsurgency Field Manual. Instead of U.S. troops sequestered in huge, heavily defended military bases, U.S. troops began to fan out into joint security bases where U.S. and Iraqi troops would live and work together as well as secure neighborhoods that had been previously abandoned to militias and insurgents.[21] Surprisingly, the surge appeared to have worked. By September 2007, Petraeus was able to report that insurgent attacks and sectarian violence had declined, although he acknowledged that the situation remained "difficult."[22] The relative peace that returned to Iraq can be partly attributed to the fact that the Mehdi Army, controlled by the Shia extremist cleric Moqtada Sadr, was ordered by Sadr himself to cease from military action including reprisals against Sunnis.

More significantly, an unexpected development that coincided with the troop surge was the revolt of Sunni tribal leaders against Al Qaeda in Iraq (AQI). This has little to do with the surge, and has been attributed to the AQI's arrogance, brutality, flouting of tribal customs, and determination to impose a Taliban-type austerity on local communities.[23] Petraeus, however, can be credited for having recognized the opportunity presented by the split and to have swiftly coopted the insurgents, offering economic incentives to do so, despite the fact that the insurgents had been responsible for attacking and killing U.S. troops. In the so-called Anbar Awakening, some 80,000 Sunnis (many ex-insurgents) joined government-sponsored militias (known as "Concerned Local Citizens") by the end of 2007. This resulted in AQI being ejected from much of the western and northern parts of Iraq, including Baghdad.[24] Some normality soon returned to Baghdad and most of Iraq.[25]

These positive developments have been facilitated by the new U.S. approach under Petraeus, which has emphasized the winning of hearts and minds, and the promotion of reconciliation. Indeed, the Commander's Counterinsurgency Guidance to all U.S. forces in Iraq was at pains to remind U.S. forces to promote reconciliation, as the United States "cannot kill our way out of this endeavor." Instead, "we and our Iraqi partners must identify and separate the 'reconcilables' from the 'irreconcilables' through engagement, population control measures, information operations, kinetic operations, and political activities . . . we must strive to make the reconcilables a part of the solution."[26]

However, despite this progress, Petraeus admitted in April 2008 that the situation was "fragile and reversible," and refused to set a timetable for withdrawal, instead recommending a process of evaluation and assessment regarding troop levels.[27] A report to U.S. Congress in June

2008 also acknowledged that while there had been gains, the environment remains "fragile, reversible and uneven."[28] This was because of a number of continuing problems and challenges in Iraq, such as the continuing threat from AQI, the lack of reconciliation between Sunnis and Shiites, the presence of armed radical Shiite militias (and Sunni militias, now that they have been armed by the United States), the lack of political consensus, the fragility of institutions, and the increased influence of Iran. The continuing threat from AQI can be seen from suicide bomb attacks, which have continued, although not with the same intensity.[29] A renewed outbreak of sectarian violence is also very possible, given the presence of armed militias, the recent history of extreme violence, and the very slow progress toward reconciliation among the Kurds, Sunnis, and Shiites. There is in fact a sense that both the Sunnis and the militant Shiite militias are only bidding their time when the United States draws down its presence. With greater strength and representation in the political process, and with its armed militias to call upon, the Sunnis could pose a serious challenge to the mainstream Shiite parties currently in government in Baghdad.

The uneven and mixed results in Iraq raises the question of whether the much touted lessons of the Malayan Emergency could be the basis for modern COIN, or as the basis for the grand strategic GCOIN strategy to deal with global terrorism as Mockaitis had advocated. Milton Osborne, in an illuminating essay in 2005, *Getting the Job Done: Iraq and the Malayan Emergency*, explained the context which made British success possible. They stemmed from the disadvantages that the Malayan Communist Party (MCP) faced. The MCP drew its membership from one ethnic minority group, the Chinese, and had to face very capable Chinese counterinsurgency officers as well as Chinese-speaking British colonial officials. Malaya's geographic isolation meant that the communists could not get supplies from any sympathetic external supporter such as China. The insurgents also failed to establish an effective presence in urban areas, which remained under the control of the competent, long-established colonial administration. In addition, the authorities possessed overwhelming superiority in terms of the ratio of its forces to the insurgents, and furthermore established "New Villages" to quarantine the Chinese squatter population from the insurgents.[30] Overall, the intensity of fighting was also much less than in Iraq today. In the 12 years of the Emergency from 1948 to 1960, 9,906 security personnel and civilians were killed or wounded.[31]

The British thus succeeded in Malaya because the circumstances were favorable. Moreover, Britain had also accepted the inevitability of the end of its empire and moves toward independence for Malaya undermined the cause of the insurgents. The British possessed a number of advantages, such as a competent colonial administration, strong military–civil relations built up over years of colonial policing, and the fact that the insurgents were much weaker than those faced by the United States in, for instance, Vietnam. All these are unique features, which are absent in present-day Iraq. Despite the many favorable circumstances in Malaya, it must also be remembered that it took 12 years for the Emergency to run its course. Even then, the communist insurgents were not defeated, giving up their struggle only in 1989 following a peace agreement with the government of Malaysia.[32]

It is thus not surprising that Osborne concluded in his 2005 study that:

> The closer one examines how this victory was achieved the clearer it becomes that it came about in circumstances that were particular, indeed unique, to Malaya...Beyond a readiness on the part of the colonial administration to pursue its goals over the long haul, there is little to suggest that the way in which the Malayan Emergency was managed offers any lessons for Iraq.[33]

Donald McKay, in his study of the Malayan Emergency in 1997, came to a similar conclusion. He ascribed British successes in Malaya to the product of a unique set of circumstances though he acknowledged that there might be some useful lessons:

> There are individual lessons to be learnt, but the unique circumstances that allowed the colonial power to deal with the terrorist campaign so effectively that it never even got as far as being a truly insurgent war were just that—unique. It seems unlikely that they will ever be replicated at another time or in another place, and those who seek in Malaya a blueprint for counterinsurgency must look elsewhere.[34]

Such assessments might have been overly harsh, as a comprehensive approach, which focuses on winning hearts and minds rather than the kinetic application of military force is surely one key lesson that can be learnt from Malaya.

Overall, however, the uneven situation in Iraq thus far has exposed the limitations of classical COIN strategy in contemporary insurgency. The greatest mistake that could be made would be to read too much into the troop surge as well as the new COIN strategy embodied in the revised Counterinsurgency Field Manual as having solved the insurgent problem. Although they have played a part in stabilizing the situation in Iraq for the moment, General Petraeus has admitted that the situation has in fact remained fragile and the gains reversible. The 15-month time frame to Host Nation effectiveness in community policing as demonstrated by the Malayan experience, and which the counterinsurgency manual cited, is clearly impractical, given the much less effective governance structures in Iraq compared to the efficient colonial Malayan Civil Service. Instead, the U.S. military would have to contend with the political realities in Iraq, which suggest that the United States might need to make a very long-term commitment if it is to maintain stability, given the real possibility of a renewed outbreak of sectarian conflict.

But the U.S. military is not going to get the long-term political commitment required to complete the job. Not only has the U.S. public grown weary of the tremendous cost of the Iraq conflict, the U.S. presence has been highly unpopular in Iraq, so much so that negotiations in 2008 over a Status of Forces Agreement regulating the U.S. military presence in Iraq became mired in confusion amidst conflicting statements by Iraqi government officials. The dilemma is that the Baghdad government needs U.S. military support until its own forces are ready to impose on extremist Shiite militias and Sunni groups but at the same time, there is popular displeasure at the U.S. presence. In the United States itself, Democratic presidential candidate Barack Obama took advantage of this to issue his own call in an Op-Ed in *The New York Times* in July 2008 for a phased withdrawal of combat troops, calling Iraq a "grave mistake" and a distraction from the fight against Al Qaeda and the Taliban. Obama stated that "ending the war (in Iraq) is essential to meeting our strategic goals, starting in Afghanistan and Pakistan, where the Taliban is resurgent and Al Qaeda has a safe haven." He added that "Iraq is not a central front in the war on terrorism, and it never has been."[35]

Ultimately, COIN strategy cannot substitute for grand strategy. COIN successes in Iraq would not remove the threat of global terrorism. As Obama assessed, the priority for the United States in the GWOT ought to be in Afghanistan and Pakistan, where Al Qaeda and its allies, the Taliban, have found refuge and rebuilt their forces. In addition, there is still the worldwide hearts and minds campaign that is needed to counter the appeal of Al Qaeda's radical ideology. Yet, exiting from Iraq is not as simple as Obama would like the U.S. public to believe. Iraq is certainly not a central front in the GWOT but it does harbor the AQI, which could thrive and potentially evolve into a broader post-Al Qaeda network to threaten the U.S. homeland should the U.S. forces depart. Thus what happens in Iraq does matter to the GWOT. Without pressure exerted in Iraq, AQI could change its attention to attacking targets in the West. Moreover, there are non-GWOT geopolitical considerations, as precipitous withdrawal will create a vacuum that can only be filled by Iran.

The Problem with Afghanistan

The emerging centrality of Afghanistan in the GWOT contrasted with the Bush administration's fixation with Iraq and Iran. As the Afghanistan Study Group Report chaired by General James Jones and Ambassador Thomas Pickering released in January 2008 made clear:

> The mission to stabilize Afghanistan is faltering. Following the rapid successes in toppling the Taliban government, passing a new constitution, and electing a president and parliament, the long road to reconstruction, reconciliation, and institutional development has grown hazardous. Despite a significant increase in the number of troops and the amount of aid to Afghanistan since 2002, violence, insecurity, and opium production have risen dramatically as Afghan confidence in their government and its international partners falls.[36]

The Report of the United Nations Secretary-General on the situation in Afghanistan in March 2008 was similarly pessimistic. It acknowledged that "despite tactical successes by national and international military forces, the anti-Government elements are far from defeated." At the same time, "poor governance and limited development efforts, particularly at the provincial and district levels, continue to result in political alienation that both directly and indirectly sustains anti-Government elements."[37]

These assessments are in stark contrast to the heady days of 2002, when the United States obtained broad international support from the international community to intervene in Afghanistan, where Al Qaeda was sheltering under the protection of the Taliban regime. At the UN conference in Bonn in December 2001, the preferred U.S. candidate, Hamid Karzai, was installed as Afghanistan's new interim leader.[38]

Karzai later won the October 2004 presidential elections. In December 2001, the UN Security Council established the International Security Assistance Force (ISAF) to maintain security in Afghanistan.[39] Initially led by Britain and other U.S. allies, ISAF came under NATO leadership in August 2003.

But the Taliban fled across the porous border into Northwest Pakistan, where it has sheltered with sympathetic tribesmen in an area only tenuously controlled by the central government of Pakistan. By 2005, they began to attack the new Karzai government as well as NATO troops in earnest. Instead of insurgent attacks, where they almost always ended up losing, the Taliban resorted to terrorist tactics, such as suicide attacks, IEDs, kidnappings, and ambushes, which began to take its toll on ISAF forces. In June 2008, Taliban insurgents killed 45 U.S. and NATO troops in Afghanistan, compared to 31 U.S. and allied troops who died in Iraq that month, an indication that the situation in Afghanistan had become much more serious.[40] By July 22, 2008, 887 coalition deaths were recorded, of which 555 were U.S. soldiers. U.S. allies too suffered, with Britain sustaining 110 deaths and Canada 87, and 2,205 U.S. troops were also wounded.[41] By January 2009, 1,055 international troops, including 637 U.S., 142 British and 107 Canadian soldiers, had been killed.[42]

The resurgence of the Taliban and the emergence of safe havens in northwest Pakistan for both the Taliban and Al Qaeda indicate that the dramatic successes in the initial phases of Operation Enduring Freedom have not translated into enduring results. The "Iraqization" of Afghanistan, with the increasing adoption of insurgent and terrorist tactics used in Iraq, has made Afghanistan a dangerous place for NGOs and aid agencies operating there. Indeed, the UN Secretary-General reported that in 2007, over 40 food convoys for the World Food Program were attacked and looted, 130 attacks were made on humanitarian programs, and 129 aid workers were either killed or abducted.[43] As a result, assistance programs, which depend on security and stability, have been seriously hampered as some aid agencies have withdrawn their staff, either to the relative safety of Kabul or out of the country altogether.[44]

What had happened? The clue lies in President Bush's assertion that the objective of Operation Enduring Freedom was to "disrupt the use of Afghanistan as a terrorist base of operations, and to attack the military capability of the Taliban regime."[45] Thus, the U.S. approach in Afghanistan has mirrored that in Iraq—an overwhelming emphasis on the use of military firepower to attack the enemy. As in Iraq, there was no effective Phase IV stabilization plan and little thought paid to the aftermath of "victory." Afghanistan is a very complex society, with historic tribal divisions and rivalries making not just stabilization but also reconstruction and nation-building extremely difficult challenges, for which the United States was unprepared and indeed failed to pay sufficient attention to.

Indeed, since its intervention in 2002, the U.S. spending in Afghanistan has been predominantly military, with 93% of the $163 billion spent until 2007 being used for military operations, and just 7% for reconstruction.[46] Moreover, as in Iraq, the United States again failed to commit sufficient troops that could secure the vast country. The United States did not have enough of its own forces in 2002, thus failing to seal the border between Afghanistan and Pakistan, which enabled top Al Qaeda and the Taliban leaders to escape to safe havens in Northwest Pakistan. After that, it failed to commit sufficient troops to secure the entire country, especially the southern provinces where the Taliban had its power base, as it was distracted by the insurgency in Iraq. Thus, the Taliban's reemergence has been attributed to a power vacuum in the south as well as the failure to begin meaningful reconstruction and state-building operations.[47]

The failure of U.S.-led strategy has led to doubts and the uncertain support and commitment of its NATO allies. A number of key NATO countries such as Germany, France, and Italy are not prepared to participate in the actual fighting, garrisoning their troops in the comparative safety of the north.[48] This led to the complaint by U.S. Defence Secretary Robert Gates that "a handful of allies are paying the price and bearing the burdens."[49] The United States has thus rebuked its European allies and pressured them to get involved in the fighting by committing more troops as well as deploying them in the south. Many European countries, however, have had fundamental disagreements with the overall U.S. strategy in Afghanistan. They have been especially critical of the military-oriented U.S. approach, preferring greater emphasis to be paid on reconstruction and humanitarian aid, and focusing on building up the governance capacity of the government in Afghanistan. U.S. officials, on the other hand, have been critical of the European approach, believing that they have been naïve since the direct assistance they have provided have often fallen victim to corruption.[50] European allies, especially France, also disagree with the view by U.S. officials that it should build democracy in Afghanistan, in view of the complexity of Afghan society and the fact that there has been no tradition of democracy. The French therefore argue for a more realistic objective of building a more tolerant and representative society. The French also argue that the United Nations, the European Union, and other multilateral institutions are more suited to undertaking development projects and that NATO should only concentrate on its military roles.[51]

The differences over Afghanistan have had the unintended consequence of making Afghanistan a test of the NATO alliance, especially U.S. leadership of that alliance. As Paul Gallis noted in a recent study for Congress, "the ultimate outcome of NATO's effort to stabilize Afghanistan and US leadership of that effort may well affect the cohesiveness of the alliance, and Washington's ability to shape NATO's future."[52] Failure in the Afghanistan mission could thus have serious consequences for the transatlantic alliance.

The United Nations has tried to play a major role in reconstruction in Afghanistan, with the support of and at the insistence of the European allies of the United States. In January 2006, the United Nations and the government of Afghanistan signed the Afghanistan Compact following discussions in London, under which it was agreed that efforts would be directed toward three critical areas for the five years from the adoption of the Compact. These are: security; governance, the rule of law and human rights; and, economic and social development. In addition, the Compact spoke of the desire to eliminate the narcotics industry.[53]

The Compact identified security as of fundamental importance and the prerequisite for stability and development in Afghanistan. However, it recognized that security could not be achieved by military means alone. According to the Compact, "it requires good governance, justice and the rule of law, reinforced by reconstruction and development." Further, the Afghan government would need to disarm all illegal armed groups and create a secure environment by strengthening Afghan institutions.[54] The ultimate objective of the Compact is capacity-building, aimed at ensuring that the government of Afghanistan would be able to build up its own security forces, maintain them without foreign assistance, and ultimately create viable institutions in provincial areas, while at the same time eliminating the narcotics industry. The Compact envisaged a five-year time frame to achieve these lofty expectations. Thus, for instance, it is envisioned that by 2010, the Afghan National Army would expand from 49,000 to 70,000 and the national and border police forces would number 62,000.[55]

Yet, although the Compact appears to be a viable roadmap toward a stable and viable state, it is also an unusually ambitious and idealistic undertaking. In effect, the United Nations is asking the international community to fund a massive effort to build a viable unitary state where none existed before, in an impossibly short period of five years, in the expectation that this would somehow be achieved without any disruption by the Taliban insurgents. In addition, it was a plan that would require a vast increase in aid and resources, but the $10.5 billion pledged by the international community for the Compact appears inconsequential when measured against the size of the tasks and the short time frame being set.[56] The fact is that any nation-building exercise in Afghanistan, especially an attempt to build a modern Westphalian state in the mould of the West, would be an extraordinarily difficult undertaking that would require a very long-term commitment. Such a project would also need to take into account the need to win hearts and minds among the Pashtun supporters of the Taliban in the south and across the border in Pakistan, which is not something that can be achieved quickly. Indeed, the Taliban themselves believe that they have time on their side. Taliban leader Mullah Omar thus believes that the Taliban will prevail as the *mujahideen* had during the 1980s against the Soviets, as his strategy is to ensure that Afghanistan remains ungovernable and that Kabul cannot secure the entire country, a classic insurgent strategy of winning by not losing.[57] But failure in Afghanistan is surely not an option, given that it would invigorate not just the Taliban but also Al Qaeda and lead to the consolidation of safe havens in both southern Afghanistan as well as in Northwest Pakistan. This would also, in the longer term, lead to the destabilization of both key U.S. allies, namely, Afghanistan and Pakistan.

According to the Afghanistan Study Group Report, the way forward in Afghanistan for the United States is as follows:

> ...the only reasonable strategy at this point is to reinvigorate and redouble the international community's effort and return to the Afghanistan Compact vision. US and other key countries must concentrate and coordinate their efforts to beat back the insurgency, propel economic development, and build a competent and capable Afghan government.[58]

In September 2008, General Petraeus became the top commander for the Middle East and Central Asia, which included responsibility for turning around the increasingly difficult situation in Afghanistan.[59] It remains to be seen however, if the comprehensive "hearts and minds" approach in the new U.S. COIN strategy, of which Petraeus is a strong advocate, will work in Afghanistan. Moreover, real change in the overall U.S. approach had to await a change of direction in Washington following the U.S. presidential elections in 2008. The new Obama administration has clearly identified Afghanistan as a priority but whether it will be able to find the necessary resources for a renewed campaign and reconstruction at a time of deep economic recession and record deficits in the United States remains to be seen.

Moreover, the Afghanistan problem is not confined to the country itself. It is intimately linked to events in neighboring Pakistan. Indeed, General Dan McNeill, the ISAF commander in Afghanistan, laid the blame on Pakistan, stating in May 2008 that it was Pakistan's failure to act against militants in its tribal areas and its decision to hold peace talks with them that led to an increase in attacks against the U.S. and NATO forces in Afghanistan.[60]

The Problem with Pakistan

Since the 9/11 terrorist attacks, Pakistan has turned out to be an important ally and key battleground in the GWOT. Several hundred Al Qaeda operatives, including a number of key leaders, were apprehended and turned over to the United States as the Musharaff regime jettisoned its previous support for the Taliban and joined the U.S.-led GWOT.

Despite the many tactical successes however, the situation in Pakistan itself has deteriorated and has begun to alarm many in the West. The Taliban and Al Qaeda operatives who fled U.S.-led military actions in Afghanistan in 2002 went across the porous border to find sanctuary amongst sympathetic tribes-people in the northwest provinces of Pakistan, where they have proven difficult to target and uproot. Indeed, they regrouped and have been able to carry out attacks not only in Pakistan but also against NATO troops in southern Afghanistan.

Yet, the problem of growing radicalism in Pakistan did not happen overnight. It stemmed from the deliberate policies of a succession of governments, including that of General Zia ul-Haq in the 1970s and 1980s, who promoted Islamization in order to bolster his military regime's legitimacy. Radical Islamist organizations were recruited from Pakistan for the war against the Soviets in the 1980s and were able to establish a minority presence in Pakistani society. Subsequent governments, including the Musharaff regime, continued to court Islamist elements in the same manner. The Islamists have, however, been aggressive in pushing their agenda for an Islamic state, with some groups using violent terrorist tactics.

Radical groups include the following: the Tehrik-e-Taliban Pakistan (TTP) headed by Baitullah Mehsud; the Islamic Movement of

Uzbekistan (IMU); the Lashkar-e-Jhangvi (LEJ); the Tehrik-e-Nifaz-Shariat-e-Mohammadi (TNSM); and the Jaish-e-Mohammad (JEM). Apart from these groups, Al Qaeda operatives have been tracked and arrested in major cities in Pakistan. In the capital, Islamabad, there have been open challenges mounted by extremists. The most spectacular was the seizure of the Red Mosque in July 2007 by militants demanding the implementation of *sharia*. The ensuing standoff with the armed forces ended with commandoes storming the mosque, resulting in the deaths of over 100 people.[61] This led to a wave of retaliatory Taliban suicide bombings targeted at government and security forces, leading to a state of emergency being declared in November 2007.[62]

The intelligence services, especially the Inter-Services Intelligence (ISI), had deep links with the militants, having established close ties in the 1980s during the anti-Soviet conflict in Afghanistan. Some members of the intelligence services and among lower ranks of the military are believed to remain sympathetic to the militants. More importantly, participation in the U.S.-led GWOT alienated large sections of the population as well as the fundamentalist Muslim parties, which opposed the unpopular Musharraf's close ties with the United States and what they perceived to be a war against Islam.

Despite Musharraf's support for the GWOT as well as attempts by militants to assassinate him, Musharraf came under severe criticism in the West. In March 2006, for instance, President Bush arrived in Pakistan for a visit and appeared to publicly admonish Musharraf for not having done enough to root out extremists in his country. This was perceived by many Pakistanis to be a display of ingratitude and arrogance, reportedly angering even the most committed of Pakistani military officials.[63] Thus, in a visit to London in January 2008, Musharraf warned that Pakistan's success in fighting terrorism was critical and any failure would have serious consequences for the West. He called for the West's support and encouragement, not criticisms and insinuations.[64]

Under pressure from the United States and opposition political parties, Musharraf agreed to free and fair elections in February 2008. According to subsequent reports, he agreed on a deal with leading opposition leader Benazir Bhutto, in which he would grant senior opposition leaders amnesty from corruption charges and participation in free elections, in return for him becoming the civilian president of the country.[65] This paved the way former prime minister Bhutto's return to Pakistan in late 2007. However, she took a strong, principled stand against terrorism and became a key target for the militants. On December 28, 2007, she was assassinated, plunging Pakistan into deep political crisis as she was a key democratic alternative to Musharaff and the militants.[66] Al Qaeda claimed credit for her murder, though the prime suspect is an Al Qaeda affiliate, Baitullah Mehsud, the Taliban leader of the militant TPP in the northwest provinces.[67]

This latest in a string of terrorist atrocities, however, led to a backlash against the militants. In the elections in February 2008, the Pakistan's People's Party (PPP) led by Bhutto's widower husband, Asif Ali Zardari, won the most seats, with a total of 87. This was followed by another secular party, the Pakistan Muslim League (PML-N) led by former prime minister Nawaz Sharif, with 66 seats, an unexpected result. The Pakistan Muslim League (PML-Q), which supported Musharraf, came third with 38 seats.[68] This meant in effect that the fundamentalist Muslim parties were rejected, once more, by the majority of the electorate.

What was surprising about the 2007 election results was that in the supposedly militant-dominated northwest provinces, where Al Qaeda and the Taliban have found sanctuary, the fundamentalist religious alliance, the Muttehida Majlis Amal (MMA), which had gained control in the 2002 elections, lost power to secular parties. Indeed, it was the Awami National Party (ANP), a Pashtun nationalist party, which emerged as the largest party, followed by the PPP.[69] This unexpected result can only be attributed to the fact that many people in Pakistan, even in an area that is supposedly dominated by extremists, do not in fact want to be ruled by Taliban-style fundamentalist clerics.

However, rooting out the influence of militants in a region where they have become entrenched would be a daunting task for the secularists. The military has launched several offensives against the militants in the northwest provinces but resentment against the military's COIN operations has helped to strengthen the cause of the militants and led to a more general uprising. After suffering heavy casualties, the military has alternated between the use of force and the offer of peace deals and ceasefires to the Taliban. Indeed, many in the public believe that if Pakistan stopped participating in the GWOT, the terrorist attacks would stop. The secular political parties believe that dialogue, not force, is required, and that the government should focus on resolving real grievances rather than be seen to be responding to U.S. pressure.

Beyond this, however, there is a lack of political consensus over counterterrorism strategy within Pakistan. The absence of a stable political center, epitomized by months of political infighting after the February 2008 elections, has resulted in the lack of any coherent, comprehensive strategy to deal with the problem. On top of these, the United

States has been putting pressure on Pakistan to do much more to wipe out the militants, on the grounds that foreign fighters were finding sanctuary in Pakistan.[70] The increasingly frustrated U.S. military has launched attacks on Pakistan territory, but such attacks have backfired. For instance, a U.S. drone attacked a militant gathering in Bajaur in May 2008, killing 14 people, including what the United States claimed to be an Al Qaeda leader.[71] In July 2008, the U.S. air force dropped bombs that killed 11 Pakistani paramilitary troops along the border after Afghan government troops were fired upon.[72] Another attack by U.S. drones killed 12 people in Pakistan in September 2008.[73] These attacks, however, have caused outrage in Pakistan. Moreover, these unilateral attacks by the United States have been widely perceived to be attempts to derail peace agreements between the new government and the militants.

After months of political deadlock following the February 2008 elections, Asif Zardari maneuvered into the position of President, replacing Musharraf. Zardari, like his late wife, Benazir Bhutto, is pro-U.S. and is committed to the war against terrorism, but faces enormous difficulties in overcoming strong domestic anti-U.S. sentiments as well as a fractured body politic.[74]

The U.S. policy in Pakistan under the Bush administration had been bereft of ideas other than to put pressure on the Pakistan government to carry out major military offensives against militants, thus compounding an already difficult situation in Pakistan. A coherent, comprehensive, and cooperative strategy in partnership with the new Pakistan government is clearly needed. The first step is already in place, with the appointment of General Petraeus in September 2008 to oversee the Afghanistan theater. Another positive development is the inauguration of a new Democrat leadership under President Obama in January 2009. Both have promised a new, more coherent approach that would emphasize greater cooperation and a more comprehensive strategy. Whether this will work in the coming months and years remain to be seen.

Local Insurgencies and the GWOT

Can insurgencies in places such as Kashmir, Somalia, Chechnya, and those in Southeast Asia be treated as part of Al Qaeda's global insurgency? The caveat here is suggested by Barack Obama in his Op-Ed cited earlier: Afghanistan and the situation in northwest Pakistan are different. This is because the central Al Qaeda leadership led by Osama bin Laden and his deputy, Ayman Al-Zawahari, as well as the Afghan Taliban, have found safe havens in the tribal regions of northwest Pakistan, a place where the Pakistan government's control has been tenuous at best. Having regrouped, they now pose a growing threat to Afghanistan's stability and could, in time, enable Al Qaeda to plan more global terrorist attacks. Thus, the U.S. objective after 9/11—to remove Al Qaeda safe havens in Afghanistan and destroy its state sponsor, the Taliban regime—in effect remains unfulfilled. Obama is therefore probably right when he stated that Afghanistan and Pakistan are central to the GWOT.

But what about other theaters in the GWOT? Do they really have linkages with Al Qaeda and are working toward meeting its objectives? Recent work on the history and motivations of Muslim rebellions has cast doubt on some of the assumptions of the "new" terrorism model that has informed Washington on its policy choices. While the "new" terrorism model of a globalized, networked, religious terrorist threat provides a useful explanation for the changes in the terrorism phenomenon in a globalizing world, it suffers from a classic levels of analysis problem in international relations. While it accurately describes trends at the global level, it is less useful at the level of the state or the substate region, where more complex political, economic, and social variables have historically been present, and which underlie Muslim alienation and rebellion.

Recent studies on rebellions in Southeast Asia reveal the complexities of Muslim rebellion and indicate that not all local Muslim insurgencies are part of Al Qaeda's plan of global insurgency.[75] Southeast Asia, or more specifically the Malay Archipelago, has the world's largest Muslim population. It also contains the world's busiest waterway and chokepoint, the narrow and strategic Straits of Malacca, through which one quarter of the world's trade, half the world's oil, and two-thirds of its natural gas trade passes. Given the region's strategic importance in the GWOT, it is not surprising that Osama bin Laden had paid particular attention to the region. Indeed, he has provided funding, training, and indoctrination to various local Muslim groups in order to establish an Al Qaeda presence in the region.[76] There has been evidence that Southeast Asia had a significant role in a number of major terrorist attacks, such as 9/11, the abortive Singapore bomb plots of late 2001, the attack on the *USS Cole* off Yemen and Operation Bojinka, in which terrorists planned to simultaneously attack a dozen American airliners in the Asia Pacific.[77] Thus, immediately following the 9/11 events, the United States designated Southeast Asia as the "second front" in the GWOT. In 2006, President Bush revealed that regional Al Qaeda operatives in Southeast Asia had a role in the abortive plan to attack an office tower in Los Angeles.[78] David Kilcullen has also asserted that it is Southeast Asia, not the Middle East, which is crucial to the future of global *jihad*. According to him, "if Southeast Asia is allowed to 'go critical' . . . it is possible that the global *jihad* as an overall system may attain almost unstoppable momentum."[79]

After the 9/11 events, the United States was galvanized to act against the new global terror, convinced it had to take the war on terrorism to its sources, be it in Iraq against rogue dictators such as Saddam Hussein; Afghanistan, which had hosted Osama bin Laden and Al Qaeda; or the Muslim Moro rebels operating in the jungles of Mindanao in Southeast Asia. But the Bush-led GWOT has been a simplistic catch-all construct that tended to conflate every Muslim rebellion with a monolithic threat influenced or directed by Al Qaeda. It had also been heavily weighted toward the application of kinetic military force, based on the premise that killing and capturing the key operators will solve the problem of global terrorism.

The region became aware of the presence of the "new" terrorism when the covert Al Qaeda-linked terrorist network known as the Jemaah Islamiah (or JI) was uncovered following the arrest of the members of its cell in Singapore in January 2002. The JI planned to use 21 tons of a powerful fertilizer bomb, ammonium nitrate, in 7 truck bombs, to attack a number of targets in Singapore, including U.S. military personnel at a subway train station on their way to work at Sembawang (where a U.S. naval logistics facility was based), U.S. naval vessels at Changi Naval Base, key U.S. multinationals, Western and Israeli embassies, and local Singaporean military facilities.[80] The abortive attacks would, collectively, have constituted the largest terrorist attack since 9/11. Instead, the JI struck more successfully in Bali in October 2002, killing 202 people including 88 Australians. It has also been responsible for other recent terrorist attacks, such as the Marriott Hotel bombing in Jakarta, in Indonesia in 2003, the attack on the Australian High Commission in Jakarta in 2004, and a second Bali bombing in October 2005.[81] Since being uncovered in early 2002, over 400 alleged JI operatives have been arrested throughout the region, including its key operations commander and liaison with Al Qaeda, Hambali, who was arrested in Thailand and is now in U.S. custody.[82] These arrests have significantly weakened the Al Qaeda–JI nexus in the region.

The JI is active in Indonesia, Malaysia, Singapore, Philippines, and Australia, and aims to establish a pan-Islamic state in the region. The

JI, however, is not a new group, despite its links to Al Qaeda. Research by Sidney Jones has suggested links between the JI network and the abortive Darul Islam rebellion in Indonesia in the 1950s.[83] That rebellion, which aimed to establish an Islamic state in Indonesia, resulted in the loss of some 25,000 lives. After it was crushed in 1960, however, its ideals survived. Both Abu Bakar Bashir and Abdullah Sungkar, the alleged cofounders of the JI, saw themselves as its ideological successors. They founded the JI network in the early 1990s and later developed links with Al Qaeda through the ex-Afghan *mujahideen* volunteers who returned to Southeast Asia after fighting the Soviets in Afghanistan in the 1980s.

It is obvious that Al Qaeda's training and funding has had a significant impact on such local militant groups, improving their operational effectiveness and organization, and raising the lethality of terrorist attacks to a new level previously unseen in the region. Al Qaeda has also helped them to establish transnational linkages, heightening their sense of belonging to the *umma* or worldwide Muslim community.

However, is the JI really "new"? What is interesting is that all militant groups in the region are, in fact, local in origin. The JI, for instance, predated both Al Qaeda and the 9/11 events, given its origins which can be traced to the abortive Darul Islam rebellion in the 1950s. This indicates that the real catalyst for rebellion stems from the presence of deep political, economic, and social grievances in the region. These grievances have led many to seek solace in radical ideology. The reasons for Muslim alienation and rebellion in the region are therefore complex and deep-seated, and stem from conditions within Southeast Asia itself.

In contrast to the "new" terrorism, the "old" terrorism in the form of ethnonationalist separatist insurgencies have been going on for many years now, in places such as Aceh, Mindanao, and Patani. These Muslim insurgencies predated Osama bin Laden, Al Qaeda, and the 9/11 events. Their persistence and severity are indicative of the failure of the states involved to achieve legitimacy for their rule since decolonization and independence after the Second World War. As Paribatra and Samudavanija have observed, "in post-colonial SE Asia, it has been conveniently forgotten by central governments that the constructing of what is more accurately a state-nation merely means that external or western imperialism had been replaced by an internalized one, which is potentially more brutal and enduring."[84] Detailed studies of three Muslim separatist insurgencies indicate that while Al Qaeda had attempted to penetrate and build links with these local rebel groups, it has met with mixed results, as it had to battle the preexisting nationalist imperative that has so far remained stronger.[85]

A brief survey of the three main Muslim insurgencies in the Malay Archipelago illustrates the presence of fundamental grievances that have led to Muslim alienation and rebellion. The Moro rebellion centered in Mindanao in the southern Philippines has deep historical roots. Over the years, massive Catholic migration from the north overwhelmed the native Moros so much so that by the 1960s, they had become a minority in their own traditional homeland. There have also been serious problems arising from landlessness, discrimination, poverty, and unemployment. Following the Jabidah massacre of 28 Muslim recruits to the Philippine military at Corregidor in 1968, the Moros rose up in rebellion. The Moro National Liberation Front (MNLF), which was founded in 1972, fought a long civil war. Although it signed a peace accord in 1996, the failure to bring about development in the southern provinces and to resolve fundamental grievances led to a renewed separatist insurgency dominated by a more overtly Muslim group, the Moro Islamic Liberation Front (MILF).

The MILF established ties with Osama bin Laden, who provided funds through his brother-in-law then running a charity in Manila. Osama also provided instructors (such as Ramzi Yousef, the first World Trade Center bomber in 1993) to help train the insurgents as well as regional militants. But the 9/11 events, rather than galvanizing the MILF into greater fervor for the radical pan-Islamist cause, actually provided a boost to the peace process as the MILF leadership quickly distanced itself from Al Qaeda.[86] Since then, under the leadership of its present leader, Murad Ibrahim, the MILF has strongly emphasized its nationalist credentials, declaring it to be a "legitimate liberation organization," that it "counts on committed popular memberships who are not fanatical about their religion," and that it would not link up with "terrorism or any extremist groups using religious faith as a tool for terroristic activities."[87] Significantly, the Philippine government's chief negotiator for peace talks with the MILF, Jesus Dureza, stated in October 2002 that he found the MILF "friendlier than the government" in building a climate of peace and development in Mindanao, citing military officials who were intent on using force to resolve the Moro problem.[88] Nonetheless, it is also acknowledged that younger MILF commanders and their followers are more responsive to radical ideology and they have defied their leadership on occasion to offer refuge to JI rebels fleeing from the authorities. The situation in southern Philippines is also complicated by the presence of a much smaller but overtly radical Islamist group that does have close links with Al Qaeda, viz. the Abu Sayaff Group. Indeed, the Abu Sayaff Group and JI carried out a deadly joint operation when it bombed a ferry in Manila Bay in 2004, resulting in the deaths of over 100 people.[89] After the 9/11 events, the United States sent troops and advisers to train and provide technical and surveillance support for the Philippine army in its operations against the Abu Sayaff Group.

Another serious Muslim separatist insurgency had existed, until recently, in Aceh, in the northern tip of Sumatra in Indonesia. Indonesia's transmigration program under the Suharto regime led to an influx of Javanese migrants, who created much resentment from the locals as they competed for jobs and opportunities. Widespread corruption, lack of development, poverty, discrimination, and domination by the Javanese elite resulted in many grievances against Jakarta. Moreover, the people of the province did not benefit from the presence of huge gas deposits, with much of the revenue going to Jakarta. The presence of fundamental grievances resulted in armed separatist rebellion against the Indonesian state. Yet, despite the evident piety of a deeply religious province, the main rebel group in Aceh, the Gerakan Aceh Merdeka (GAM), consistently emphasized its nationalist credentials as well as territorial objectives. Thus, when Al Qaeda leaders led by its deputy chief, Al-Zawahiri, visited the province in 2000, they were rebuffed by GAM, which did not want to get involved in a wider religious war. Following the 9/11 events, GAM even sent a message of condolence to the U.S. Ambassador in Jakarta.[90]

In southern Thailand, a long-running Muslim insurgency has its roots in political, economic, and social grievances against the central government in Bangkok. The southern provinces, dominated by Malay Muslims, were incorporated into modern Thailand through the Anglo-Siamese Treaty of 1909. In subsequent years, the influx of Thai Buddhists and a policy of assimilation (abandoned in 1977) alienated the Malays. The centralization of the bureaucracy eroded the power of Malay royalty and the religious elite, while Thai education and language challenged traditional Malay Muslim culture. There have thus been numerous small-scale revolts. However, the situation worsened after the Thaksin government came to power in 2002.[91] The Thaksin government emphasized a tough military approach to the insurgency, which led to some deadly, and unnecessary, incidents, which have contributed to a worsening of the insurgency. In April 2004, for instance, 108 Muslims were killed by security forces in a single day, with 32 killed while sheltering at a historic mosque.[92] In October 2004, at Tak

Bai, 85 unarmed Muslim protesters died after they suffocated in police vans.[93] Despite claims by the Thai authorities that the insurgents had deep links with Al Qaeda, there has been little evidence although JI and Al Qaeda operatives have found shelter amongst coreligionists in southern Thailand.[94] Although the level and organization of violence dramatically increased from 2001, Western tourists and interests have not been targeted. The insurgency has, for the time being, remained local and nationalist in orientation, as well as largely confined to the four southern Muslim provinces. Indeed, according to key Al Qaeda–JI commander, Hambali, now in U.S. custody, the insurgents had rebuffed Al Qaeda when approached for assistance to carry out bombings in Thailand.[95] However, there is the danger that the global *jihadists* would eventually be able make inroads if the situation continues to be mismanaged by the government.

From this brief survey of Muslim insurgencies in the Malay Archipelago, it is evident that the nature of Muslim alienation and rebellion in the region is historical and complex, involving long-standing fundamental grievances against the state. There are also clear tensions between the "new" radical pan-Islamism advocated by Al Qaeda and the preexisting "old" ethnonationalism. The region thus demonstrates a complex mix of new and old terrorism, with change existing side by side with continuity. However, despite the presence of Al Qaeda affiliates such as the JI, which has carried out terrorist attacks against Western targets, this brief survey also suggests that the "old" ethnonationalism impulse has remained more dominant for the time being, although it is entirely possible that further mismanagement and poor strategy in managing the problem in Mindanao and southern Thailand could lead to a change. What is clear is that local Muslims have complex, long-standing, and homegrown political, economic, and social grievances that dates back before 9/11 and Al Qaeda. Thus, not every Muslim rebel in the region has turned out to be a dedicated Al Qaeda operative striving to achieve pan-Islamist religious objectives.

This suggests that there are much more complex variables at work in various Muslim regions, and while Osama bin Laden has sought to link them together as part of the global religious war, it would be foolhardy for Washington to treat them all as part of the GWOT, because many local Muslim rebels themselves may not, in fact, see themselves as being part of the global *jihad*. Like Sunni insurgents in Iraq, their objectives could in fact differ quite markedly from Al Qaeda. The examples from Southeast Asia also suggest that many existing Muslim insurgencies have at their root long-standing socioeconomic grievances, which cannot be redressed solely through the use of force. Thus, understanding the complexity of such rebellions is important if an appropriate and effective counterterrorism strategy is to be devised, and if local Muslims are to be prevented from signing up to Al Qaeda's global *jihad*.

In turn, this suggests the need for caution in treating local Muslim insurgencies as part of Al Qaeda's global insurgency. At the very least, the premise of a global insurgency needs qualification. But this raises questions over the efficacy of a grand strategic approach based on a GCOIN strategy.

The New Global Counterinsurgency Strategy

The question of a global insurgency could be posed in another way. Should the global threat from Al Qaeda's violent *jihadist* ideology mean that it should be treated as a global insurgency, with the logical strategy to counter it being a strategy of GCOIN?

In 2003, American historian Thomas Mockaitis argued that the whole concept of the GWOT should be abandoned, since war, in international law, has a precise definition and does not readily lend itself to a gray-area phenomenon like terrorism.[96] Al Qaeda's transformation into a generalized global threat necessitates the reconceptualization of the GWOT not as a war but as a GCOIN operation, in which there is a change in emphasis from a direct military to an indirect comprehensive approach, with the military taking a more supporting role in a predominantly ideological, political, and diplomatic response, with the objective of containing the problem.[97] This GCOIN strategy should focus on winning hearts and minds, the same strategy that was used to defeat communist guerrillas during the Malayan Emergency.[98]

In his testimony before U.S. Congress in February 2006, Bruce Hoffman too called for a new approach built around a GCOIN approach, utilizing many of the classic lessons of comprehensive counterinsurgency used in dealing with cold war insurgencies. According to Hoffman:

> ...rather than viewing the fundamental organizing principle of American national defence strategy in this unconventional realm as a global war on terrorism (GWOT) as it has been to date, it may be more useful to re-conceptualize it in terms of a global counter-insurgency (GCOIN). Such an approach would a priori knit together the equally critical political, economic, diplomatic,

and developmental sides inherent to the successful prosecution of counterinsurgency to the existing dominant military side of the equation.[99]

Both Mockaitis and Hoffman advocate a comprehensive approach to counterterrorism, the objective being not victory in the conventional sense but containment of an age-old social phenomenon within acceptable boundaries.[100] This containment strategy is similar in some ways to that used during the cold war to counter global communism.

However, there has been the problem of defining what this comprehensive GCOIN strategy should entail. A number of analysts have tried to explain how a comprehensive grand strategic approach should work, without resorting to COIN models. For instance, Daniel Byman advocates a Five Front War, focusing on: a more effective military that can help allies fight insurgents rather than doing so directly; a war on ideas focusing on the *jihadists'* unpopular deeds and theology; better intelligence, which requires working effectively with local partners; homeland defense based on realistic threat assessments rather than the unrealistic goal of hardening all possible targets; and finally, promoting democratic reform throughout the Muslim world while recognizing the limits of reform. Byman also argued against unilateralism, advocating instead multilateral approaches based on cooperation with allies.[101]

Similarly, Rohan Gunaratna and Michael Chandler argue in their collaborative book *Countering Terrorism* that defeating global terrorism requires a coordinated, collaborative effort from the international community. They are critical of the failure of the United States in using its considerable economic instruments, and strengths in diplomacy and public affairs, and fault it for preferring a kinetic, military approach to dealing with global terrorism. They argue that while investment in operational counterterrorism is still essential to reduce the immediate threat, it is necessary to craft a long-term strategic response. This would entail a "multi-pronged approach against a multi-dimensional threat," i.e., a comprehensive approach.[102] Interestingly, they also cited the Malayan Emergency in justifying the need for a hearts and minds strategy.[103] Although they reserve their harshest criticisms for the failure of the United Nations in providing the necessary global leadership against terrorism, they see no alternative to the United Nations in taking the lead for the multilateral comprehensive global approach that is required. Only the United Nations could find the necessary international consensus to meeting the challenges of protracted regional conflicts (the breeding ground for terrorism), global terrorism, and the proliferation of weapons of mass destruction.[104]

Similarly, while Jason Burke recognizes that there must be a military component to countering terrorism, he argues in favor of strategies that are broader and more sophisticated. We must, according to him, "eliminate our enemies without creating new ones."[105] He correctly identifies the center of gravity in the war on terrorism as residing in the "courage, decency, humor and integrity of the vast proportion of the world's 1.3 billion Muslims."[106] Burke adds that it is this that is restricting the spread of Al Qaeda and its warped worldview, not the activities of counterterrorist experts or the military strategists.[107] In doing so however, Burke panders to neo-left academe, which has treated counterterrorist experts and realist academics as a monolithic group of right-wing, warmongering adversaries who have somehow come to underpin the Bush administration's unilateral military-oriented approach that has spawned abuses such as torture, rendition, and Guantanamo Bay. But the decency and professional integrity of realist-oriented academic experts need to be recognized for their important contribution to the policy debate, and for the honesty of their critique of the failures of the Bush-led GWOT.

Contrasting with Mockaitis, Hoffman, Byman, Gunaratna, and Burke is the more narrow counterterrorism and COIN approach in the work of military-oriented analysts who focus on how the military could do better against insurgent adversaries. James Corum, for instance, tries to explain how modern COIN strategies could be updated through aiding and training allies and local forces to fight insurgents, fighting a better psychological war focused on winning hearts and minds, and the establishment of good intelligence.[108] Corum also argues for a whole of government, interagency approach to suppressing insurgencies, as doing so requires a large amount of civilian expertise that the military simply does not have, and cites the need for some sort of a Marshall Plan that had been instrumental in defeating communism. According to Corum, "we cannot build a military strategy around the hope that the United States will carry out the major conventional military operations, and then turn missions such as nation-building over to coalitions and international organizations."[109] He reserves his harshest criticism for the U.S. military, calling for reform and restructuring in the wake of its failures since 9/11.[110]

Corum's military-oriented, COIN approach is not surprising given his credentials as a professor at the U.S. Army Command and General Staff College, an institution that trains senior commanding officers of the U.S. armed forces. His prescriptions read very much like an update of British COIN doctrine, but they are unrealistic for several reasons.

Firstly, the military-oriented prescriptions obscure the complex nature of insurgencies, which require attention to its underlying political, economic, and social causes. Secondly, the United States can today no longer afford to fund a Marshall Plan as it did in the early days of the cold war and therefore cannot engage effectively in nation-building on its own, if the experiences in Iraq and Afghanistan are any guide. Moreover, the idea of the United States rebuilding entire countries is a chimera in the context of the severe economic recession that emerged in late 2008 as a result of the subprime lending crisis in the United States and record deficits. Finally, Corum's work raises an important issue. Can COIN strategy be used to counter global terrorism?

Austin Long has argued that it can because the key starting point is the state. Whether the goals of a local insurgency end at the nation-state level or transcend it, the nation-state is the battleground for insurgents. If nation-sates can defeat insurgents within their own borders, then sporadic and localized terrorism will be the best that Al Qaeda could possibly hope for. Thus, the successful application of COIN in local theaters among local allies would be the best hope of countering the global terrorism waged by Al Qaeda.[111]

This line of argument has been evident in the work of arguably the best articulated and cogent construction of the newly evolving GCOIN strategy. David Kilcullen is an unlikely source, being an Australian army officer who wrote a PhD thesis on the Darul Islam rebellion in Indonesia in the 1950s. An expert on COIN who served and taught in a number of countries, his *Twenty-Eight Articles: Fundamentals of Company-level Counterinsurgency* is a short article used by a number of armed forces including the United States to train junior military officers in the operational art of COIN.[112] As a nonpartisan analyst from Australia, Kilcullen's careful and sophisticated ideas articulated in straightforward language found a ready audience within the U.S. military that has been searching for answers to the problem of containing the insurgency in Iraq. He began with identifying the key future challenge facing the U.S. military, which is in fighting adversaries using asymmetric tactics. According to Kilcullen:

> Any smart enemy has watched what is happening in Iraq and Afghanistan and they would have worked out how to beat the West, so this kind of thing is not going to go away. We could leave Iraq tomorrow, but until we demonstrate an ability to win this kind of campaign, any smart enemy is going to adopt these tactics.[113]

Kilcullen's assessment stems from his view that globalization has changed the nature of security threats, and that the United States' continued military dominance will force others to adopt asymmetric strategies against it.

In 2004, Kilcullen called for a reconceptualization of counterterrorism strategy in view of the changed nature of the threat. According to Kilcullen, the threat from Al Qaeda has been transformed into a dispersed and amorphous global insurgency. The GWOT is therefore in reality a campaign to counter a globalized Islamist insurgency. Accordingly, COIN theory would be more relevant in countering it than traditional counterterrorism. However, he acknowledged that classical COIN was designed to defeat insurgency in one country and thus, what is needed is a new, updated COIN paradigm that could address the problem of globalized insurgency.[114]

Central to Kilcullen's construct is his premise that globalization and other forces have resulted in "new" forms of insurgencies that are different from those during the cold war era. In doing so, Kilcullen cleverly uses a dichotomy similar to the old versus new terrorism dichotomy in his analysis. Kilcullen departs from Mockaitis in that he is critical of efforts at rediscovering and revisiting "classical COIN" as an answer to the conundrum in Iraq even though he is himself revising an old paradigm. His critique of the old COIN models contrasts with the "new" features of insurgencies in our post–cold war era of globalization, such as the fact that today's Internet-based virtual sanctuary is beyond the reach of counterinsurgent forces and the fact that modern communications has so compressed the operational level of war that almost any tactical action can have immediate strategic impact.[115]

He argues that the transnational character of modern insurgency is a new feature, given the ability of insurgents in various theaters to cooperate with each other. They are also harder to defeat, as religiously motivated insurgents may not really want to achieve any practical objective but rather be a *mujahid*, earning God's favor by sacrificing himself on the battlefield.[116] These arguments are less convincing, given that during the cold war communist insurgencies did try to work together as, for instance, they did to some extent in Indochina. In many cases, left-wing terrorists adopted a transnational mode of operation as well as engaged in cooperation with like-minded groups. Examples include the worldwide terrorist attacks and the cooperation between the Palestinian Liberation Organization, the Japanese Red Army, and the Baadar Meinhoff Gang. It can also be argued that today's insurgents and terrorists, despite their religious motivation and the desire for *mujahid* status among many foot soldiers, do have a political agenda. Al Qaeda might operate much like the Communist International (or Comintern) in coordinating and instigating uprisings around the world but ultimately, the objective is the overthrow of current regimes in the Middle East and other Muslim lands and replacing them with a greater caliphate ruled by the *sharia*. Amongst local Muslim insurgents, such as those in Southeast Asia, there are also tangible and concrete political and territorial objectives that they are fighting for.

More convincingly, Kilcullen argues that modern insurgencies operate like a "self-synchronizing swarm of independent, but cooperating cells," and that this diffused, cell-based structure creates mass movements without mass organisation to target, thus rendering classical COIN measures ineffective.[117] Thus, security forces must now control a complex "conflict ecosystem" rather than defeat a single, specific enemy. The unity of effort that classical COIN prescribes cannot be achieved in the modern era because of the explosion of nonstate actors such as NGOs, global media, and religious leaders; instead, a collaborative effort based on a common diagnosis of the problem might work for modern insurgencies. Kilcullen also argued that modern COIN "may be 100% political," given that comprehensive media coverage has made any combat action a political warfare engagement. More importantly, he argued that in modern COIN, there is no victory in the traditional sense; instead, "permanent containment" may be needed to prevent defeated insurgents transforming into terrorist groups. Finally, instead of secret intelligence, situational awareness matters more; instead of an organization that can be penetrated, a cultural and demographic knowledge of the population would be required.[118]

An important idea that Kilcullen has discussed is the need to understand the numerous cultures present in an insurgent ecosystem. Cultural awareness and cultural understanding leads to cultural leverage. Thus, "every key operator in the War on Terrorism needs a comprehensive understanding of Islam, jihad, Islamist ideology and Muslim culture."[119] Understanding them helps COIN forces understand the divisions among insurgent groups and to exploit them. Thus, according to Kilcullen:

> The bottom line is that no handbook relieves a professional counterinsurgent from the personal obligation to study, internalize and interpret the physical, human, informational and ideological setting in which the conflict takes place. Conflict ethnography is key...you have to be a participant observer. And the key is to see

beyond the surface differences between our societies and these environments...to the deeper social and cultural drivers of conflict, drivers that locals would understand on their own terms.[120]

This need for cultural understanding has been translated into the controversial policy of embedding anthropologists and other social scientists with U.S. combat teams in Iraq and Afghanistan. While praised by the U.S. military for helping to reduce the number of combat operations by their ability to resolve problems due to their understanding of local culture and subtleties, the Human Terrain Team program has been attacked by many academics uneasy with fellow academics contributing to a brutal war of occupation.[121] Yet, Montgomery McFate, for instance, has been unrepentant, penning a self-explanatory article "The Military Utility of Understanding Adversary Culture."[122] Those who defend the likes of McFate would argue that military anthropologists have contributed to a more comprehensive, and more humane, approach by the U.S. military in implementing COIN.

Central to Kilcullen's new COIN paradigm is the use of systems analysis. He argued that "traditional reductionist systems analysis cannot handle the complexity of insurgency." On the other hand, "complex adaptive systems modeling shows that the global nature of the present Islamist *jihad*...derives from the links in the system—energy pathways that allow disparate groups to function in an aggregated fashion across intercontinental distances." Therefore, countering global insurgency does not demand the destruction of every Islamist insurgent from the Philippines to Chechnya.[123] Instead, Kilcullen argued, counterterrorism response should revolve around a GCOIN strategy he called "disaggregation," which focuses on "interdicting links between theaters, denying the ability of regional and global actors to link and exploit local actors, disrupting flows between and within *jihad* theaters, denying sanctuary areas, isolating Islamists from local populations, and disrupting inputs from sources of Islamism in the greater Middle East."[124] He defined "disaggregation" as delinking or dismantling, the objective of which is to prevent the dispersed and disparate elements of the *jihad* movement from functioning as a global system. Just as the containment strategy was central to the cold war, this new, updated global COIN strategy, Kilcullen argued, would provide a "unifying strategic conception," or Grand Strategy, that has been lacking in the war on global terrorism.[125]

Specifically, Kilcullen's strategy of disaggregation focuses on the following: interdicting links between Islamist theaters of operation within the global insurgency; denying the ability of regional and global actors to link and exploit local actors; interdicting flows of information, personnel, finance, and technology between and within *jihad* theaters; denying sanctuary areas within theaters; isolating Islamists from the local populations through theater-specific measures to win hearts and minds; disrupting inputs (personnel, finance, information) from sources of Islamism in the Middle East to dispersed *jihad* theaters worldwide; and finally, preventing or ameliorating communal and sectarian conflicts, which create the grievances on which the *jihadists* can prey.[126]

Although Kilcullen acknowledged that the new COIN approach which the United States is gradually adopting is really a British Commonwealth approach, it is intellectually more sophisticated and certainly more appropriately articulated for a globalized era.[127] As a grand strategy, it imbibes the lessons of not just classical COIN, but also the lessons of Iraq and the evolving nature of Al Qaeda on the global stage, and provides the unifying paradigm to the comprehensive approach that is needed to replace the failed kinetic, military-oriented approach of the Bush-led GWOT that followed 9/11.

What is immediately striking, however, is the fascination with adapting classical COIN strategy to meet present-day threats, which should come as no surprise, given that after 2003, insurgency and terrorism became conflated in the way global terrorism and Iraq somehow became conflated. Though Iraq and global terrorism had no linkages, U.S. actions in Iraq have made this a self-fulfilling prophecy. Thus, fighting local insurgencies and fighting Al Qaeda at the global level have become intertwined due to the Iraq experience. Kilcullen, and other military officers around General David Petreaus, have been strongly influential in revamping U.S. COIN strategy in Iraq, as contained in the revised Counterinsurgency Field Manual. But has the new approach actually worked in Iraq? In 2008, the fall in terrorist attacks and the reduction in the scale of the insurgency could be partly attributed to the success of the new COIN approach. But more significant factors, such as the unexpected falling out between Sunni nationalist insurgents and Al Qaeda, and the restraint shown by Moqtada Al-Sadr, the leader of the Mehdi Army, have been at work. Various groups in Iraq also appear to be strengthening their positions through political maneuvering ahead of an ultimate U.S. drawdown or pullout. In Afghanistan, the new U.S. COIN strategy has either not been properly implemented, or has been faring poorly. It will be interesting to see if the appointment of General Petraeus to oversee that theater in September 2008 would make a difference.

A number of questions could also be legitimately asked about the evolving GCOIN. The obvious ones to begin with are: Do classic COIN models (such as those from the success of the Malayan Emergency) hold any lessons for dealing with modern-day Iraq? Are there lessons from such models for a GCOIN strategy at the global level?

But the more interesting questions are these: should the global insurgency be dealt with by a GCOIN strategy built in part by an understanding of classic COIN, which was meant to apply at a much lower level—i.e., the level of a state or a subregion of a state? Conversely, how much of the newly evolving GCOIN should guide strategy at the local level in countering insurgents operating in Iraq and similar theaters? These questions are important because the variables operating at one level, for instance, the global level, might be different from the much more complex variables operating at the local level, i.e., what is referred to in International Relations as the "levels of analysis" problem. Will a GCOIN strategy work at various levels of analysis, i.e., the global, the region, the state, and the substate? We have seen in the case study of Southeast Asia above that it would require an exceedingly sophisticated level of understanding in order to manage and contain the complex problem of Muslim rebellion. But as sophisticated as Kilcullen's formulation is, does the United States have the intellectual capacity and resources to manage a global theater in the culturally sensitive, deeply knowledgeable manner that Kilcullen advocates?

GCOIN also assumes a certain level of consensus domestically and more importantly, globally, amongst key allies. Domestically, with a fractured body politic divided along partisan lines and in the context of deep mistrust of Washington, will a GCOIN strategy command the requisite political will and consensus that is required for it to succeed? Globally, in a more fluid and complex world, with U.S. soft power at a nadir, building a global consensus against terrorism will be a serious challenge. Moreover, the suspicion of peer challengers and rivals has already prevented effective global cooperation with Russia and China, where their militant Islamist problem is actually more acute.

Furthermore, can we conflate insurgency at the local level with the global insurgency? Is the "new" insurgency really "new" or have we made too much of the changes to what is in effect a more efficient local insurgency albeit with transnational linkages? The examples from Southeast Asia earlier in this chapter illustrate the complexity of Muslim alienation and rebellion. The new–old debate here parallels the new–old debate in terrorism studies, but the same criticisms could be levied. The new-old debate is important, because in emphasizing the new characteristics, we might in fact miss the fact that the old ethnonationalist issues and motivations are still more salient. This has important implications of how we approach insurgencies at the local level and raises questions over the wisdom of conflating it with a strategy meant to apply at the global level.

Questions can also be raised regarding the present quest for grand strategy, which has evolved toward a GCOIN strategy. Does a grand strategy based on GCOIN work in today's very complex world with its uneven penetration of globalization and a complex mixture of old and new security challenges? Are we missing something here in the quest for another quick fix in the form of a grand strategic solution to the problem of global terrorism? Is there not a great danger of GCOIN aggregating instead of disaggregating various theaters and separate strategic issues? For instance, Iran could become a subject of GCOIN, even though it is not a participant in Al Qaeda's global *jihad*. And, is Iraq really the center of gravity in the war against global terrorism, a premise that David Kilcullen accepts but which is surely not the case?[128]

Moreover, even if a GCOIN grand strategy is the answer, it would require a fundamental reconfiguration of U.S. military and security institutions. But would this be a wise course of action, given that peer state competitors and conventional military deterrence remain needed? Even if the United States decided to adopt such a strategy, can it overcome the deeply ingrained American Way of War within the U.S. military and security establishments? For instance, what is needed is a learning and adaptive bureaucratic culture that encourages flexibility and adaptability. This is what Al Qaeda has achieved through force of circumstances, as it has been dealt a weak hand with much less humanpower and resources than a state, let alone a superpower such as the United States. Yet, too much resources has hobbled the U.S. response, which has relied too much on technology, mass, resources, and military capabilities, resulting in the lack of imagination and the ability to adapt in the face of a smart and nimble adversary. Can the United States overcome its ingrained cultural habit of using force as an easy option? While a consensus could plausibly be found regarding the key elements of a GCOIN strategy based on the mistakes and failures of the GWOT, it is far from clear if any GCOIN strategy could work precisely because it would require fundamental organizational and cultural changes to the ingrained American Way of War. Finding the political will to overcome bureaucratic barriers to changing a long-established political culture will be a daunting challenge.

Besides, the intellectual resources needed, firstly, to achieve clarity in understanding the nature of the complex security challenges; secondly, in devising a range of options to deal with these challenges; and thirdly, in implementing these options, depend crucially on intellectual, linguistic, and analytical abilities as well as a deep empirical understanding of the world. This requires expertise in a range of area studies disciplines, and most crucially the ability to think within a positivist framework. The United States is simply not equipped intellectually for the task, including the implementation of a GCOIN strategy however it is conceptualized, given the fact that positivist empirical social science has given way since the end of the cold war to dominant neo–Marxist postpositivist approaches in academe and social science research. Postpositivism asks the question "what ought to be" rather than "what is" but this prescriptive, normative approach has led to ideological crusades, for instance, and ironically, in the form of right-wing neoconservatism. Within universities and academe, it has led to neo–left dominance and the marginalization of realist-oriented academics. But existential problems require deep empirical knowledge in order for solutions to be framed in a way that better corresponds to reality as can be verified. Without the language and cultural training, area studies expertise and intellectual knowledge based on a deep empiricism, the tools to put GCOIN strategy to work are absent.

Finally, there are legitimate questions that can be asked regarding the seemingly obvious objective of winning hearts and minds. This implies that there is a neutral population whose loyalty is to be won. But winning hearts and minds in the Muslim world, particularly in the wake of Iraq and eight years of the Bush administration's hard military approach may prove well nigh impossible, even with a fresh start amid high hopes for the Obama administration that was inaugurated in January 2009. How can the anger and hostility at the United States be so easily dissipated? How can the United States regain its moral legitimacy after frittering it away so quickly in Iraq, Guantanamo, Abu Ghraib, renditions, and the use of torture?

Ultimately, there are no easy answers. A comprehensive approach focusing on winning hearts and minds; disaggregating local conflicts from the global *jihad*; using a range of military and nonmilitary instruments; building a global consensus against terrorism; and achieving a whole of government approach to dealing with terrorism and insurgency, all takes time and effort to bear fruit. No matter how cogently a GCOIN grand strategy might be constructed, it will have to overcome many obstacles in the United States itself. For instance, can it overcome the contending domestic pressure groups and political partisanship to enable it to get the necessary political consensus and support? Even if this is possible, does the United States have the resources to fight a GCOIN on a global scale, particularly given its own parlous economic state at the end of the Bush presidency in early 2009? Has its decline in absolute power and moral legitimacy left the United States unable to lead such a global strategy? Finally, can there be a global consensus on such a strategy, particularly one led by the United States?

Thus, the conclusion must be that the U.S. quest for grand strategy is probably a chimera. Instead, what is likely to happen is that the GWOT will be a long-term ideological struggle that will likely be dealt with by "muddling through," suggesting that patience and a long-term perspective will be required.

CHAPTER EIGHT

The Future for Counterterrorism

The Challenges for Counterterrorism

Since the seminal 9/11 terrorist attacks, Al Qaeda has failed to carry out a single attack in the United States. Indeed, except for attacks in Saudi Arabia, no major terrorist operation around the world since 9/11 can be directly attributed to Al Qaeda. Unprecedented worldwide security action by the United States and its allies appears to have decimated the bulk of Al Qaeda's leadership and operatives. Thus, a U.S. National Intelligence Council report, *Global Trends 2025*, concluded in November 2008 that Al Qaeda's weaknesses, such as its unachievable strategic objectives, inability to attract broad-based support, and self-destructive actions, would cause it to decay.[1] Given that terrorism is an historical social phenomenon, Al Qaeda would ultimately turn out to be no different from established, historical patterns of the terrorist problem.

Yet, despite the decline of Al Qaeda, the organization, it is also clear that there remains considerable unease and apprehension over the threat of catastrophic mass casualty terrorism begun by Al Qaeda on 9/11 and which many believe will remain a feature of global society. Another reason for the unease is the sense of strategic failure since 9/11, which stems from the many terrorist attacks around the world since then and which appear to suggest that the global terrorist problem has grown exponentially despite the U.S. and international counterterrorism actions. Initial counterterrorism successes, such as the arrest of Al Qaeda operatives throughout the world and the swift ouster of Al Qaeda and its Taliban allies from its sanctuaries in Afghanistan in late

2001, have given way to growing doubts and criticism at the evolving U.S. strategy in the light of the continuing threat of global terrorism.

There is also growing consensus that the terrorist attacks since 9/11 have been heavily influenced or inspired by Al Qaeda's radical ideology as well as enabled by U.S. strategic mistakes. This suggests that Al Qaeda and its associates worldwide have not only weathered unprecedented security operations by military and security forces all over the world, but they have also, in fact, adapted, evolved, and grown into an even deadlier global insurgency. As Bruce Hoffman noted in his testimony in the U.S. Congress in February 2006, the current Al Qaeda exists more as an ideology than as an identifiable, unitary terrorist organization. He observed that it has become "an international franchise with like-minded local representatives...today there are many Al Qaedas rather than the single Al Qaeda of the past."[2]

The transformation of Al Qaeda into a global insurgency, with a much greater geographical footprint and much greater support for its radical, violent agenda than in the past by local regional groups and individuals around the world, represents remarkable strategic success in the light of considerable tactical losses suffered by Al Qaeda since 9/11. Despite the deaths and arrests of many of its leaders and operatives, the Al Qaeda radical agenda has survived and outgrown the organization itself. The proof lies in the many deadly Al Qaeda-linked attacks across the globe since 9/11 and the many radical groups, which have adopted its radical pan–Islamist agenda. Hoffman in fact goes further to argue that although Al Qaeda today constitutes an ideological threat, the Al Qaeda core remains dangerous, as it has found safe haven in Pakistan's lawless northwestern provinces bordering Afghanistan.[3] A U.S. National Intelligence Estimate in July 2007 also warned that Al Qaeda is reconstituting its global network and planning attacks on the West while sheltering in those areas.[4] According to another recent assessment, Al Qaeda's intent to attack the U.S. homeland remains undiminished, as it continues to identify, train, and position operatives to mount attacks in the West. Despite setbacks in Iraq, Al Qaeda in Iraq (AQI) remains Al Qaeda's most prominent and lethal regional affiliate. More seriously, since early 2006, Pakistani militant groups have increased their collaboration with Al Qaeda.[5] In conjunction with the worsening security situation in Afghanistan as a result of the Taliban resurgence, there has thus been a growing body of opinion that the United States needs to refocus the Global War on Terror (GWOT) from Iraq to Afghanistan and Pakistan, a line of thinking, which has been embraced by the new Obama administration in the United States.

Al Qaeda's global influence will be hard to counter or eliminate. Many of the techniques and skills required for the many deadly contemporary terrorist attacks that have taken place around the world since 9/11 have been imparted by Al Qaeda to its own operatives and many more through its training manuals, as well as training camps in Afghanistan in the 1990s. For instance, although suicide bombings as a terrorist tactic is not new, Al Qaeda has played an important role in its spread, facilitating its adoption by local groups and radical associates around the world, including in the Philippines and Indonesia.[6] Al Qaeda has succeeded in justifying it ideologically and glorifying it to such a degree that there have been many willing volunteers. The success of suicide bombings as a terrorist tactic has led to many terrorist attacks since 9/11.

The disastrous U.S. decision to invade Iraq in 2003, an unnecessary war in the context of the GWOT as it turned out, has also turned Iraq into a vast training center for terrorists. Serious mistakes, such as the lack of a postconflict plan to stabilize the country, and the incompetent manner in which the country was run under the United States, led to the outbreak of the anti-U.S. insurgency as well as a deadly civil conflict. The heavy loss of civilian life in Iraq, and the use of extrajudicial measures such as renditions, torture, and indefinite detention at Guantanamo Bay also shocked and outraged the Muslim world. Such strategic missteps have helped in recruitment to the radical cause, even though the overwhelming majority of Muslims worldwide do not subscribe to radical ideology and do not wish to be ruled by Al Qaeda or the Taliban.

The insurgency in Iraq thus attracted foreign *mujahideen* fighters. More seriously, Iraq has proved to be a very useful training ground for honing all the necessary skills in urban terrorism, such as the use of improvised explosive devices (IEDs), car and truck bombs, suicide attacks, ambushes, assassinations, kidnapping, sniper attacks, and sabotage. The application of these newly learned capabilities to urban centers elsewhere could result in the escalation of violence, reaching into countries and regions that hitherto have experienced little organized *jihadist* violence.[7] Al Qaeda's training, funding, and its ideological propaganda has had a significant impact on local militant groups, in terms of improving their motivation, operational effectiveness, and organization, and raising the lethality of terrorist attacks to a new level previously unseen in many regions. For instance, this has happened in Southeast Asia, in the case of the deadly Bali bombing in 2002 that killed 202 people. In southern Thailand, insurgents have, since 2005, begun to use weapons and tactics that appear to have been imported from Iraq and Afghanistan, such as the use of mobile phones to trigger bombs, and IEDs as roadside bombs.[8]

Al Qaeda's radical cause has been helped by advanced communication technologies in an age of globalization, which have helped to facilitate the spread of radical ideology. The phenomenon of self-radicalization means that even without the efforts of local radical groups, individuals could still become radicalized to join militant terrorist groups or set up cells themselves. Thus, Marc Sageman has argued that the threat now emanates from the grassroots, such as radicalized individuals and groups who meet and plot in their neighborhoods and on the Internet.[9]

However, this inevitably leads to the question as to why some people might be attracted to militant ideology. According to Jason Burke, the root causes of modern militancy lie in a complex mix of grievances that are the first step on the road to terrorism. He observed that "social and economic problems, though the link to terrorism is indirect, are critical as a pre-condition," and that "such problems are growing more, not less, widespread and profound throughout the Islamic world."[10] For those who feel angry and disempowered, radical Islam provides an answer, a message that, as Burke ruefully observed, is easy to pick up in an age of globalization.[11]

Yet, the GWOT has taken place in the backdrop of a more fundamental change in the nature of the new security challenges from nonstate actors. In Jeffrey Norwitz's groundbreaking volume, *Armed Groups: Studies in National Security, Counterterrorism and Counterinsurgency,* the concept of "armed groups" is used to describe the complex security challenges by such groups in a globalized but fractured post–cold war world. Armed groups, according to Norwitz, includes classic insurgents, terrorists, guerillas, militias, police agencies, criminal organizations, warlords, privatized military organizations, mercenaries, pirates, drug cartels, apocalyptic religious extremists, orchestrated rioters and mobs, and tribal factions.[12] These armed groups, empowered by globalization, operate not just in many weak and failed states but have also found sustenance in the strongest ones. They epitomize the complex security challenges that governments and the international community face in building global governance and security in the post–cold war era. Writing in the same volume, Peter Curry has argued, from his experience with Afghan tribal politics, that armed groups are living organisms, not mechanistic organizational structures. Thus, when considering long-term strategy to counter armed groups, it is wise to remember that "small wars are local."[13] In a similar vein, David

Kilcullen's seminal observations on Iraqi tribal mores in his personal blog have also exposed the difficulties of applying strategy to such theaters.[14] Given the complex nature of local small wars in places such as Afghanistan, how do you deal with them? How do you incorporate local dynamics and variables into the strategy needed to counter such small wars?

P. H. Liotta has identified a fundamental weakness in the U.S. approach to countering armed groups. U.S. national security decision making is essentially a rational process but can the United States adapt to the irrational chaos of an adversary, which aims to achieve victory by avoiding defeat? How do you deal with this chaotic "new" asymmetry?[15] It is this broader evolution toward "armed groups," newly empowered by globalization to pose a serious challenge to states, which suggests the need to think beyond terrorism and insurgency to examine more holistically the manner in which globalization, religion, and other factors are fundamentally transforming armed groups and the nature of conflict. After all, it is in this context that Al Qaeda has evolved, adapted, and survived.

Improving Counterterrorism

How then can counterterrorism efforts be improved? After several years of numerous strategic missteps since the seminal 9/11 terrorist attacks, the outlines of what needs to be done have been emerging.

The first step is to acknowledge the complexity of the challenge. The complex, globalizing world of the post–cold war era is simply not amenable to the simplistic and contradictory mix of idealistic democratic principles and the forceful application of U.S. military power that are part of the neoconservative worldview. As Gareth Evans of the International Crisis Group correctly noted, global terrorism is a "complex, multi-dimensional phenomenon, which demands a complex, multi-layered response." Thus, good policy requires "not simplification but complexification." According to Evans, the struggle against violent extremism can be won, but it would not be easy, requiring "a lot more thought and application and persistence, a lot more balanced approach, and a lot more attention to underlying causes and currents as distinct from surface manifestations."[16]

There is thus a growing consensus that an effective counterterrorism approach requires a comprehensive approach at the global, regional, and local levels. At the global strategic level, there is a need for a multilateral and comprehensive approach designed to contain the new global terrorism through the winning of hearts and minds of the Muslim world, where the true center of gravity lies. Most analysts agree that what has to be abandoned is the unilateral and unidimensional military-oriented approach that has characterized the U.S. approach. Indeed, there has been growing recognition that there can be no battlefield solution to terrorism and that military force instead usually has the opposite effect from what it is intended. A recent RAND study, reflecting this growing opinion, thus pointed out that the military instrument "is often overused, alienates the local population by its heavy-handed nature, and provides a window of opportunity for terrorist-group recruitment."[17]

Thomas Mockaitis has therefore argued persuasively that the whole concept of the GWOT has to be abandoned.[18] War is a problematic concept because it implies the emphasis on military force as well as an end-state of "victory," which is difficult to define in nonconventional conflicts. Instead, Al Qaeda's transformation into a generalized global threat akin to a global insurgency requires a "long war" approach in which containment, not victory, may be the only realistic objective. Thus, it is necessary to reconceptualize the GWOT not as a war but as a global counterinsurgency (GCOIN) operation. This means a comprehensive strategy, which focuses predominantly on ideological, political, and diplomatic responses, with the military taking on a more supporting role.[19]

An important focus of this new strategy has to be a battle for hearts and minds. As Jason Burke correctly pointed out, "the greatest weapon available in the war on terrorism is the courage, decency, humour and integrity of the vast proportion of the world's 1.3 billion Muslims...it is this that is restricting the spread of Al Qaeda and its warped worldview."[20] Indeed, long-term success can only come in countering the appeal of radical ideology, but this can only be done if the overwhelming majority of Muslims themselves find radical ideology unappealing. Ultimately, the problem of radicalism can only be won with the support and through the effort of the Muslim communities themselves. The center of gravity, therefore, lies within the Muslim world. However, the unilateral, military-oriented approach promoted by the Bush administration to dealing with global terrorism has put moderate Muslims who disagree with radical ideology on the backfoot.

This new strategy also has to be multilateral in nature if it is to succeed. This invariably means relying on international institutions, laws, and norms, which offers the best chance of building an international consensus on countering global terrorism. In effect, the United States has to learn to work with its allies and friends, in particular those from the Muslim world. For the United States to succeed in the GWOT, it will have to measure success not just in the decline in the number and scope of attacks, the collapse of terrorist morale, and a growing sense of safety among ordinary people, but also in the significant improvement in the political standing and general reputation of the United States in the eyes of the international, and particularly Muslim, communities. It is legitimacy that the United States and its allies, including those in the Muslim world, need in order to marginalize the radical ideologues. To begin to reclaim that legitimacy, however, the United States must somehow find a way to exit from Iraq, for as long as it remains there, Muslim rage will not be assuaged, radical Islam will continue to find recruits, and the problem of global terrorism will remain serious.

Finally, there is a need to fix the deep-seated domestic roots of Muslim rage and alienation in Muslim countries. It is important to recognize that the roots of Muslim rage and alienation lie fundamentally in local political, economic, and social issues and conflicts, whether in Palestine, Chechnya, Kashmir, Mindanao, or southern Thailand. The failure of postconflict rebuilding in Iraq and Afghanistan indicates the need for a proper postsettlement strategy that involves governance, security, and economic development. Without basic services, jobs, rehabilitation, and effective local government, the alienated will not be placated and will have little to lose in resorting to arms. Thus, addressing fundamental grievances has been another lesson from the missteps since 9/11.

A comprehensive approach focusing on winning hearts and minds; disaggregating local conflicts from the global *jihad*; employing a range of military and nonmilitary instruments; building a global consensus against terrorism; and, achieving a whole of government approach to dealing with terrorism and insurgency will take a long time and enormous effort to bear fruit. Patience and a long-term perspective will therefore be required. There is thus growing consensus that this would be a "long war," as well as a long-term ideological struggle. Optimists believe that in the long-run, the United States would ultimately emerge victorious. According to Philip Gordon, "ultimately, violent Islamism is not likely to win enduring support...with time and experience, and if the United States and its allies make the right choices, Muslims will themselves turn against the extremists in their midst."[21]

The evolution toward a GCOIN grand strategic approach has been a natural consequence of this emerging consensus over how to counter the global terrorist challenge. The best articulated construction of the emerging GCOIN strategy has come from David Kilcullen, the influential Australian adviser to the U.S. government on counterinsurgency and counterterrorism. Kilcullen has advocated a GCOIN strategy called "disaggregation," which focuses on "interdicting links between theatres, denying the ability of regional and global actors to link and exploit local actors, disrupting flows between and within *jihad* theatres, denying sanctuary areas, isolating Islamists from local populations, and disrupting inputs from sources of Islamism in the greater Middle East."[22] In other words, delinking these localized grievances from the global *jihad* must thus be the key objective. "Disaggregation" is a sophisticated strategy based on complex systems analysis. Cogent and well-structured, it is postulated as a new form of grand strategy, much like containment during the cold war, but infused with the lessons of classic counterinsurgency albeit adapted to the modern evolution of the "new" insurgency that parallels the emergence of the "new" terrorism. This fascination with adapting counterinsurgency strategy to meet present-day threats should come as no surprise, given that after 2003, insurgency and terrorism have became conflated in the way global terrorism and Iraq somehow became conflated. Though Iraq and global terrorism had no linkages, the U.S. actions in Iraq have made this a self-fulfilling prophecy.

In 2003, Mockaitis complained that "the Al Qaeda attacks have produced no serious reassessment of US foreign policy nor even the recognition that the soft core of support surrounding bin Laden's extremists might have roots in legitimate grievances...calls for change have been easily brushed aside with the cliché that any alteration of US goals amounts to 'giving in to terrorism.'"[23] Further, he decried the fragmentation of terrorism research instead of drawing expertise from a variety of fields, and called for the breaking down of "the walls of rhetoric that have caused soldiers and scholars to view each other with suspicion if not disdain."[24]

Five years later, the U.S. National Defense Strategy released in June 2008 provided some serious reassessments regarding the U.S. approach and reflected all the painful lessons arising from the missteps in U.S. grand strategy since those seminal events of 9/11. The new strategy incorporated the many criticisms and lessons pointed out by military and civilian analysts since then. It was made possible by the departure of Donald Rumsfeld as defense secretary and his replacement by Robert Gates. This resulted in much greater openness to critical assessment as well as a change in emphasis. Chastened by the failure of the United States to deal with asymmetric insurgent and terrorist threats,

Gates has deemphasized military transformation as the key to a New American Way of War and instead stressed the need for more and better trained soldiers rather than expensive weapons systems that cannot be employed in dealing with the "new" insurgencies or in battling the many armed groups that now challenge U.S. power throughout the globe.[25]

The new U.S. National Defense Strategy of 2008 thus acknowledges that "US dominance in conventional warfare has given prospective adversaries, particularly non-state actors and their state sponsors, strong motivation to adopt asymmetric methods to counter our advantages." The United States must therefore "display a mastery of irregular warfare comparable to that which we possess in conventional combat." Meeting these challenges, however, would require "better and more diverse capabilities in both hard and soft power, and greater flexibility and skill in employing them."[26] The National Defense Strategy also echoed the GCOIN strategy espoused by Mockaitis, Hoffman, Kilcullen, and others, when it proclaimed that the United States is now facing a global struggle against extremist ideology. This conflict is a prolonged irregular campaign and a "violent struggle for legitimacy and influence over the population," that is, winning over hearts and minds. The National Defense Strategy also acknowledged the need for a comprehensive approach:

> The use of force plays a role, yet military efforts to capture or kill terrorists are likely to be subordinate to measures to promote local participation in government and economic programs to spur development, as well as efforts to understand and address the grievances that often lie at the heart of insurgencies.[27]

Thus, according to the National Defense Strategy, reflecting the priorities in Iraq and Afghanistan, "the most important military component of the struggle against violent extremists is not the fighting we do ourselves, but how well we help prepare our partners to defend and govern themselves." Reflecting a more multilateral, as opposed to a unilateral, military-oriented approach, the National Defense Strategy also advocated greater collaboration with interagency and international partners to assist vulnerable states and local populations in ameliorating the conditions that foster extremism and dismantling the structures that support the growth of extremist groups.[28] Reflecting Kilcullen's call for disaggregation, the United States would also now "adopt approaches tailored to local conditions that will vary considerably across regions."[29]

The National Defense Strategy also acknowledged the crucial importance of ideological warfare in its reference to "discrediting extremist ideology." It echoed the revised U.S. Army Counterinsurgency Field Manual when it advocated "creating fissures between and among extremist groups and reducing them to the level of nuisance groups that can be tracked and handled by law enforcement capabilities."[30] The National Defense Strategy against terrorism has thus been to take an indirect approach in the "long war," a lesson of the Malayan Emergency.[31]

The National Defense Strategy also called for greater "jointness," as the emerging security challenges require the seamless combination of civil and military options. The United States must, according to the document, "consider further realigning Department structures, and interagency planning and response efforts, to better address these risks and to meet the new needs."[32] Recognizing that the United States could not meet all possible security threats all the time, the document paid special attention to "Managing Risk," in other words, the adoption of a risk management approach to security. According to the document:

> We cannot do everything, or function equally well across the spectrum of conflict. Ultimately, we must make choices. With limited resources, our strategy must address how we assess, mitigate and respond to risk.[33]

The National Defense Strategy under Robert Gates is thus an impressive document, one which has intelligently incorporated the "best-practice" recommendations of those who have studied the U.S. failures and strategic missteps since 9/11. It reflected a rational, objective approach to diagnosing the problems and finding the solutions, an approach made possible by the departure of Donald Rumsfeld and the diminution of neoconservative ideological approaches in the Department of Defense. It also reflected a sober appreciation of the limits of U.S. military power, the need for allies in the context of a more multilateral approach, the employment of a comprehensive approach that would much better utilize nonkinetic instruments, and, in acknowledging the need to manage risk, displayed a keen awareness of the limits of resources compared to the complex security landscape, one that included not just nonstate actors such as terrorist groups but also emerging peer competitors such as China.

There is thus nothing much wrong with the new U.S. National Defense Strategy and much to admire about it. The document complements well the much more sophisticated, comprehensive approach contained in the revised Counterinsurgency Field Manual. It is also an impressive demonstration of the capacity of the United States for the necessary critical self-reflection to learn from previous mistakes and missteps. Despite being responsible for many strategic mistakes through the incoherence and lack of clarity of its strategy, the Bush administration has ironically bequeathed the new Obama administration with the outlines of a coherent grand strategy to counter global terrorism.

However, the problem is that the U.S. pursuit of a grand strategy is a chimera. In practice, significant obstacles remain in its effective implementation. The United States faces significant political, bureaucratic, and other constraints to engage in the thorough overhaul of policy and whole-of-government approach that the new strategy demands. The new approach also demands an intellectual and cultural sophistication coupled with a pragmatic, adaptable mindset that runs counter to the deep-seated bureaucratic value system that has developed around the military-kinetic American Way of War.

But the greatest obstacle is the fact that the United States no longer has the economic resources nor the moral legitimacy (or soft power) to be able to lead a global grand strategy against the threat of global terrorism. Unlike during the cold war in the aftermath of the Second World War, the United States' unipolar moment in the wake of the fall of the Berlin Wall lasted only until around 2005, about 16 years to be precise, when the Iraqi insurgency got under way and exposed the United States' vulnerability to asymmetric challenges to its much vaunted military power. Then, North Korea appeared to have gotten away with its nuclear test in 2006 without any serious consequences. NATO's postwar cohesion under U.S. leadership has been in serious danger in the wake of allied disquiet over the U.S. invasion of Iraq, and the bickering in Afghanistan over strategy and who should do the fighting. This bickering would have paled in comparison if the United States did actually attack Iran, a course of action that was seriously considered in around 2006 by neoconservatives in Washington. Fortunately, the Bush administration did not follow through on this as the realization sunk in that the proposed solution would cause more problems than it would solve. Indeed, the consequences of such a course of action would have been dire not for Iran but for the United States. As Gwynne Dyer observed:

If the United States attacked Iran, most European countries would be scrambling to dissociate themselves from the American action, and it could even spell the end of the NATO alliance...for the

Russians, it would be the final evidence that the United States is a reckless country whose actions can only be constrained by counterbalancing force, and that conclusion would push them into a military understanding with the Chinese...at the end of it, America's power in the world would be greatly diminished.[34]

In other words, if the United States used nuclear weapons in a preemptive strike on Iran or any other state, it would be an exceptional turning point; the United States would become the world's "rogue state" and would have been seen as such, even by its closest allies.

The U.S. pursuit of a grand strategic approach will also not effectively address the very serious and complex problems in Iraq and Afghanistan. The U.S. invasion of Iraq has been, in hindsight, ill-conceived given the boost it has given to Al Qaeda's cause. More seriously, it rewrote the strategic map of the Middle East in a manner that is likely to turn out to be inimical to the strategic interests of the United States in a pivotal region. The U.S. conundrum in Iraq has been summed up by Daniel Byman:

> Every additional day that the United States remains in Iraq is a boon for Al Qaeda and the broader jihadist movement. On the other hand, a US withdrawal that left Iraq in chaos would also be a boon for Al Qaeda.[35]

But the Iraq conundrum has extends beyond this. The United States evicted the Sunnis from power in Iraq with the removal of the secular regime of Saddam Hussein. This power vacuum has now been filled by pro-Iranian Shiite religious parties. As they bide their time while consolidating their position of power in the post-Saddam era, in the long run, they can be expected to come under the increasing sway of the regional power in propinquity, that is, Iran, given that they are not the natural allies of the United States. In the long run, this also opens up the possibility of Iran destabilizing the rest of the Arabian peninsula through Shiites residing there. If this was done with the tacit support of Russia and China, it would lead to strategic retreat for the United States in a region of pivotal importance to it since the United States relies heavily on energy supplies from the Middle East.

Just as seriously, one lesson of Iraq is that the United States should not in fact be in the business of counterinsurgency except under the most pressing of circumstances, as it must in Afghanistan. Not only does the United States historically and in contemporary times demonstrated its lack of ease and competence in fighting such wars, there is simply no political will to be able to sustain a long war of counterinsurgency where the human and economic costs are high. This should constrain any more overseas adventures except in the most pressing of cases. But this also means a diminution of U.S. global power and its ability to defend its interests where it really matters.

The United States in a Changing World

The vicissitudes of U.S. strategy since the pivotal events of 9/11 have been overtaken by fundamental changes in the international system. It is this context that has been missing in the debates about Iraq and the GWOT. As the United States fiddled and Iraq burned, the world has marched on. The shape of the post–cold war world since 9/11 has become clearer. The inability of the United States to stamp its authority in Iraq and Afghanistan, or on "rogue states" such as Iran and North Korea, nor in 2008 to do much about the Russia–Georgia conflict has exposed the limits of the U.S. power in the post–cold war era. Much of this has to do with the march of globalization—the emergence of a global interlinked economy and the free flow of technology and resources have done much to foster a more egalitarian world order, one in which states have never been so powerful yet at the same time so vulnerable. The rise of nonstate actors in the form of armed groups, enabled by globalization, is posing a serious challenge to security and stability not only in weak and failed states but even in the strongest ones, where terrorist groups may find sustenance in the globalized economy and where the discourse on the terrorist threat has now turned its attention to the possible use of weapons of mass destruction in the "new" terrorist quest for mass casualties.

Yet, the events of 9/11 have also strengthened the agency of the state in that it proved that states, and their actions, matter in the GWOT as only the institutions and agencies of states, or what the states can meaningfully provide multilateral bodies such as the United Nations, can provide security against the newly emerging global security threats.

But in a world where states still matter, the position of the United States has diminished under the watch of the Bush administration. The United States would still be a power of note, but in the post-9/11 era, it would only be one among equals. The world as it is evolving will not be unipolar dominated by a single superpower hegemon but will be a multipolar order. According to *Global Trends 2025*, this will consist of rising powers and peer competitors such as China, India, and Brazil, as well as a revitalized Russia, Japan, and the European Union.[36] In time, this will be something akin to a Concert of Powers, characterized by shifting alliances designed to maintain a balance of power. The end of superpower domination and unipolarity is probably a positive development but there are signs that the United States might not take to this reduced status quite so kindly or gracefully, given the inevitable consequences for its strategic interests in energy, access to markets, and global economic interests. As *Global Trends 2025* warned, "historically, the rise of new powers...presented stiff challenges to the existing international system, all of which ended in worldwide conflict."[37] Much will depend on the leadership in the White House in the years and decades following the Bush administration. How successful the United States will be in adjusting to a more multilateral world and how it will be able to influence and work with others toward a global consensus on containing the threat of global terrorism are other important variables.

The Bush administration will be remembered for its hubris and its unrealistic expectations of being able to consolidate unipolar U.S. hegemony against all challengers, state and nonstate, for the foreseeable future. The conflation of counterterrorism with the objective of ensuring U.S. global supremacy would be remembered as the greatest strategic misstep of the Bush administration. The failure of this unilateral project undertaken in the face of global norms and society has eroded U.S. soft power, the one thing that could have ensured U.S. power and influence for a long time to come, in the manner that Britain retained its influence long after its relative decline and the end of empire. Not only that, U.S. unilateralism has severely set back the emergence of a global society with functioning norms, laws, and institutions that could have been beneficial in building multilateral approaches to dealing with the complex security challenges of the post–cold war era. The fact that a discussion on U.S. strategy against global terrorism since 9/11 should lead to a discussion of U.S. strategic failures and an accelerated decline in U.S. global power in terms of influence and prestige is a stunning indictment of the failure of leadership under the Bush administration. The United States, Middle East, and the rest of the world will have to live with the reverberations of the failed strategic policies of the Bush era, such as dealing with the long-term consequences on the GWOT due to the self-inflicted problems in Iraq.

Without U.S. leadership, are we therefore condemned to "muddling through" in the long-term ideological struggle with Al Qaeda? Not necessarily. The answer to the threat of global terrorism would not lie in U.S. grand strategy that implicitly serves only U.S. interests but in multilateral, global efforts among equals. This is where the quest for strategy might more fruitfully lie. The United States and its allies would need great leadership and wisdom to establish a leading voice in this new multilateral, as opposed to unilateral, endeavor, but because this would take time and effort to evolve, it seems that patience and a long-term perspective will be required. This would truly turn out to be a long, and quite messy, war, which could yet be overtaken by new interstate strategic rivalries between the United States on the one hand, and China and Russia on the other.

NOTES

1   The United States and Global Terrorism

1. Andrew T. H. Tan (ed.), *The Politics of Terrorism* (London: Routledge, 2006), pp. 211–212.
2. "Bin Laden Voice on Channel, Says TV Channel: Al Qaeda Tape Finally Claims Responsibility for Attacks," *The Guardian*, September 10, 2002, http://www.guardian.co.uk/media/2002/sep/10/alqaida.september112001
3. "After the Abadan Fire," *Time*, September 4, 1978, http://www.time.com/time/magazine/article/0,9171,912118–1,00.html
4. See Bruce Hoffman, *Inside Terrorism* (New York: Columbia University Press, 2006). For a more succinct description of the New Terrorism, see Bruce Hoffman, "The New Terrorism," in Andrew Tan and Kumar Ramakrishna (eds.), *The New Terrorism: Anatomy, Trends and Counter-Strategies* (Singapore: Times Academic/Eastern Universities Press, 2003).
5. Remarks by the president, September 12, 2001, http://www.americanrhetoric.com/speeches/gwbush911cabinetroomaddress.htm
6. Radio address of the president to the nation, September 15, 2001, http://www.americanrhetoric.com/speeches/gwbush911radioaddress.htm
7. *The 9/11 Commission Report*, p. 336, http://www.gpoaccess.gov/911/pdf/fullreport.pdf
8. *The 9/11 Commission Report*, p. 66.
9. The National Security Strategy of the United States of America, September 2002, http://www.lib.umich.edu/govdocs/pdf/nss02.pdf
10. National Strategy for Combating Terrorism, February 2003, http://www.globalsecurity.org/security/library/policy/national/counter_terrorism_strategy.pdf, p. 10.
11. National Strategy for Combating Terrorism, February 2003, p. 2.
12. National Strategy for Combating Terrorism, February 2003, pp. 15–28.
13. National Strategy for Combating Terrorism, February 2003, p. 30.
14. National Strategy for Combating Terrorism, September 2006, http://www.globalsecurity.org/security/library/policy/national/nsct_sep2006.pdf
15. National Strategy for Combating Terrorism, September 2006, pp. 1–4.
16. National Strategy for Combating Terrorism, September 2006, pp.11–17.
17. "All Change at the Pentagon," *Strategic Comments*, 14(6), August 2008, pp. 1–2. See also National Defense Strategy, June 2008, http://www.defenselink.mil/news/2008%20National%20Defense%20Strategy.pdf
18. National Defense Strategy, June 2008, p. 8.
19. National Defense Strategy, June 2008, p. 8.

20. National Defense Strategy, June 2008, pp. 8–9.

21. National Defense Strategy, June 2008, p. 20.

22. See Nadine Gurr and Benjamin Cole, *The New Face of Terrorism: Threats from Weapons of Mass Destruction* (London: IB Taurus, 2000).

23. See Walter Lacqueur, *The New Terrorism: Fanaticism and the Arms of Mass Destruction* (New York: Oxford University Press, 1999).

24. David C. Rapoport, "Modern Terror: History and Special Features," in Andrew T. H. Tan (ed.), *The Politics of Terrorism*, p. 23.

25. See David C. Rapoport, "The Four Waves of Rebel Terror and September 11," in Charles W Kegley Jr., *The New Terrorism: Characteristics, Causes and Controls* (New Jersey: Prentice Hall, 2003), pp.37–45. See also David C. Rapoport, "Modern Terror: History and Special Features," and David C Rapoport, "The Fourth Wave: September 11 in the History of Terrorism," *Current History*, December 2001.

26. David C. Rapoport, "The Four Waves of Rebel Terror and September 11," p. 50.

27. See Bruce Hoffman, *Inside Terrorism* (New York: Columbia, 1998). An expanded and revised version appeared in 2006. A more concise exposition of Hoffman's ideas can be found in Bruce Hoffman, "The New Terrorism," in Andrew Tan and Kumar Ramakrishna (eds.), *The New Terrorism: Anatomy, Trends and Counter-Strategies* (Singapore: Times Academic/Eastern Universities Press, 2003). See also Bruce Hoffman, "The Congruence of International and Domestic Trends in Terrorism," *Terrorism and Political Violence*, 9(2), summer 1997, pp. 8–9.

28. Back-cover summation, Rohan Gunaratna, *Inside Al Qaeda* (London: Hurst, 2002).

29. Rohan Gunaratna, *Inside Al Qaeda*, p. 238.

30. Jason Burke, *Al Qaeda* (London: Penguin, 2003), p. 312.

31. Jason Burke, *Al Qaeda*, p. 313.

32. Jason Burke, *Al Qaeda*, p. 313.

33. Ahmed S Hashim, *Insurgency and Counterinsurgency in Iraq* (London: Hurst, 2006), p. 365.

34. Ali A. Allawi, *The Occupation of Iraq: Winning the War, Losing the Peace* (New Haven: Yale University Press, 2007), pp. 459–460.

35. See Peter W. Galbraith, *The End of Iraq: How American Incompetence Created a War Without End* (New York: Simon and Schuster, 2006), and Thomas E. Ricks, *Fiasco: The American Military Adventure in Iraq* (New York: Penguin, 2006).

36. Isaiah Wilson, *New Thoughts on War and Peace*, prologue, http://www.thinkbeyondwar. com/Documents/Prologue_New_Thoughts_on_War_and_Peace.pdf (accessed February 1, 2008)

37. Austin Long, *On "Other War": Lessons from Five Decades of RAND Counterinsurgency Research* (Santa Monica: RAND, 2006), pp. 19–20.

38. See, for instance, Bruce R. Pirnie and Edward O'Connell, *Counterinsurgency in Iraq: 2003–2006* (Santa Monica: RAND, 2008), and Seth G. Jones, *Counterinsurgency in Afghanistan* (Santa Monica: RAND, 2008).

39. See James S. Corum, *Fighting the War on Terror: A Counterinsurgency Strategy* (St. Paul, MN: Zenith Press, 2007), pp. 257–265.

40. David Kilcullen, "Twenty-Eight Articles: Fundamentals of Company-Level Counterinsurgency," http://www.au.af.mil/info-ops/iosphere_summer06_kilcullen.pdf

41. Rebecca Weisser, "Strategist Behind War Gains," *The Australian*, August 18, 2007, http://www.theaustralian.news.com.au/story/0,25197,22263435–31477,00.html

42. Daniel Byman, *The Five Front War* (Hoboken, NJ: John Wiley and Sons, 2008), pp. 3–4.

43. Michael Chandler and Rohan Gunaratna, *Countering Terrorism: Can We Meet the Threat of Global Violence?* (London: Reaktion Books, 2007), p. 14.

44. See Audrey K. Cronin, *Ending Terrorism: Lessons for Defeating Al Qaeda*, Adelphi Paper 394, International Institute for Strategic Studies, London, 2008.

45. Bruce Hoffman, "Combating Al Qaeda and the Militant Islamic Threat," Testimony Before the Committee on Armed Services Subcommittee on Terrorism, Unconventional Threats

and Capabilities, United States House of Representatives, February 16, 2006, p. 14, http://www.rand.org/pubs/testimonies/2006/RAND_CT255.pdf

46. Thomas R. Mockaitis, "Winning Hearts and Minds in the War on Terrorism," in Thomas R. Mockaitis and Paul B Rich (eds.), *Grand Strategy in the War against Terrorism* (London: Frank Cass, 2003), p. 21.

47. See the executive summary of David Kilcullen, "Countering Global Insurgency."

48. David Kilcullen, "Countering Global Insurgency," pp. 1–2.

49. Linda J. Bilmes and Joseph E. Stiglitz, "The Iraq War Will Cost Us $3 Trillion, and Much More," *Washington Post*, March 9, 2008, http://www.washingtonpost.com/wp-dyn/content/article/2008/03/07/AR2008030702846.html

50. "US Is Studying Military Strike Options in Iran," *Washington Post*, April 9, 2006, http://www.washingtonpost.com/wp-dyn/content/article/2006/04/08/AR2006040801082_pf.html

51. Gwynne Dyer, *After Iraq: Where Next for the Middle East?* (New Haven: Yale University Press, 2008), p. 78.

52. See Coral Bell, *The End of the Vasco da Gama Era: The Next Landscape of World Politics* (Sydney: Lowy Institute, 2007).

53. See Jeffrey H. Norwitz (ed.), *Armed Groups: Studies in National Security, Counterterrorism and Counterinsurgency* (Newport: U.S. Naval War College, 2008).

2   The Failure of the GWOT

1. *North Atlantic Treaty Organization—Chronology Update*, September 10–16, 2001.

2. Christopher Bennett, "Combating Terrorism," *NATO Review*, Spring 2003, http://www.nato.int/docu/review/2003/issue1/english/art2.html

3. Condemnation of Terrorist Attacks in the United States, United Nations General Assembly, September 12, 2001, http://www.un.org/documents/ga/docs/56/agresolution.htm

4. Background Note: Australia, U.S. State Department, http://www.state.gov/r/pa/ei/bgn/2698.htm

5. United Nations Security Council Resolution 1373, September 28, 2001, http://www.un.org/Docs/scres/2001/sc2001.htm

6. UN Security Council Counter Terrorism Committee, http://www.un.org/sc/ctc

7. See Zahid Hussain, *Frontline Pakistan: The Struggle Within Militant Islam* (London: I. B. Taurus, 2007), pp. 119–140.

8. "Terror Suspect Hambali Quizzed," BBC News, August 15, 2003, http://news.bbc.co.uk/2/hi/asia-pacific/3152755.stm See also "Confessions of an Al Qaeda Terrorist," *Time*, September 15, 2002, http://www.time.com/time/world/article/0,8599,351169,00.html

9. "How Much of Al Qaeda's Leadership has been Captured or Killed," News Center for the Study of Terrorism and Political Conflict, http://www.borrull.org/e/noticia.php?id=40842

10. *The Guardian*, November 19, 2001.

11. "US Kills Al Qaeda Suspects in Yemen," *USA Today*, May 11, 2002 http://www.usatoday.com/news/world/2002-11-04-yemen-explosion_x.htm

12. UN Security Council Resolution 1390, January 16, 2002 http://daccessdds.un.org/doc/UNDOC/GEN/N02/216/02/PDF/N0221602.pdf?OpenElement

13. "Bush Delivers Ultimatum," CNN.com, September 21, 2001, http://edition.cnn.com/2001/WORLD/asiapcf/central/09/20/ret.afghan.bush/index.html

14. Presidential Address to the Nation, The White House, October 7, 2001, http://www.whitehouse.gov/news/releases/2001/10/20011007–8.html accessed February 1, 2008.

15. "Afghan Opposition Leader's Fate Unclear," BBC News, September 10, 2001, http://news.bbc.co.uk/2/hi/south_asia/1534629.stm

16. Donald H. Rumsfeld, "Transforming the Military," *Foreign Affairs*, May/June 2002, p. 20.

17. Afghan Bonn Agreement, http://www.afghangovernment.com/AfghanAgreementBonn.htm

18. UN Security Council Resolution 1386, December 20, 2001, http://daccessdds.un.org/doc/UNDOC/GEN/N01/708/55/PDF/N0170855.pdf?OpenElement

19. UN Security Council Resolution 1401, March 28, 2002, http://daccessdds.un.org/doc/UNDOC/GEN/N02/309/14/PDF/N0230914.pdf?OpenElement

20. NATO in Afghanistan: Factsheet, http://www.nato.int/issues/afghanistan/040628-factsheet.htm

21. Julianne Smith, "NATO Battles the Taliban and Tests Its Future in Afghanistan," *China and Eurasia Forum Quarterly*, 4(4) (2006) 25.

22. International Security Assistance Force, http://web.archive.org/web/20070628124507/http://www.nato.int/isaf/media/pdf/placemat_isaf.pdf

23. "The Taliban: Regrouped and Rearmed," *Washington Post*, September 10, 2006, http://www.washingtonpost.com/wp-dyn/content/article/2006/09/08/AR2006090801614_2.html

24. "US and Coalition Casualties," CNN.com, http://www.cnn.com/SPECIALS/2004/oef.casualties (accessed on January 29, 2009).

25. "Rift in NATO Over Afghanistan Forces," CBS News, February 26, 2008, http://www.cbsnews.com/stories/2008/02/02/world/main3782460.shtml

26. "The Taliban: Regrouped and Rearmed," *Washington Post*, September 10, 2006.

27. "Afghanistan: The Taliban Resurgent and NATO," The Brookings Institute, February 25, 2008, http://www.brookings.edu/opinions/2006/1128globalgovernance_riedel.aspx

28. "Military Flags All-out Onslaught in Badlands," *The Australian*, January 7, 2008.

29. "Al Qaeda's Profile: Slimmer but More Menacing," *Christian Science Monitor*, September 9, 2003.

30. Revi Bhalla, "Beyond the Post 9/11 World," STRATFOR, October 8, 2008.

31. *Global Trends 2025: A Transformed World*, National Intelligence Council, November 2008, pp. 69–70, http://www.acus.org/files/publication_pdfs/3/Global-Trends-2025.pdf

32. See David C. Rapoport, "The Four Waves of Rebel Terror and September 11," in Charles W. Kegley Jr, *The New Terrorism: Characteristics, Causes and Controls* (Englewood Cliffs, NJ: Prentice Hall, 2003), pp. 37–45, and David C. Rapoport, "The Fourth Wave: September 11 in the History of Terrorism," *Current History*, December 2001.

33. See Bruce Hoffman, "The New Terrorism," in Andrew Tan and Kumar Ramakrishna (eds), *The New Terrorism: Anatomy, Trends and Counter-Strategies* (Singapore: Times Academic/Eastern Universities Press, 2003), and Bruce Hoffman, "The Congruence of International and Domestic Trends in Terrorism," *Terrorism and Political Violence*, 9(2) (Summer 1997).

34. *Global Trends 2025: A Transformed World*, National Intelligence Council, November 2008, p. 70.

35. *Global Trends 2025: A Transformed World*, National Intelligence Council, November 2008, p. 70.

36. See Marc Sageman, *Leaderless Jihad: Terror Networks in the Twenty-First Century* (Philadelphia, PA: Pennsylvania University Press, 2008).

37. "Homeland Security's 5-Year Threat Picture," *Washington Times*, December 25, 2008, http://www.washingtontimes.com/news/2008/dec/25/homeland-securitys-5-year-threat-picture/?popup=false

38. The Terrorist Threat to the U.S. Homeland, National Intelligence Estimate, July 2007, http://www.dni.gov/press_releases/20070717_release.pdf

39. Bruce Hoffman, "Al Qaeda Dangerous as Ever," *The National Interest*, September 10, 2008, http://www.nationalinterest.org/Article.aspx?id=19846

40. Bruce Hoffman, "Terrorism's Twelve Step Program," *The National Interest*, January 13, 2009, http://www.nationalinterest.org/Article.aspx?id=20592" See also, "A Not Very

Private Feud Over Terrorism," *New York Times*, June 8, 2008, http://www.nytimes.com/2008/06/08/weekinreview/08sciolino.html?_r=2&oref=slogin&partner=rssnyt&emc=rss&pagewanted=print

41. "Bush Details Foiled 2002 Al Qaeda Attack on L.A," CNN.com, February 9, 2006, http://www.cnn.com/2006/POLITICS/02/09/bush.terror/index.html

42. "Plot to Destroy Brooklyn Bridge," Telegraph.co.uk, June 20, 2003, http://www.telegraph.co.uk/news/main.jhtml?xml=/news/2003/06/20/wterr20.xml

43. "Shoe Bomb Suspect to Remain in Custody," CNN.com, December 25, 2001, http://archives.cnn.com/2001/US/12/24/investigation.plane

44. "U.S. Attorney General Says Terrorist Threats to U.S. Very Real," GlobalSecurity.org, December 2, 2005, http://www.globalsecurity.org/security/library/news/2005/12/sec-051202-usia01.htm

45. Fred Burton and Scott Stewart, "Grassroots Jihadists and the Thin Blue Line," STRATFOR, February 27, 2008

46. "Seven Charged Over Chicago Plot," BBC News, June 23, 2006, http://news.bbc.co.uk/2/hi/americas/5110342.stm

47. "Suspect in Tunnel Bombing Plot Had Maps, Beirut Official Says," *New York Times*, July 10, 2006, http://www.nytimes.com/2006/07/10/nyregion/10plot.html

48. "Agent Infiltrated Terror Cell, U.S. Says," CNN.com, August 11, 2006, http://www.cnn.com/2006/US/08/10/us.security/index.html

49. Rohan Gunaratna, *Inside Al Qaeda* (London: Hurst, 2002), pp. 175–176.

50. "Six Charged in Plot To Attack Fort Dix," *Washington Post*, May 9, 2007, http://www.washingtonpost.com/wp-dyn/content/article/2007/05/08/AR2007050800465.html

51. "Four Charged Over JFK Bomb Plot," BBC News, June 3, 2007, http://news.bbc.co.uk/2/hi/americas/6715443.stm

52. Interview with Lee Hamilton, Council on Foreign Relations, September 7, 2006, http://www.cfr.org/publication/11319

53. Andrew T. H. Tan, *A Political and Economic Dictionary of Southeast Asia* (London: Routledge, 2004), p. 44.

54. "Bali Bomber Sentenced to Die," CNN.com, February 26, 2004, http://www.cnn.com/2003/WORLD/asiapcf/southeast/08/07/bali.verdict/index.html

55. "Jemaah Islamiyah in Southeast Asia: Damaged But Dangerous," Asia Briefing, No. 63, August 26, 2003, International Crisis Group, Executive Summary and pp. 2–3.

56. "Al Qaeda in Southeast Asia: The Case of the Ngruki Network in Indonesia," Asia Briefing, No. 20, August 8, 2002, International Crisis Group, p. 7.

57. "Jemaah Islamiyah in Southeast Asia: Damaged But Dangerous," Asia Briefing, No. 63, August 26, 2003, International Crisis Group, Executive Summary

58. Andrew T. H. Tan, *A Political and Economic Dictionary of Southeast Asia* (London: Europa, 2004), pp. 136–137.

59. "In the Spotlight: The Special Purpose Islamic Regiment," Center for Defence Information, Terrorism Project, May 2, 2003, http://www.cdi.org/terrorism/spir.cfm

60. Andrew T. H. Tan (ed), *The Politics of Terrorism*, p. 208.

61. Andrew T. H. Tan (ed), *The Politics of Terrorism*, p. 184. See also "Gas Killed Moscow Hostages," BBC News, October 27, 2002, http://news.bbc.co.uk/2/hi/europe/2365383.stm

62. "Putin Vows to Destroy Chechin Rebels," BBC News, July 7, 2003, http://news.bbc.co.uk/2/hi/europe/3050806.stm

63. "Terror Blasts Rock Casablanca," BBC News, May 17, 2003, http://news.bbc.co.uk/2/hi/africa/3035803.stm

64. "Moscow Blasts Blamed on Chechin Rebels," BBC News, July 6, 2003 http://news.bbc.co.uk/2/hi/europe/3048486.stm

65. "Russia Mourns Hospital Victims," BBC News, http://news.bbc.co.uk/2/hi/europe/3122385.stm

66. "Four Bomb Attacks in Saudi Arabia," *The Telegraph*, May 13, 2003, http://www.telegraph.co.uk/news/main.jhtml?xml=/news/2003/05/13/wsaud13.xml

67. Anthony H. Cordesman and Nawaf Obaid, "Al-Qaeda in Saudi Arabia: Asymmetric Threats and Islamist Extremists," Center for Strategic and International Studies, Washington, January 26, 2005, p. 8.

68. Anthony H. Cordesman and Nawaf Obaid, "Al-Qaeda in Saudi Arabia: Asymmetric Threats and Islamist Extremists," pp. 9–10.

69. "Why the War on Terror Will Never End," *Time*, May 20, 2003.

70. "French Busts in Morocco Bombing," CBS News, April 5, 2004, http://www.cbsnews.com/stories/2004/03/03/world/main603720.shtml

71. Andrew T. H. Tan, *The Politics of Terrorism*, pp. 183–184.

72. *Time*, May 26, 2003, p. 19.

73. Andrew T. H. Tan, *A Political and Economic Dictionary of Southeast Asia*, p. 177. See also "Bomb Rips Through Indonesia Hotel: Kills Ten," Reuters, August 5, 2003.

74. "UN Marks Iraq Attack Anniversary," BBC News, August 19, 2004, http://news.bbc.co.uk/2/hi/europe/3578734.stm

75. "Istanbul Rocked by Double Bombing," BBC News, November 20, 2003, http://news.bbc.co.uk/2/hi/europe/3222608.stm

76. Al Qaeda Statement: Full Text, BBC News, November 17, 2003, http://news.bbc.co.uk/2/hi/in_depth/3276859.stm

77. Andrew T. H. Tan (ed), *The Politics of Terrorism*, p. 216.

78. "Scores Die in Madrid Bomb Carnage," BBC News, March 11, 2004, http://news.bbc.co.uk/2/hi/europe/3500452.stm

79. Editorial, *Arab News* (Saudi Arabia), March 12, 2004.

80. Andrew T. H. Tan (ed), *The Politics of Terrorism*, p. 179.

81. "Russian Media Unsurprised by Train Bombing," BBC News, December 6, 2003, http://news.bbc.co.uk/2/hi/europe/3296219.stm

82. Roman Kupchinsky, "Who Downed The Russian Jets," Radio Free Europe, August 30, 2004, http://www.rferl.org/featuresarticle/2004/08/76A7767C-540C-4626-9AD6-549DCC8F4BD3.html

83. Andrew T. H. Tan (ed), *The Politics of Terrorism*, pp. 138–139. See also "Beslan School Siege," BBC News, undated, http://news.bbc.co.uk/2/shared/spl/hi/world/04/russian_s/html/1.stm

84. "Russia School Siege Ends in Carnage," *Washington Post*, September 4, 2004, http://www.washingtonpost.com/wp-dyn/articles/A58381–2004Sep3_2.html

85. "Eleven Killed in Embassy Bombing," *The Age*, September 9, 2004, http://www.theage.com.au/articles/2004/09/09/1094530752760.html

86. "Bali Terrorist Blasts Kill at Least 26," CNN.com, October 2, 2005, http://www.cnn.com/2005/WORLD/asiapcf/10/01/bali.blasts

87. Andrew T. H. Tan (ed), *The Politics of Terrorism*, pp. 176–177.

88. "Al Qaeda Warns of More Destruction in London Over Blair Policy on Iraq", *Financial Times*, August 5, 2005.

89. "Suicide Bomber's Video Confession Blames Iraq War," *Times Online*, September 2, 2005, http://www.timesonline.co.uk/article/0,,22989–1761688,00.html

90. "Death Toll Rises in Egypt Blasts," BBC News, October 9, 2004, http://news.bbc.co.uk/2/hi/middle_east/3728436.stm

91. "Sharm el-Sheik Attack Probe Widens," CNN.com, July 25, 2005, http://edition.cnn.com/2005/WORLD/meast/07/25/egypt.explosions/index.html

92. "Bombs Kill Scores in Egyptian Resort Town," CNN.com, July 25, 2005, http://edition.cnn.com/2005/WORLD/meast/07/23/egypt.explosions

93. "Three Bombs Rip Through Egyptian Resort," CNN.com, April 25, 2006, http://edition.cnn.com/2006/WORLD/meast/04/24/egypt.blasts/index.html

94. "Egypt Probes Same Sinai Bombers," BBC News, April 26, 2006, http://news.bbc.co.uk/2/hi/middle_east/4948886.stm

95. "Zarqawi's Network Asserts it Launched Attacks in Amman," *Washington Post*, November 11, 2005, http://www.washingtonpost.com/wp-dyn/content/article/2005/11/10/AR2005111002074.html

96. "Jordan was Chemical Bomb Target," BBC News, April 17, 2004, http://news.bbc.co.uk/2/hi/middle_east/3635381.stm

97. "Al Qaeda Claims Algeria Blasts," Channel Four News, April 12, 2007, http://www.channel4.com/news/articles/world/al%20qaida%20claims%20algeria%20blasts/422657

98. "11 UN Workers Among 26 Killed in Algeria Blasts," CBS News, December 11, 2007, http://www.cbc.ca/world/story/2007/12/11/algeria.html

99. "Al Qaeda Strikes in Algeria," *The Long War Journal*, April 11, 2007, http://www.longwarjournal.org/archives/2007/04/al_qaeda_strikes_in.php

100. "Pakistan Role in Mumbai Attacks," BBC News, September 30, 2006, http://news.bbc.co.uk/2/hi/south_asia/5394686.stm

101. "As it Happened: Mumbai Attacks 29 Nov," BBC News, November 29, 2008, http://news.bbc.co.uk/2/hi/south_asia/7756073.stm See also "India Police Name Mumbai Gunmen," BBC News, December 9, 2008, http://news.bbc.co.uk/2/hi/south_asia/7773927.stm

102. "Pakistan Holds 71 Over Mumbai," BBC News, January 15, 2009, http://news.bbc.co.uk/2/hi/south_asia/7830276.stm

103. B. Raman, "Bin Laden's Fatwa Against Musharraf and Pakistani Army," South Asia Analysis Group, Paper No. 2388, September 22, 2007, http://www.southasiaanalysis.org/papers24/paper2388.html

104. Zahid Hussain, *Frontline Pakistan: The Struggle with Militant Islam* (London: I. B. Taurus, 2007), p. 99.

105. Evagoras C. Leventis, "The Waziristan Accord," *The Middle East Review of International Affairs*, 11(4), December 2007.

106. Zahid Hussain, *Frontline Pakistan: The Struggle With Militant Islam*, p. 150.

107. "Bhutto Attack Was Suicide Bombing: Death Toll 134," *International Herald Tribune*, October 19, 2007, http://www.iht.com/articles/2007/10/19/asia/20pakistan.3.php

108. "Bhutto Killed in Suicide Attack," News.com, December 28, 2007, http://www.news.com.au/story/0,23599,22979273-2,00.html

109. "Pakistan: Al Qaeda Claims Bhutto's Death," Adnkronos International, December 27, 2007 http://www.adnkronos.com/AKI/English/Security/?id=1.0.1710322437

110. "Zardari Takes Office as President," *International Herald Tribune*, September 9, 2008, http://www.iht.com/articles/2008/09/09/asia/pakistan.php

111. Adam Dolnik and Rohan Gunaratna, "Dagger and Sarin: The Evolution of Terrorist Weapons and Tactics," in Andrew T. H. Tan (ed), *The Politics of Terrorism* (London: Routledge, 2006), p. 33.

112. Adam Dolnik and Rohan Gunaratna, "Dagger and Sarin: The Evolution of Terrorist Weapons and Tactics," in Andrew T. H. Tan (ed), *The Politics of Terrorism*, pp. 35–36.

113. Bruce Hoffman, "Combating Al Qaeda and the Militant Islamic Threat," Testimony presented to the House Armed Services Committee, Subcommittee on Terrorism, Unconventional Threats and Capabilities on February 16, 2006 (Santa Monica: RAND, 2006), p. 3.

3 The U.S. Invasion of Iraq

1. "Rumsfeld Offered to Help Saddam," *The Guardian*, December 31, 2002, http://www.guardian.co.uk/world/2002/dec/31/iraq.politics

2. For instance, President Ahmadinejad vowed that Israel should be "wiped off the face of the earth." See "Israel Should be Wiped Off Map, Says Iran's President," Guardian.co.uk, October 27, 2005, http://www.guardian.co.uk/world/2005/oct/27/israel.iran

3. "Neocons on the Line", *Newsweek*, June 23, 2003, pp. 15–18.

4. Donald H. Rumsfeld, "Transforming the Military," *Foreign Affairs*, May–June 2002, p. 31.

5. "The Twelve Year Itch," *Newsweek*, March 31, 2003, p. 54.

6. "The Spies Who Pushed for War," *The Guardian*, July 17, 2003.

7. "Iran's Continuing Programs for Weapons of Mass Destruction," National Intelligence Estimate, October 1, 2002, http://homepage.ntlworld.com/jksonc/docs/nie-iraq-wmd.html

8. "Overselling the World on War," *Newsweek*, June 9, 2003, p. 14.

9. "Follow the Yellow Cake Road," *Newsweek*, July 28, 2003, p. 13.

10. "Overselling the World on War," *Newsweek*, June 9, 2003, p. 14.

11. Sidney Blumenthal, "Washington's Chalabi Nightmare," Salon.com, May 27, 2004, http://dir.salon.com/story/opinion/blumenthal/2004/05/27/chalabi/index.html See also Russ Hoyle, *How Misinformation, Disinformation, and Arrogance Led America into Iraq* (New York: Thomas Dunne Books, 2008).

12. The President's State of the Union Address, January 29, 2002, http://www.mtholyoke.edu/acad/intrel/bush/stateoftheunion.htm

13. "Al Qaeda–Hussein Link is Dismissed," *Washington Post*, June 17, 2004, http://www.washingtonpost.com/wp-dyn/articles/A47812-2004Jun16.html

14. "A Decade of Deception and Defiance: Saddam Hussein's Defiance of the United Nations," White House Background Paper, September 12, 2002, http://webharvest.gov/peth04/20041101060918/www.whitehouse.gov/news/releases/2002/09/iraqdecade.pdf

15. See, for instance, "Rice Lays Out Case for War in Iraq," *Washington Post*, August 2002.

16. See John J. Mearsheimer and Stephen M. Walt, "Can Saddam be Contained? History Says Yes" (Occasional Paper, Belfer Center for Science and International Affairs, Kennedy School of Government, Harvard University, 2002).

17. Brent Scowcroft, "Don't Attack Saddam," Editorial, *Wall Street Journal*, August 15, 2002.

18. "Taking on the Doubters," *The Economist*, September 2, 2002.

19. President's Remarks at the United Nations General Assembly, September 12, 2002, http://www.johnstonsarchive.net/terrorism/bushiraqun.html

20. Joint Resolution to Authorize the Use of United States Armed Forces Against Iraq, October 16, 2002, http://www.c-span.org/resources/pdf/hjres114.pdf

21. United Nations Security Council Resolution 1441, November 8, 2002, http://daccessdds.un.org/doc/UNDOC/GEN/N02/682/26/PDF/N0268226.pdf?OpenElement

22. *New York Times*, January 28, 2003.

23. Michael F. Glennon, "Why the Security Council Failed," *Foreign Affairs*, May/June 2003, pp. 16–18.

24. Michael F. Glennon, "Why the Security Council Failed," p. 21.

25. "Iraq War Unjustified: Putin," *The Times of India*, December 18, 2003.

26. "Chirac Expresses Regret After US Attack on Iraq," VOA News, March 20, 2003, http://www.voanews.com/english/archive/2003–03/a-2003–03-20–27-Chirac.cfm

27. "Saddam Rejects Bush Ultimatum," BBC News, March 18, 2003, http://news.bbc.co.uk/2/hi/middle_east/2861029.stm

28. "Millions Join Global Anti-War Protests," BBC News, February 17, 2003, http://news.bbc.co.uk/2/hi/europe/2765215.stm

29. "War Coming to Close After Key Town Taken," BBC News, April 14, 2003, http://news.bbc.co.uk/cbbcnews/hi/world/newsid_2945000/2945417.stm

30. Max Boot, "The New American Way of War," *Foreign Affairs*, July–August 2003, p. 2, http://www-stage.foreignaffairs.org/20030701faessay15404-p10/max-boot/the-new-american-way-of-war.html

31. "Analysis: Three Stages to a New Iraq," BBC News, April 8, 2003, http://news.bbc.co.uk/2/hi/middle_east/2929365.stm

32. "Army Report: U.S. Lost Control in Iraq Three Months After Invasion," World Tribune.com, March 7, 2005, http://www.worldtribune.com/worldtribune/05/breaking2453436.980555556.html

33. Peter W. Galbraith, *The End of Iraq: How American Incompetence Created a War Without End* (New York: Simon & Schuster, 2006), p. 83.

34. Steve Bowman, "Iraq: US Military Operations," CRS Report for Congress, Updated May 9, 2006, http://italy.usembassy.gov/pdf/other/RL31701.pdf

35. Steve Bowman, "Iraq: U.S. Military Operations and Costs," CRS Report for Congress, Updated November 20, 2004, http://www.fas.org/man/crs/RL31701.pdf

36. "Can Anyone Govern This Place?" *Time*, May 26, 2003.

37. "Jobless Iraqi Soldiers Issue Threats," *Christian Science Monitor*, June 5, 2003, http://www.csmonitor.com/2003/0605/p06s01-woiq.html

38. See, for instance, "Abuse of Iraqi POWs by GIs Probed," CBS News, April 28, 2004, http://www.cbsnews.com/stories/2004/04/27/60II/main614063.shtml

39. Ahmed S. Hashim, *Insurgency and Counter-Insurgency in Iraq* (London: Hurst, 2006), p. 107.

40. Ahmed S. Hashim, *Insurgency and Counter-Insurgency in Iraq*, p. 136.

41. Andrew T. H. Tan (ed), *The Politics of Terrorism* (London: Routledge, 2006), pp. 162–165.

42. "Iraqis Mourn Shia Massacre Dead," BBC News, March 3, 2004, http://news.bbc.co.uk/2/hi/middle_east/3527221.stm

43. "Al Qaeda Denies Link to Iraq Blasts as US Says Group Responsible," *Muslim American Society*, March 4, 2004, http://www.masnet.org/news.asp?id=1011

44. "Al Zarqawi Group Claims Allegiance to bin Laden," CNN.com, October 17, 2004, http://www.cnn.com/2004/WORLD/meast/10/17/al.zarqawi.statement

45. "Insurgent Leader Al Zarqawi Killed in Iraq," *Washington Post*, June 8, 2006.

46. Casualties in Iraq, Antiwar.com, http://www.antiwar.com/casualties (accessed February 22, 2008).

47. "National Strategy for Victory in Iraq," http://www.globalsecurity.org/military/library/policy/national/ns-victory-iraq_051130.htm

48. *The Iraq Study Group Report*, http://www.usip.org/isg/iraq_study_group_report/report/1206/iraq_study_group_report.pdf

49. *The Iraq Study Group Report*, p.41.

50. "Newsweek Poll: Americans Back Baker-Hamilton," MSBC.com, December 9, 2006, http://www.msnbc.msn.com/id/16122983/site/newsweek/print/1/displaymode/1098/

51. See Frederick W. Kagan, "Choosing Victory: A Plan for Success in Iraq," American Enterprise Institute, January 5, 2007, http://www.aei.org/publications/pubID.25396,filter.all/pub_detail.asp

52. Text of President Bush's Speech, in "Bush: We Need to Change Our Strategy in Iraq," CNN.com, January 11, 2007, http://www.cnn.com/2007/POLITICS/01/10/bush.transcript/index.html

53. See Interview with General David Petraeus, PBS Frontline, November 23, 2003, http://www.pbs.org/wgbh/pages/frontline/shows/beyond/interviews/petraeus.html

54. "US Surge Plan in Iraq Working," BBC News, September 12, 2007.

55. General David Petraeus "Report to Congress on the Situation in Iraq," September 10–11, 2007, http://www.defenselink.mil/pubs/pdfs/Petraeus-Testimony20070910.pdf, p. 2.

56. General David Petraeus "Report to Congress on the Situation in Iraq," p. 5.

57. General David Petraeus "Report to Congress on the Situation in Iraq," p. 2.

58. General David Petraeus "Report to Congress on the Situation in Iraq," p. 6.

59. "US Surge Plan in Iraq Working," BBC News, September 10, 2007, http://news.bbc.co.uk/2/hi/americas/6986461.stm

60. "Is Iraq Getting Better?" BBC News, November 11, 2007, http://news.bbc.co.uk/2/hi/middle_east/7089168.stm

61. "Will Petraeus Strategy be the Last?" The Atlantic.com, September 17, 2007, http://www.theatlantic.com/doc/200709u/petraeus-bing-west

62. David Kilcullen, "Anatomy of a Tribal Revolt," Blog, August 29, 2007, *Small Wars Journal*, http://smallwarsjournal.com/blog/2007/08/anatomy-of-a-tribal-revolt/

63. "Is Iraq Getting Better?" BBC News, November 13, 2007.

64. "Al Qaeda Leaders Admit: We are in Crisis. There is Fear and Panic," *The Times*, February 11, 2008, http://www.timesonline.co.uk/tol/news/world/iraq/article3346386.ece

65. "Bush to Announce Iraq Troop Cut," BBC News, September 11, 2007, http://news.bbc.co.uk/2/hi/americas/6990361.stm

66. General David H. Petraeus, Testimony to Senate Armed Services Committee, April 8, 2008, http://www.realclearpolitics.com/articles/2008/04/gen_petraeus_testimony_to_the.html

67. "Reports on Iraq to Congress," BBC News, September 14, 2007, http://news.bbc.co.uk/2/hi/americas/6984210.stm

68. General David Petraeus "Report to Congress on the Situation in Iraq," p. 5.

69. "Sheikh Sattar, Leader of the Anbar Awakening, Killed in Bombing," *The Long War Journal*, September 13, 2007, http://www.longwarjournal.org/archives/2007/09/sheikh_sattar_leader.php

70. "Iraq Civilian Deaths Down in 2008," BBC News, December 29, 2008, http://news.bbc.co.uk/1/hi/world/middle_east/7802545.stm

71. "Al Qaeda in 2008: The Struggle for Relevance," *STRATFOR*, April 2, 2008, http://www.stratfor.com/weekly/al_qaeda_2008_struggle_relevance

72. "Suicide Bomb Kills Many in Iraq," BBC News, January 2, 2009, http://news.bbc.co.uk/2/hi/middle_east/7808354.stm

73. "Intelligence Chief Cites Qaeda Threat to US," *New York Times*, February 6, 2008, http://www.nytimes.com/2008/02/06/washington/06intel.html?hp

74. "Zarqawi's Network Asserts it Launched Attacks in Amman," *Washington Post*, November 11, 2005, http://www.washingtonpost.com/wp-dyn/content/article/2005/11/10/AR2005111002074.html

75. "Jordan was Chemical Bomb Target," BBC News, April 17, 2004, http://news.bbc.co.uk/2/hi/middle_east/3635381.stm

76. See, for instance, Andrew T. H. Tan (ed), *The Politics of Terrorism*, p. 164.

77. "Turkey Hits Rebel Targets in Iraq," BBC News, March 29, 2008, http://news.bbc.co.uk/2/hi/europe/7320508.stm

78. "Iraq Troop Withdrawal Baffles Turks," BBC News, February 29, 2008, http://news.bbc.co.uk/2/hi/europe/7272108.stm

79. "Who Are the Mehdi Army?" BBC News, May 30, 2007, http://news.bbc.co.uk/2/hi/middle_east/3604393.stm

80. "Shia Call on Mehdi Army to Take Up Arms Again in Iraq," *The Independent*, February 7, 2008, http://www.independent.co.uk/news/world/middle-east/shia-call-on-mehdi-army-to-take-up-arms-again-in-iraq-779160.htm

81. Andrew T. H. Tan (ed), *The Politics of Terrorism*, p. 181.

82. "Iraq: Fighting Over, But Shi'ite Power Struggle Continues," Radio Free Europe, March 31, 2008, http://www.rferl.org/featuresarticle/2008/03/01dd1947-746a-4bbb-bb68-e3d047627687.html

83. Casualties in Iraq, Antiwar.com, http://www.antiwar.com/casualties (accessed January 30, 2009).

84. "Iraq's Provincial Elections: The Stakes," Middle East Report No. 82, International Crisis Group, January 27, 2009, p. ii, http://www.crisisgroup.org/library/documents/middle_east___north_africa/iraq_iran_gulf/82_iraqs_provincial_elections___the_stakes.pdf

4 The Iraq Conundrum and Its Implications

1. President George Bush, "Address to a Joint Session of Congress and the American People," September 20, 2001, http://www.historycentral.com/documents/Bushjoint.html

2. "Views of a Changing World 2003: War With Iraq Further Divides Global Politics," June 3, 2003, Pew Research Center for the People and the Press, p.5, http://people-press.org/reports/print.php3?PageID=712

3. Jason Burke, *Al Qaeda: The True Story of Radical Islam* (London: Penguin, 2007), p. 306.

4. See Andrew T. H. Tan, "Terrorism and Insurgency in Southeast Asia," in Andrew T. H. Tan (ed), *A Handbook of Terrorism and Insurgency in Southeast Asia* (Cheltenham: Edward Elgar, 2007), p. 14.

5. Jitka Maleckova, "Impoverished Terrorists: Stereotype or Reality?" in Tore Bjorgo (ed), *Root Causes of Terrorism: Myths, Reality and Ways Forward* (New York: Routledge, 2005), pp. 41–42.

6. Jason Burke, *Al Qaeda: The True Story of Radical Islam*, p. 308.

7. Bruce Hoffma, *Inside Terrorism* (New York: Columbia University Press, 2006), p. 285.

8. Bruce Hoffma, *Inside Terrorism*, pp. 285–288.

9. Daniel Byman, *The Five Front War: The Better Way to Fight Global Jihad* (Hoboken, NJ: John Wiley and Sons, 2008), pp. 10–12.

10. Osama bin Laden, "Declaration of War Against the Americans Occupying the Land of the Two Holy Places," http://www.pbs.org/newshour/terrorism/international/fatwa_1996.html (accessed May 21, 2009).

11. Gareth Evans, "The Global Response to Terrorism," 2005 Wallace Wurth Lecture, University of New South Wales, Sydney, September 27, 2005, p. 13.

12. The President's State of the Union Address, January 29, 2002, http://www.johnstonsarchive.net/policy/bushstun2002.html

13. "Bush Hopeful New Report Will Link Iraq to Al Qaeda," *Sydney Morning Herald*, December 13, 2002, http://www.smh.com.au/articles/2002/12/12/1039656171115.html

14. Francis Fukuyama, "The Neoconservative Moment," *The National Interest*, July 1, 2004, http://www.tvo.org/goingglobal/readings/The_Neoconservative_Moment.pdf

15. See Charles Krauthammer, "The Unipolar Moment", *Foreign Affairs*, 70(1), 1990/91.

16. See Charles Krauthammer, "The Unipolar Moment Revisited", *The National Interest*, Winter 2002/2003.

17. Charles Krauthammer, "Democratic Realism: An American Foreign Policy for a Unipolar World," February 27, 2004, American Enterprise Institute, http://www.aei.org/books/bookID.755,filter.all/book_detail.asp

18. Charles Krauthammer, "Democratic Realism: An American Foreign Policy for a Unipolar World," p. 16.

19. Charles Krauthammer, "Democratic Realism: An American Foreign Policy for a Unipolar World," p. 8.

20. Charles Krauthammer, "The Unipolar Moment Revisited", p. 16.

21. Charles Krauthammer, "Democratic Realism: An American Foreign Policy for a Unipolar World," p. 11.

22. "Neocons on the Line", *Newsweek*, June 23, 2003, pp. 15–18.

23. Francis Fukuyama, "The Neoconservative Moment," *The National Interest*, July 1, 2004, http://www.tvo.org/goingglobal/readings/The_Neoconservative_Moment.pdf

24. Michael Mandelbaum, "The Inadequacy of American Power," in *Foreign Affairs*, Sep–Oct 2002, p. 61. See also Charles Krauthammar, "The Unipolar Movement Revisited," in *The National Interest*, Winter 2002/3.

25. "The Twelve Year Itch," *Newsweek*, March 31, 2003, p. 54.

26. See John Mearsheimer and Stephen Walt, "The Israel Lobby and US Foreign Policy," *Middle East Policy*, 13(3), Fall 2006, 53–58.

27. "Neocons on the Line", *Newsweek*, June 23, 2003, pp. 15–18.

28. "Saddam Had No Link to Al Qaeda," BBC News, September 9, 2006, http://news.bbc. co.uk/2/hi/americas/5328592.stm

29. "Iran's Continuing Programs for Weapons of Mass Destruction," National Intelligence Estimate, October 1, 2002, http://homepage.ntlworld.com/jksonc/docs/nie-iraq-wmd.html

30. Paul Wolfowitz, "Iraq, What Does Disarmament Look Like?" Council on Foreign Relations, January 23, 2003, http://www.cfr.org/publication.html?id=5454

31. BBC News, http://news.bbc.co.uk, March 22, 2003.

32. President George Bush, "Address to a Joint Session of Congress and the American People," September 20, 2001.

33. "Japanese Soldiers Head Home As Iraq Mission Ends", AFP, July 7, 2006, http://www. spacewar.com/reports/Japanese_Soldiers_Head_Home_As_Iraq_Mission_Ends_999.html

34. "Myers Thanks Mongolians for Iraqi Freedom Help," Armed Forces Press Service, U.S. Department of Defense, January 13, 2004, http://www.defenselink.mil/news/newsarticle. aspx?id=27505

35. "The Insurgency," Operation Iraqi Freedom, August 20, 2007, http://www.mnf-iraq.com/ index.php?option=com_content&task=view&id=729&Itemid=45

36. "Study Claims Iraq's 'Excess' Death Toll Has Reached 655,000," *The Washington Post*, October 11, 2006, http://www.washingtonpost.com/wp-dyn/content/article/2006/10/10/ AR2006101001442.html

37. Transcript: Bin Laden Accuses the West, Aljazeera.net, April 25, 2006, http://english. aljazeera.net/English/archive/archive?ArchiveId=22235

38. Daniel Byman, *The Five Front War: The Better Way to Fight Global Jihad*, p. 240.

39. Daniel Byman, *The Five Front War: The Better Way to Fight Global Jihad*, p. 240.

40. "Scarier Than Bin Laden," *Washington Post*, September 9, 2007, http://www.washingtonpost. com/wp-dyn/content/article/2007/09/07/AR2007090702056_pf.html

41. Murad Batal Al-Shishani, "The Salafi-Jihadist Movement in Iraq: Recruitment Methods and Arab Volunteers," in *Terrorism Monitor*, 3(23), December 2, 2005, pp.5–6.

42. "Iraq War Hurt Al-Qaeda Fight," Associated Press, August 1, 2003.

43. Marc Sageman, "Leaderless Jihad: Radicalization in the West," New America Foundation, pp. 31–32. http://www.newamerica.net/files/Microsoft%20PowerPoint%20-%20Sageman. pdf

44. "President Bush Announces Major Combat Operations in Iraq Have Ended," May 1, 2003, http://www.americanrhetoric.com/speeches/wariniraq/gwbushiraq5103.htm

45. "Views of a Changing World 2003: War With Iraq Further Divides Global Politics," June 3, 2003, Pew Research Center for the People and the Press, p. 3, http://people-press.org/ reports/print.php3?PageID=712

46. "Failure to find weapons in Iraq leads to intelligence scrutiny," McClatchy, June 2, 2003, http://www.mcclatchydc.com/128/story/9706.html

47. "Forget Saddam's Missing Weapons," *Straits Times*, July 11, 2003.

48. "Senate Intel Chairman Suggests Proof Coming on Iraqi WMD," CNN.com http://www. cnn.com/2003/allpolitics/07/03/sprj.nitop.senator, August 11, 2003.

49. "Banned Weapons: Where are They?" BBC News, http://news.bbc.co.uk, April 15, 2003.

50. Casualties in Iraq, Antiwar.com, http://www.antiwar.com/casualties (accessed January 30, 2009).

51. Michael F. Glennon, "Why the Security Council Failed," *Foreign Affairs*, May–June 2003, 34.

52. "Chirac Expresses Regret After US Attack on Iraq," VOA News, March 20, 2003, http:// www.voanews.com/english/archive/2003–03/a-2003–03-20–27-Chirac.cfm

53. "Millions Join Global Anti-War Protests," BBC News, February 17, 2003, http://news.bbc.co.uk/2/hi/europe/2765215.stm

54. "America's Image Further Erodes, Europeans Want Weaker Ties," Pew Research Center for the People and the Press, March 18, 2003, p. 1, http://people-press.org/reports/display.php3?ReportID=175

55. "America's Image Further Erodes, Europeans Want Weaker Ties," Pew Research Center for the People and the Press, p. 2.

56. Summary of Findings, "A Year After Iraq War," Pew Research Center for the People and the Press, March 16, 2004, http://people-press.org/reports/display.php3?ReportID=206

57. The Secretary-General Address to the General Assembly, New York, September 23, 2003, http://www.un.org/webcast/ga/58/statements/sg2eng030923.htm

58. "The Democratic Domino Theory," BBC News, April 10, 2003, http://news.bbc.co.uk

59. Mike Shuster, "IAEA Fears Iran Actively Seeking Nuclear Weapons," NPR News, June 16, 2004, http://www.npr.org/templates/story/story.php?storyId=1960229

60. "Rumsfeld Offered to Help Saddam," *The Guardian*, December 31, 2002, http://www.guardian.co.uk/world/2002/dec/31/iraq.politics

61. "Iran Leader in Landmark Iraq Trip," BBC News, March 2, 2008, http://news.bbc.co.uk/2/hi/middle_east/7273431.stm

62. "Evidence of Iran-Shiite Arms Link Cited by US," *International Herald Tribune*, February 11, 2007, http://www.iht.com/articles/2007/02/12/africa/web.0212weapons.php

63. "Mehdi army commanders withdraw to Iran to lie low during security crackdown," Guardian.co.uk, February 15, 2007, http://www.guardian.co.uk/world/2007/feb/15/iraq.iran

64. "Iraq: Fighting Over, But Shi'ite Power Struggle Continues," Radio Free Europe, March 31, 2008, http://www.rferl.org/featuresarticle/2008/03/01dd1947-746a-4bbb-bb68-e3d047627687.html

65. Cited in Alfred B. Prados and Christopher M. Blanchard, "Saudi Arabia: Current Issues and US Relations," CRS Report for Congress, August 2, 2006, p. 10, http://www.fas.org/sgp/crs/mideast/RL33533.pdf

66. Memo of Alberto R. Gonzales, Counsel to the President, to President George W. Bush, "Decision Re Application of the Geneva Convention on Prisoners of War to the Conflict with al Qaeda and the Taliban," January 25, 2002, http://texscience.org/reform/torture/gonzales-bush-25jan02.pdf

67. Text of Bush's Order on Treatment of Detainees, February 7, 2002, http://www.kron.com/global/story.asp?s=1962000&ClientType=Printable

68. "Bush Puts CIA Prisons Under Geneva Conventions," Reuters, July 20, 2007, http://dandelionsalad.wordpress.com/2007/07/20/bush-puts-cia-prisons-under-geneva-conventions-by-david-morgan/

69. "Working Group Report on Detainee Interrogations in the Global War on Terrorism: Assessment of Legal, Historical, Policy, and Operational Considerations," Department of Defense, March 6, 2003 http://texscience.org/reform/torture/dod-detainee-interro-6mar03.pdf

70. Memo from Secretary of Defense Donald H. Rumsfeld to Gen. James T. Hill, "Counter-Resistance Techniques in the War on Terrorism," April 2, 2003 http://texscience.org/reform/torture/rumsfeld-hill-2april03.pdf

71. Fact Sheet: Extraordinary Rendition, 12 June 2005, American Civil Liberties Union, http://www.aclu.org/safefree/extraordinaryrendition/22203res20051206.html

72. CIA Holds Terror Suspects in Secret Prisons, *Washington Post*, November 2, 2005, p. A01, http://www.washingtonpost.com/wp-dyn/content/article/2005/11/01/AR2005110101644.html

73. "Behind the Walls of Abu Ghraib," *Newsweek*, May 22, 2004, http://www.truthout.org/cgi-bin/artman/exec/view.cgi/9/4598

bu Ghraib Photos, http://www.cnn.com/interactive/world/0405/gallery.iraq. buse/frameset.exclude.html

75. "Beneath the Hoods: Many of the Tortured at Abu Ghraib Were Common Criminals, Not Terrorists," *Newsweek*, July 19, 2004, http://www.newsweek.com/id/54447

76. "Abu Ghraib: Dark Stain on Iraq's Past," BBC News, May 25, 2005, http://news.bbc.co.uk/2/hi/americas/3747005.stm

77. "Obama Orders Guantanamo Closure," BBC News, January 22, 2009, http://news.bbc.co.uk/2/hi/americas/7845585.stm

78. Joseph S. Nye, Jr., "US Power and Strategy After Iraq," *Foreign Affairs*, July/August 2003, p. 73.

5 The Continuing Threat and Why the United States Failed

1. Annual Threat Assessment of the Intelligence Community for the Senate Armed Services Committee, February 27, 2008, pp. 4–5, http://armed-services.senate.gov/statemnt/2008/February/McConnell%2002-27-08.pdf

2. Annual Threat Assessment of the Intelligence Community, February 27, 2008, p. 5.

3. Bruce Hoffman, "Combating Al Qaeda and the Militant Islamic Threat," Testimony Presented to the House Armed Services Committee, Subcommittee on Terrorism, Unconventional Threats and Capabilities, February 16, 2006, http://www.au.af.mil/au/awc/awcgate/congress/hoffman_testimony16feb06.pdf

4. Annual Threat Assessment of the Intelligence Community, February 27, 2008, p. 6.

5. "Jordan was Chemical Bomb Target," BBC News, April 17, 2004, http://news.bbc.co.uk/2/hi/middle_east/3635381.stm

6. "Zarqawi's Network Asserts it Launched Attacks in Amman," *The Washington Post*, November 11, 2005, http://www.washingtonpost.com/wp-dyn/content/article/2005/11/10/AR2005111002074.html

7. Annual Threat Assessment of the Intelligence Community, February 27, 2008, p. 8.

8. Greg Grant, "Analyst Warns of Third Islamic Terrorist Wave, Enabled by Internet," Government Executive.com, February 25, 2008, http://www.govexec.com/dailyfed/0208/022508g1.htm See also Marc Sageman, *Leaderless Jihad: Terror Networks in the Twenty-First Century* (University of Pennsylvania Press, 2007).

9. "Seven Charged Over Chicago Plot," BBC News, June 23, 2006, http://news.bbc.co.uk/2/hi/americas/5110342.stm

10. "Six Charged in Plot To Attack Fort Dix," *The Washington Post*, May 9, 2007, http://www.washingtonpost.com/wp-dyn/content/article/2007/05/08/AR2007050800465.html

11. "Terrorism Probe Points to Reach of Web Networks," *Washington Post*, January 24, 2008.

12. "Radicalization in the West: The Homegrown Threat," New York City Police Department, August 2007, http://www.nyc.gov/html/nypd/downloads/pdf/public_information/NYPD_Report-Radicalization_in_the_West.pdf

13. See Marvin J. Cetron, "Defeating Terrorism: Is it Possible? Is it Probable?" *The Futurist*, May–June 2007, http://www.versaterm.com/about_vtm/advisory/DefeatingTerrorism18-25_MJ2007_Cetron.pdf

14. Iraq Coalition Casualty Count, http://icasualties.org/oif/ (assessed January 30, 2009). See also Joseph Stiglitz and Linda Bilme, "The Three Trillion War," *The Times*, February 23, 2008, http://www.timesonline.co.uk/tol/comment/columnists/guest_contributors/article3419840.ece

15. Francis Fukuyama, "The End of History?" *The National Interest*, Summer 1989, http://www.wesjones.com/eoh.htm

16. Francis Fukuyama, "Self-Defeating Forays," *The Straits Times*, October 25, 2007.

17. Francis Fukuyama, "Self-Defeating Forays," *The Straits Times*, October 25, 2007.

18. Isaiah Wilson, New Thoughts on War and Peace, Prologue, http://www.thinkbeyondwar.com/Documents/Prologue_New_Thoughts_on_War_and_Peace.pdf (assessed January 1, 2008).

19. Isaiah Wilson, New Thoughts on War and Peace.

20. Russell R Weigley, *The American Way of War: A History of United States Military Strategy and Policy* (Bloomington: Indiana University Press, 1973).

21. Russell R Weigley, *The American Way of War*, p. xxii.

22. Autolio J. Echevarria, *Toward An American Way of War* (Strategic Studies Institute Monograph, March 2004), p. 1, http://www.strategicstudiesinstitute.army.mil/pdffiles/PUB374.pdf

23. Autolio J. Echevarria, *Toward An American Way of War*, pp. 2–3.

24. Robert M. Cassidy, *Counterinsurgency and the Global War on Terror: Military Culture and Irregular War* (Westport, CT: Praeger, 2006), p. 99.

25. For a study of Dupuy's role in producing the AirLand Battle doctrine, which was embodied in Field Manual (FM) 100-5, Operations, of 1986, and guided U.S. strategy in the Gulf War of 1990–91, see Richard M Swain, "AirLand Battle," in George F. Hoffman and Donn Albert Starry (eds), *Camp Colt to Desert Storm: The History of US Armoured Forces* (Lexington: University Press of Kentucky, 1999), pp. 360–402.

26. See, for instance, Harry Summers, *On Strategy: A Critical Analysis of the Vietnam War* (Novato, CA: Presidio, 1982).

27. See Caspar W. Weinberger, *Fighting for Peace: Seven Critical Years in the Pentagon* (New York: Warner, 1990), pp. 433–448.

28. Andrew Krepinevich, "Cavalry to Computer: The Pattern of Military Revolutions," *The National Interest*, August 1994, p. 30.

29. Lawrence Freedman, "The Revolution in Strategic Affairs," Adephi Paper No. 318 (London: International Institute for Strategic Studies, 1998), p. 32.

30. Thomas Keaney and Eliot Cohen, *Revolution in Warfare?* (Annapolis: Naval Institute Press, 1995), p. 211.

31. Remarks by the President at U.S. Naval Academy Commencement, U.S. Naval Academy Stadium, Annapolis, Maryland, May 25, 2001, The White House, http://www.whitehouse.gov/news/releases/2001/05/20010525-1.html (accessed June 1, 2008).

32. Donald H. Rumsfeld, "Transforming the Military," *Foreign Affairs*, May–June 2002, 20–21.

33. Donald H. Rumsfeld, "Transforming the Military," p. 26.

34. Donald H. Rumsfeld, "Transforming the Military," p. 31.

35. "2003: US Launches Missiles Against Saddam," BBC News, March 20, 2003, http://news.bbc.co.uk/onthisday/low/dates/stories/march/20/newsid_3495000/3495453.stm

36. "Pentagon Contradicts General on Iraq Occupation Force's Size," *New York Times*, February 28, 2003.

37. Thomas E. Ricks, *Fiasco: The American Military Adventure in Iraq* (London: Penguin, 2007), p. 156.

38. Thomas E. Ricks, *Fiasco: The American Military Adventure in Iraq*, p. 157.

39. Max Boot, "The New American Way of War," *Foreign Affairs*, July-August 2003, p.2, http://www-stage.foreignaffairs.org/20030701faessay15404-p10/max-boot/the-new-american-way-of-war.html

40. Max Boot, "The New American Way of War," p. 1.

41. Max Boot, "The New American Way of War," p. 7.

42. International Security Assistance Force, http://web.archive.org/web/20070628124507/http://www.nato.int/isaf/media/pdf/placemat_isaf.pdf (assessed June 8, 2008).

43. "US and Coalition Casualties," CNN.com, http://www.cnn.com/SPECIALS/2004/oef.casualties (accessed on January 29, 2009).

44. Casualties in Iraq, Antiwar.com, http://www.antiwar.com/casualties (accessed January 30, 2009).

45. Steven Metz, "Strategists and the Revolution in Military Affairs," in Hugh Smith (ed), *The Strategists* (Canberra: Australian Defence Force Academy, 2001), p. 117.

46. Carl von Clausewitz, *On War* (London: Plain Label Books), pp. 31–32, http://books.google.com.au/books?id=fXJnOde4eYkC.

47. Jeffrey Record, "The American Wary of War: Cultural Barriers to Successful Counterinsurgency," Cato Institute Policy Analysis No. 577, September 1, 2006, p. 7, http://www.cato.org/pubs/pas/pa577.pdf

48. "US Describes Confrontation with Iranian Boats," *New York Times*, January 8, 2008, http://www.nytimes.com/2008/01/08/washington/08military.html

49. Steven Metz, "Learning from Iraq: Counterinsurgency Strategy in American Strategy," Monograph, Strategic Studies Institute, January 2007, p. 25, http://www.strategicstudiesinstitute.army.mil/pdffiles/PUB752.pdf

50. Brigadier Nigel Aylwin-Foster, "Changing the Army for Counterinsurgency Operations," *Military Review*, November–December 2005, p. 9.

51. Brigadier Nigel Aylwin-Foster, "Changing the Army for Counterinsurgency Operations," pp. 14–15.

52. Carl von Clausewitz, *On War*, p. 30.

53. Thomas R. Mockaitis, "Counter Terrorism," in Andrew T. H. Tan (ed), *The Politics of Terrorism* (London: Routledge, 2006), p. 103.

54. Thomas R. Mockaitis, "Winning Hearts and Minds in the War on Terrorism," in Thomas A. Mockaitis and Paul B. Rich (eds), *Grand Strategy in the War Against Terrorism* (London: Frank Cass, 2003), p. 31.

55. Thomas R. Mockaitis, "Counter Terrorism," p. 112.

56. David Omand, "Countering International Terrorism: The Use of Strategy," *Survival*, Winter 2005–6, p. 107.

57. J. Robinson West, "Saudi Arabia, Iraq and the Gulf," in Jan H. Kalicki and David L. Goldwin (eds), *Energy and Security: Toward a New Foreign Policy Strategy* (Washington: Woodrow Wilson Center Press, 2005), p. 207.

58. George Friedman, "War Psychology and Time," *Strategic Forecasting*, September 11, 2007.

6 The Evolution of U.S. Counterterrorism Strategy: From GWOT to COIN

1. Bruce Hoffman, Combating Terrorism: In Search of a National Strategy, Testimony Presented to the Subcommittee on National Security, Veterans Affairs, and International Relations, House Committee on Government Reform, March 27, 2001, http://www.rand.org/pubs/testimonies/2005/CT175.pdf, p. 7.

2. Bruce Hoffman, Combating Terrorism: In Search of a National Strategy, Testimony Presented to the Subcommittee on National Security, Veterans Affairs, and International Relations, House Committee on Government Reform, March 27, 2001, http://www.rand.org/pubs/testimonies/2005/CT175.pdf, p. 8.

3. The National Security Strategy of the United States of America, September 2002, http://www.lib.umich.edu/govdocs/pdf/nss02.pdf

4. National Strategy for Combating Terrorism, February 2003, http://www.globalsecurity. org/security/library/policy/national/counter_terrorism_strategy.pdf, p. 1.
5. National Strategy for Combating Terrorism, February 2003, p. 2.
6. National Strategy for Combating Terrorism, February 2003, p. 10.
7. National Strategy for Combating Terrorism, February 2003, p. 2.
8. National Strategy for Combating Terrorism, February 2003, p. 1.
9. See Bruce Hoffman, *Inside Terrorism* (New York: Columbia University Press, 2006). For a more succinct description of the New Terrorism, see Bruce Hoffman, "The New Terrorism," in Andrew Tan and Kumar Ramakrishna (eds), *The New Terrorism: Anatomy, Trends and Counter-Strategies* (Singapore: Times Academic/Eastern Universities Press, 2003).
10. National Strategy for Combating Terrorism, February 2003, pp. 7–8.
11. Rohan Gunaratna, *Inside Al Qaeda: Global Network of Terror* (London: Hurst, 2002), p. 54.
12. Rohan Gunaratna, *Inside Al Qaeda: Global Network of Terror*, p. 1.
13. National Strategy for Combating Terrorism, February 2003, p. 12.
14. National Strategy for Combating Terrorism, February 2003, pp. 15–28.
15. National Strategy for Combating Terrorism, February 2003, p. 30.
16. National Strategy for Combating Terrorism, September 2006, http://www.globalsecurity. org/security/library/policy/national/nsct_sep2006.pdf
17. National Strategy for Combating Terrorism, September 2006, pp. 1–4.
18. National Strategy for Combating Terrorism, September 2006, p. 1.
19. National Strategy for Combating Terrorism, September 2006, p. 10.
20. National Strategy for Combating Terrorism, September 2006, pp. 11–17.
21. National Strategy for Combating Terrorism, September 2006, pp. 19–20.
22. Project for the New American Century, http://www.newamericancentury.org/
23. National Strategy for Combating Terrorism, September 2006, p. 21.
24. Bruce Hoffman, Combating Al Qaeda and the Islamic Militant Threat, Testimony Presented to the House Armed Services Committee, Subcommittee on Terrorism, Unconventional Threats and Capabilities on February 16, 2006, http://www.rand.org/ pubs/testimonies/2006/RAND_CT255.pdf, p. 1.
25. Bruce Hoffman, *Combating Al Qaeda and the Islamic Militant Threat*, pp. 2–3.
26. Peter W. Galbraith, *The End of Iraq: How American Incompetence Created a War Without End* (New York: Simon and Schuster, 2006), pp. 83–84.
27. "Lost in Translation," Government Executive.com, May 1, 2002, http://www.govexec. com/features/0502/0502s4.htm
28. "Lack of Arabic Translators Hurting US," ABC News, November 19, 2003, http://abcnews. go.com/wire/World/ap20031119_102.html
29. Anne H. Betteridge, *A Case Study in Higher Education International and Foreign Area Needs: Changes in the Middle East Studies Association Membership from 1990 to 2002*, http://www.jhfc. duke.edu/ducis/globalchallenges/pdf/betteridge1.pdf, p. 1, 9.
30. Anne H. Betteridge, *A Case Study in Higher Education International and Foreign Area Needs*, pp. 9–10.
31. Rima Merriman, "Middle East Studies Seen as Against American Interests," *Jordan Times*, March 11, 2004, http://www.arab2.com/n/newspaper/jordan-jordan-times.htm
32. Whalid Phares, *The War of Ideas* (New York: Palgrave Macmillan, 2007), p. 194. See Terry Hartle's defense against such criticism, in Terry W. Hartle, "International Programs in Higher Education and Questions of Bias," Testimony Before the U.S. House of Representatives Committee on Education and the Workforce Subcommittee on Select Education, June 19, 2003, http://republicans.edlabor.house.gov/archive/hearings/108th/ sed/titlevi61903/hartle.htm
33. See John J. Mearsheimer, "E.H. Carr vs. Idealism: The Battle Rages On," *International Relations*, 19(2), 2005.

34. David Martin Jones and Carl Ungerer, "Delusion Reigns in Terror Studies," *The Australian*, September 15, 2006, http://www.theaustralian.news.com.au/story/0,20867,20413449–7583,00.html

35. Bruce Hoffman, *Combating Al Qaeda and the Islamic Militant Threat*, p. 2.

36. Whalid Phares, *The War of Ideas*, p. 66.

37. Jason Burke, *Al Qaeda* (London: Penguin, 2007), p. 311.

38. Bin Laden's Fatwa, http://www.pbs.org/newshour/terrorism/international/fatwa_1996.html, p. 1.

39. Bin Laden's Fatwa, p. 9, 16.

40. Transcript: Bin Laden Accuses the West, Aljazeera.net, http://english.aljazeera.net/News/aspx/print.htm, p. 1.

41. Transcript: Bin Laden Accuses the West, p. 4.

42. Transcript: Bin Laden Accuses the West, p.4.

43. Whalid Phares, *The War of Ideas*, p. 15.

44. See, for instance, "Views of a Changing World 2003: War With Iraq Further Divides Global Politics," June 3, 2003, Pew Research Center for the People and the Press, p. 3, http://people-press.org/reports/print.php3?PageID=712

45. See Brynjar Lia, "Al Qaeda's Appeal: Understanding its Unique Selling Points," *Perspectives on Terrorism*, 2(8), May 2008.

46. Jason Burke, Al Qaeda, p. 295.

47. Jason Burke, Al Qaeda, p. 297.

48. "Public Diplomacy After September 11," Charlotte Beers, Under Secretary for Public Diplomacy and Public Affairs, Remarks to the National Press Club, Washington, December 18, 2002, http://www.state.gov/r/us/16269.htm

49. See Gallup Center for Muslim Studies, http://www.gallup.com/tag/Muslim%2bWorld.aspx A summary of findings also appears in "What do a Billion Muslims Really Think?" *Christian Science Monitor*, May 16, 2008, http://www.csmonitor.com/2008/0517/p12s01-wogi.html

50. "Is Islam Compatible with Democracy?" *Christian Science Monitor*, May 16, 2008, http://www.csmonitor.com/2008/0517/p12s05-wogi.html

51. See Omar Ashour, "De-Radicalization of Jihad? The Impact of Egyptian Islamist Revisionists on Al Qaeda," *Perspectives on Terrorism*, 2(5), March 2008.

52. See John J. Mearsheimer and Stephen M. Walt, "Can Saddam Be Contained? History Says Yes" (Occasional Paper, Belfer Center for Science and International Affairs, Kennedy School of Government, Harvard University, 2002).

53. See, for instance, Noam Chomsky's monograph which appeared after September 11, 2001 to some surprising popularity and acclaim but elicited shock and outrage in official circles, in which he concluded that the United States is a terrorist state. Noam Chomsky, *9–11* (Seven Stories, 2001).

54. Thomas R. Mockaitis and Paul B. Rich (eds), *Grand Strategy in the War Against Terrorism* (London: Frank Cass, 2003).

55. Thomas R. Mockaitis, "Winning Hearts and Minds in the War on Terrorism," in Thomas R. Mockaitis and Paul B. Rich (eds), *Grand Strategy in the War Against Terrorism*, p. 21.

56. Thomas R. Mockaitis, "Winning Hearts and Minds in the War on Terrorism," p. 36.

57. Thomas R. Mockaitis, "Winning Hearts and Minds in the War on Terrorism," p. 21.

58. Thomas R. Mockaitis, "Winning Hearts and Minds in the War on Terrorism," p. 21.

59. Thomas R. Mockaitis, "Winning Hearts and Minds in the War on Terrorism," p. 22, 27.

60. Thomas R. Mockaitis, "Winning Hearts and Minds in the War on Terrorism," p. 31.

61. Thomas Mockaitis, "Counter-Terrorism," in Andrew T. H. Tan (ed), *The Politics of Terrorism* (London: Routledge, 2006), p. 106.

62. Thomas Mockaitis, "Counter-Terrorism," p. 109.

63. Thomas Mockaitis, "Counter-Terrorism," p. 110.

64. Thomas Mockaitis, "Counter-Terrorism," p. 112.

65. Stephen Biddle, *American Grand Strategy After 9/11: An Assessment* (Monograph, April 2005, Strategic Studies Institute, U.S. Army War College), pp. 31–32, http://www.strategicstudiesinstitute.army.mil/pdffiles/PUB603.pdf

66. Thomas Mockaitis, *The "New" Terrorism: Myths and Reality* (Westport, CT: Praeger, 2007), p. 125.

67. See, for instance, David C. Rapoport, "The Fourth Wave: September 11 in the History of Terrorism," in *Current History*, December 2001, and David C. Rapoport, "Modern Terror: History and Special Features," *The Politics of Terrorism* (London: Routledge, 2006).

68. Steven Metz, "Learning From Iraq: Counterinsurgency in American Strategy" (Monograph, January 2007, Strategic Studies Institute), p. vi, http://www.strategicstudiesinstitute.army.mil/pdffiles/PUB752.pdf

69. Steven Metz, "Learning From Iraq: Counterinsurgency in American Strategy," p. 23.

70. Cited in Steven Metz, "Learning From Iraq: Counterinsurgency in American Strategy," p. 24. Isaiah Wilson is also cited in Thomas E Ricks, "Army Historian Cites Lack of Postwar Plan: Major Calls Effort in Iraq Mediocre," *The Washington Post*, 25 December 2004, p. A01.

71. Steven Metz, "Learning From Iraq: Counterinsurgency in American Strategy," pp. 77–78.

72. Steven Metz, "Learning From Iraq: Counterinsurgency in American Strategy," p. 79.

73. Steven Metz, "New Challenges and Old Concepts: Understanding 21st Century Insurgency," in *Parameters*, Winter 2007–8, 21–22.

74. Steven Metz, "New Challenges and Old Concepts: Understanding 21st Century Insurgency," p. 31.

75. Steven Metz, "Learning From Iraq: Counterinsurgency in American Strategy," p. 74.

76. Steven Metz, "New Challenges and Old Concepts: Understanding 21st Century Insurgency," pp. 30–31.

77. Department of Defence Dictionary of Military Terms, http://www.dtic.mil/doctrine/jel/doddict/data/t/05488.html (accessed June 1, 2008).

78. For a more detailed discussion and survey, see Dennis Pluchinsky, "Ethnic Terrorism: Themes and Variations," David W. Brannan, "Left and Right Wing Political Terrorism," Mark Juergensmeyer, "Religion and the New Terrorism," and Adam Dolnik and Rohan Gunaratna, "On the Nature of Religious Terrorism," in Andrew T. H. Tan, *The Politics of Terrorism* (London: Routledge, 2006).

79. *Army Doctrine Publications: Land Operations*, p. 17.

80. Andrew T. H. Tan, "Terrorism and Insurgency in Southeast Asia," in Andrew T. H. Tan (ed), *A Handbook of Terrorism and Insurgency in Southeast Asia* (Cheltenham: Edward Elgar, 2007), p. 4.

81. Steven Metz, "Learning From Iraq: Counterinsurgency in American Strategy," p. 88.

82. President Addresses Nation, Discusses Iraq, War on Terror, June 28, 2005, http://merln.ndu.edu/MERLN/PFIraq/archive/wh/20050628-7.pdf

7 The Evolution of U.S. Counterterrorism Strategy: From COIN to Global Counterinsurgency

1. Army Doctrine Publications: Land Operations, p. 17.

2. Army Doctrine Publications: Land Operations, pp. 18–19.

3. Robert Thompson, *Defeating Communist Insurgency: Experiences from Malaya and Vietnam* (London: Chatto and Windus, 1972), p. 51.

4. Richard Stubbs, *Hearts and Minds in Guerilla Warfare: The Malayan Emergency 1948–1960* (Singapore: Oxford University Press, 1989), p. 264.

5. Commanding General Biography, U.S. Army Combined Arms Center, http://www.dodig. osd.mil/IGInformation/archives/LTG_Petreaus.pdf

6. "Iraq's Repairman," *Newsweek*, July 5, 2004, http://www.newsweek.com/id/54322/

7. Counterinsurgency Field Manual 1–20 to 1–24 FM 3–24/MCWP 3–33.5, December 15, 2006, Headquarters, Department of the Army, Chapter 1–20 to 1–24, http://www.fas.org/ irp/doddir/army/fm3-24.pdf

8. Counterinsurgency Field Manual 1–29 FM 3–24/MCWP 3–33.5, December 15, 2006.

9. Counterinsurgency Field Manual 1–2 FM 3–24/MCWP 3–33.5, December 15, 2006.

10. Counterinsurgency Field Manual 2–14 FM 3–24/MCWP 3–33.5, December 15, 2006.

11. Counterinsurgency Field Manual 2–2 FM 3–24/MCWP 3–33.5, December 15, 2006.

12. Counterinsurgency Field Manual 1–27 to 1–28 FM 3–24/MCWP 3–33.5 15, December 15, 2006.

13. Counterinsurgency Field Manual, Appendix A, A-8 FM 3–24/MCWP 3–33.5, December 15, 2006.

14. Counterinsurgency Field Manual 1–27 FM 3–24/MCWP 3–33.5, December 15, 2006.

15. Counterinsurgency Field Manual 1–28 FM 3–24/MCWP 3–33.5, December 15, 2006.

16. Counterinsurgency Field Manual 6–22 FM 3–24/MCWP 3–33.5, December 15, 2006.

17. Counterinsurgency Field Manual 5–2 FM 3–24/MCWP 3–33.5, December 15, 2006.

18. Counterinsurgency Field Manual 6–21 to 6–22 FM 3–24/MCWP 3–33.5, December 15, 2006.

19. See Frederick W. Kagan, "Choosing Victory: A Plan for Success in Iraq," American Enterprise Institute, January 5, 2007, http://www.aei.org/publications/pubID.25396,filter. all/pub_detail.asp

20. "US Surge Plan in Iraq Working," BBC News, September 12, 2007.

21. Joe Klein, "David Petraeus," *Time*, December 17, 2007, http://www.time.com/time/ specials/2007/personoftheyear/article/0,28804,1690753_1695388_1695379,00.html See also General David Petraeus "Report to Congress on the Situation in Iraq," September 10–11, 2007, http://www.defenselink.mil/pubs/pdfs/Petraeus-Testimony20070910.pdf, p. 2.

22. General David Petraeus "Report to Congress on the Situation in Iraq," p. 2.

23. "Will Petraeus Strategy be the Last?" The Atlantic.com, September 17, 2007, http://www. theatlantic.com/doc/200709u/petraeus-bing-west

24. "Is Iraq Getting Better?" BBC News, November 13, 2007.

25. "Baghdad Sees Tentative Rebirth," BBC News, June 30, 2008, http://news.bbc.co.uk/2/ hi/middle_east/7482307.stm

26. Multi-National Force-Iraq Commander's Counterinsurgency Guidance, Headquarters, Multi-National Force, Baghdad, June 21, 2008, http://www.mnf-iraq.com/images/ CGs_Messages/080621_coin_%20guidance.pdf

27. General David H. Petraeus, Testimony to Senate Armed Services Committee, April 8, 2008, http://www.realclearpolitics.com/articles/2008/04/gen_petraeus_testimony_to_ the.html

28. "Measuring Stability and Security in Iraq," Report to Congress, June 2008, p. vi, http:// www.defenselink.mil/pubs/pdfs/Master_16_June_08_%20FINAL_SIGNED%20.pdf

29. In July 2008, for instance, at least 35 people were killed in a suicide bombing at an Iraqi army recruitment base. See "Bombers Kill Iraq Army Recruits," BBC News, July 17, 2008, http://news.bbc.co.uk/2/hi/middle_east/7506749.stm In January 2009, 23 people were killed and 110 wounded in a suicide bombing of a meeting of Sunni tribal leaders in Yusufiya, just outside Baghdad. See "Suicide Bomb Kills Many in Iraq," BBC News, January 2, 2009, http://news.bbc.co.uk/2/hi/middle_east/7808354.stm

30. Milton Osborne, "Getting the Job Done: Iraq and the Malayan Emergency," Perspectives, Lowy Institute, February 2005, pp. 6, 8–9, http://www.lowyinstitute.org/Publication. asp?pid=215

31. Milton Osborne, "Getting the Job Done: Iraq and the Malayan Emergency," p. 9.

32. A pertinent point made by Ian Beckett, "Forward to the Past: Insurgency in Our Midst," Harvard International Review, Summer 2001, p. 63.

33. Milton Osborne, "Getting the Job Done: Iraq and the Malayan Emergency," p. 12.

34. Donald Mackay, *The Malayan Emergency, 1948–60: The Domino That Stood* (London: Brassey's, 1997), pp.152–153.

35. Barack Obama, "My Plan for Iraq," *The New York Times*, July 14, 2008.

36. *Afghanistan Study Group Report*, January 30, 2008, p. 17, http://www.thepresidency.org/pubs/Afghan_Study_Group_final.pdf

37. "The Situation in Afghanistan and its Implications for International Peace and Security," Report of the Secretary-General, March 6, 2008, p. 1.

38. Afghan Bonn Agreement, http://www.afghangovernment.com/AfghanAgreement Bonn.htm

39. UN Security Council Resolution 1386, December 20, 2001, http://daccessdds.un.org/doc/UNDOC/GEN/N01/708/55/PDF/N0170855.pdf?OpenElement

40. "Afghanistan Troop Deaths Outnumber Those in Iraq," Guardian.co.uk, July 1, 2008, http://www.guardian.co.uk/world/2008/jul/jul/01/afghanistan.iraq/print

41. "US and Coalition Casualties," CNN.com, http://edition.cnn.com/SPECIAS/2004/oef.casualties/ (accessed July 23, 2008).

42. US and Coalition Casualties, CNN.com, http://www.cnn.com/SPECIALS/2004/oef.casualties (accessed on January 29, 2009).

43. "The Situation in Afghanistan and its Implications for International Peace and Security," Report of the Secretary-General, March 6, 2008, p. 5.

44. "Afghan Insurgency Still a Potent Force," United States Institute of Peace Briefing, February 2006, http://www.usip.org/pubs/usipeace_briefings/2006/0223_afghan.html

45. President George W. Bush's Address to the Nation, October 7, 2001, http://www.johnstonsarchive.net/terrorism/bush911d.html

46. "Afghan Opium Fields Show Failure of US Economic Aid Efforts," Bloomberg.com, February 11, 2008, http://taraqee.wordpress.com/2008/02/13/afghan-opium-fields-show-failure-of-us-economic-aid-efforts/

47. "The Situation in Afghanistan: A Re-evaluation Needed," United States Institute Peace Briefing, April 2007, http://www.usip.org/pubs/usipeace_briefings/2007/0419_koenigs_afghanistan.html

48. "Rift in NATO Over Afghanistan Forces," CBS News, February 26, 2008, http://www.cbsnews.com/stories/2008/02/02/world/main3782460.shtml

49. "Afghanistan: Gates Doubts Europeans' War Commitment," *New York Times*, October 26, 2007, http://www.nytimes.com/2007/10/26/world/asia/26briefs-gates.html

50. Paul Gallis, "NATO in Afghanistan: A Test of the Transatlantic Alliance," Congressional Research Service Report for Congress, May 6, 2008, p. 17,

51. Paul Gallis, "NATO in Afghanistan: A Test of the Transatlantic Alliance," pp. 21–22.

52. Paul Gallis, "NATO in Afghanistan: A Test of the Transatlantic Alliance," p. 27.

53. The Afghanistan Compact, London, 31 January–1 February 2006, p. 2, http://www.nato.int/isaf/docu/epub/pdf/afghanistan_compact.pdf

54. The Afghanistan Compact, p. 3.

55. The Afghanistan Compact, p. 6.

56. "Afghanistan in the Crosshairs: Broad Agreement on the Problems, No Consensus on the Solutions," United States Institute of Peace, April–May 2006, p. 2, http://www.usip.org/peacewatch/2006/april_may/afghanistan.html

57. "Afghanistan: The Taliban Resurgent and NATO," The Brookings Institute, February 25, 2008, http://www.brookings.edu/opinions/2006/1128globalgovernance_riedel.aspx

58. Afghanistan Study Group Report, January 30, 2008, p. 18.

59. "General Petraeus Takes on Afghanistan," *The Times Online*, September 16, 2008, http://www.timesonline.co.uk/tol/news/world/iraq/article4761445.ece

60. "NATO Chief in Afghanistan Says Pakistan's Tack on Militants is Not What as Expected," *New York Times*, May 30, 2008, http://www.afghanistannewscenter.com/news/2008/may/may302008.html

61. "Red Mosque Rebel Cleric, 50 Others Killed in Raid," CNN.com, July 10, 2007, http://www.cnn.com/2007/WORLD/asiapcf/07/10/pakistan.mosque/index.html

62. "Pakistani Islamists Rally on Red Mosque Anniversary," ABC.net, July 6, 2008, http://www.abc.net.au/news/stories/2008/07/06/2295786.htm

63. As recounted by Zahid Hussain, *Frontline Pakistan: The Struggle with Militant Islam* (London: I.B. Taurus, 2007), pp. 185–186.

64. "Musharaff Issues Warning to West," BBC News, January 25, 2008, http://news.bbc.co.uk/2/hi/south_asia/7209611.stm

65. "What to do with Pakistan's Judges," BBC News, May 12, 2008, http://news.bbc.co.uk/2/hi/south_asia/7393078.stm

66. "Bhutto Killed in Suicide Attack," News.com, December 28, 2007, http://www.news.com.au/story/0,23599,22979273-2,00.html

67. "Pakistan: Al Qaeda Claims Bhutto's Death," Adnkronos International, December 27, 2007, http://www.adnkronos.com/AKI/English/Security/?id=1.0.1710322437

68. Pakistan Elections 2008 Summary, http://www.elections.com.pk/summary.php

69. "All Change in Pakistan's Wild West," BBC News, February 21, 2008, http://news.bbc.co.uk/2/hi/south_asia/7255642.stm

70. "US Military in Pakistan Warning," BBC News, July 11, 2008.

71. "Pak Army Protests US Drone Attack in Bajaur," The Indian.com, May 17, 2008, http://www.thaindian.com/newsportal/health/pak-army-protests-us-drone-attack-in-bajaur_10049702.html

72. "US-Pakistan at Odds Over Strike in Tribal Area," *Washington Post*, June 12, 2008, http://www.washingtonpost.com/wp-dyn/content/article/2008/06/11/AR2008061100719.html?nav=rss_world/asia

73. "Pakistani Fury as Suspected US Drone Attack Kills 12," Telegraph.co.uk, September 12, 2008, http://www.telegraph.co.uk/news/worldnews/asia/pakistan/2827257/Pakistani-fury-as-suspected-US-drone-attack-kills-12.html

74. "Zardari Takes Office as President," *International Herald Tribune*, September 9, 2008, http://www.iht.com/articles/2008/09/09/asia/pakistan.php

75. See Andrew T. H. Tan (ed), *A Handbook of Terrorism and Insurgency in Southeast Asia* (Cheltenham: Edward Elgar, 2006); a collaborative work of 19 scholars.

76. As documented by Rohan Gunaratna, *Inside Al Qaeda* (London: Hurst, 2002). See Chapter 4.

77. See Rohan Gunaratna, *Inside Al Qaeda*, pp. 175–176.

78. "Bush Details Foiled 2002 Al Qaeda Attack on Los Angeles," CNN News, February 9, 2006, http://www.cnn.com

79. David Kilcullen, "Countering Global Insurgency," *Small Wars Journal*, November 30, 2004, p. 32, http://www.smallwarsjournal.com/documents/kilcullen.pdf

80. Summary of Case Against Jemaah Islamiah in Singapore, NEFA Foundation, http://nefafoundation.org/miscellaneous/FeaturedDocs/SingMHA_JISummary.pdf (accessed February 1, 2009).

81. Andrew T. H. Tan (ed), *The Politics of Terrorism* (London: Routledge, 2006), pp. 164–165.

82. Andrew T. H. Tan, *A Political and Economic Dictionary of Southeast Asia* (London: Europa, 2004), pp. 136–137.

83. See Al Qaeda in Southeast Asia: The Case of the Ngruki Network in Indonesia, Asia Briefing No. 20, August 8, 2002, International Crisis Group, http:/www.crisisgroup.org

84. Sukhumbhand Paribatra and Chai-Anan Samudavanija, Chai-Anan, quoted in Lim Joo Jock and S. Vani (eds), *Armed Separatism in Southeast Asia* (Singapore: Institute of Southeast Asian Studies), p. 32.

85. See Paul A. Rodell, "Separatist Insurgency in the Southern Philippines," Kamarulzaman Askandar, "The Aceh Conflict: Phases of Conflict and Hope for Peace," and Thitinan Pongsudhirak, "The Malay-Muslim Insurgency in Southern Thailand," in Andrew T. H. Tan (ed), *A Handbook of Terrorism and Insurgency in Southeast Asia.*

86. Rohan Gunaratna, *Inside Al Qaeda*, p. 185. See also *Straits Times*, November 4, 2002, p. A6, which reported the denials of the MILF of alleged links with Al Qaeda.

87. Mindanao Times Interactive News, mindanaotimes.com.p/news, March 2, 2002.

88. Mindanao Times Interactive News, mindanaotimes.com.p/news, October 22, 2002.

89. Andrew T. H. Tan (ed), *The Politics of Terrorism*, pp. 116–117.

90. Andrew T. H, Tan, *Security Perspectives of the Malay Archipelago* (Cheltenham: Edward Elgar, 2004), pp. 178–179.

91. Andrew T. H. Tan (ed), *The Politics of Terrorism*, p. 198.

92. "Who Was Behind Thai Attacks?" BBC News, April 30, 2004. See also "Grieving Begins in Thailand's South," BBC News, April 29, 2004, http://news.bbc.co.uk/2/hi/asia-pacific/3669353.stm

93. "Deadly Demo Puts Thais on Tightrope," *The Age*, October 30, 2004, http://www.theage.com.au/articles/2004/10/29/1099028209065.html?from=storylhs

94. See, for instance, "The Thai Connection", *Al Ahram Weekly*, Issue No. 689, May 6–12, 2004, http://weekly.ahram.org (accessed on October 5, 2006).

95. "Targeting Thailand," *Time*, January 19, 2003.

96. Thomas Mockaitis, "Counter-Terrorism," in Andrew T. H. Tan (ed), *The Politics of Terrorism*, p. 110.

97. Bruce Hoffman, "Combating Al Qaeda and the Militant Islamic Threat," Testimony Before the Committee on Armed Services Subcommittee on Terrorism, Unconventional Threats and Capabilities, United States House of Representatives, February 16, 2006, p. 14, http://www.rand.org/pubs/testimonies/2006/RAND_CT255.pdf

98. Thomas R. Mockaitis, "Winning Hearts and Minds in the War on Terrorism," in Thomas R. Mockaitis and Paul B. Rich (eds), *Grand Strategy in the War Against Terrorism* (London: Frank Cass, 2003), p. 21.

99. Bruce Hoffman, "Combating Al Qaeda and the Militant Islamic Threat," p. 14.

100. See Thomas R. Mockaitis, "Counter-Terrorism," p. 107.

101. Daniel Byman, *The Five Front War* (Hoboken, NJ: John Wiley and Sons, 2008), pp. 3–4.

102. Michael Chandler and Rohan Gunaratna, *Countering Terrorism: Can We Meet the Threat of Global Violence?* (London: Reaktion Books, 2007), p. 14.

103. Michael Chandler and Rohan Gunaratna, *Countering Terrorism: Can We Meet the Threat of Global Violence?* pp. 88–90.

104. Michael Chandler and Rohan Gunaratna, *Countering Terrorism: Can We Meet the Threat of Global Violence?* p. 220. Loretta Napleoni, arguably one of the world's leading experts on terrorism financing, endorsed this book on the backcover as "required reading for Number 10 and the White House."

105. Jason Burke, *Al Qaeda* (London: Penguin, 2003), p. 312.

106. Jason Burke, *Al Qaeda*, p. 312.

107. Jason Burke, *Al Qaeda,* pp. 312–313.

108. See James S. Corum, *Fighting the War on Terror: A Counterinsurgency Strategy* (St Paul, MN: Zenith Press, 2007), pp. 257–265.

109. James S. Corum, *Fighting the War on Terror: A Counterinsurgency Strategy*, p. 113, 238.

110. See James S. Corum, *Fighting the War on Terror: A Counterinsurgency Strategy*, pp. 233–255.

111. Austin Long, On "Other War": Lessons from Five Decades of RAND Counterinsurgency Research (Santa Monica, CA: RAND, 2006), pp. 19–20.

112. David Kilcullen, "Twenty-Eight Articles: Fundamentals of Company-level Counterinsurgency," http://www.au.af.mil/info-ops/iosphere_summer06_kilcullen.pdf

113. Quoted in Rebecca Weisser, "Strategist Behind War Gains," *The Australian*, August 18, 2007, http://www.theaustralian.news.com.au/story/0,25197,22263435-31477,00.html

114. David Kilcullen, "Countering Global Insurgency," p. 1, http://www.smallwarsjournal.com/documents/kilcullen.pdf

115. David Kilcullen, "Counterinsurgency Redux," *Survival*, 48(4), December 2006, http://smallwarsjournal.com/documents/kilcullen1.pdf, pp. 3, 6–7.

116. David Kilcullen, "Counterinsurgency Redux," pp. 3–6.

117. David Kilcullen, "Counterinsurgency Redux," pp. 6–7.

118. David Kilcullen, "Counterinsurgency Redux," pp. 9–11.

119. David Kilcullen, "Countering Global Insurgency," pp. 29–30, 44–45.

120. David Kilcullen, "Religion and Insurgency," *Small Wars Journal* Blog, May 12, 2007, http://smallwarsjournal.com/blog/2007/05/religion-and-insurgency/

121. "Army Enlists Anthropology in War Zones," *New York Times*, October 5, 2007, p. 1.

122. Montgomery McFate, "The Military Utility of Understanding Adversary Culture," in *Joint Forces Quarterly*, Issue 38, July 2005, http://www.au.af.mil/au/awc/awcgate/jfq/1038.pdf

123. David Kilcullen, "Countering Global Insurgency," p. 2.

124. See the Executive Summary of David Kilcullen, "Countering Global Insurgency."

125. David Kilcullen, "Countering Global Insurgency", pp. 1–2.

126. David Kilcullen, "Countering Global Insurgency," pp. 37–38.

127. Rebecca Weisser, "Strategist Behind War Gains," *The Australian*, August 18, 2007, http://www.theaustralian.news.com.au/story/0,25197,22263435-31477,00.html

128. David Kilcullen, "Countering Global Insurgency," p. 47.

8   The Future for Counterterrorism

1. *Global Trends 2025: A Transformed World,* National Intelligence Council, November 2008, pp. 69–70, http://www.acus.org/files/publication_pdfs/3/Global-Trends-2025.pdf

2. Bruce Hoffman, "Combating Al Qaeda and the Militant Islamic Threat," Testimony presented to the House Armed Services Committee, Subcommittee on Terrorism, Unconventional Threats and Capabilities on February 16, 2006 (Santa Monica, CA: RAND, 2006), p. 3.

3. Bruce Hoffman, "Al Qaeda Dangerous as Ever," *The National Interest*, September 10, 2008, http://www.nationalinterest.org/Article.aspx?id=19846

4. The Terrorist Threat to the U.S. Homeland, National Intelligence Estimate, July 2007, http://www.dni.gov/press_releases/20070717_release.pdf

5. Ted Gistaro, "Assessing the Fight Against Al Qaeda," The Washington Institute for Near East Policy, August 12, 2008, pp. 1–2, http://www.washingtoninstitute.org/print.php?template=C07&CID=414

6. Adam Dolnik and Rohan Gunaratna, "Dagger and Sarin: The Evolution of Terrorist Weapons and Tactics," in Andrew T. H. Tan (ed), *The Politics of Terrorism* (London: Routledge, 2006), pp. 35–36.

7. Bruce Hoffman, "Combating Al Qaeda and the Militant Islamic Threat," p. 12.

8. "Bloodletting in Troubled Thai South Continues," *Straits Times*, March 16, 2006.

9. See Marc Sageman, *Leaderless Jihad: Terror Networks in the Twenty-First Century* (Philadelphia: Pennsylvania University Press, 2008).

10. Jason Burke, *Al Qaeda: The True Story of Radical Islam* (London: Penguin, 2007), p. 306.

11. Jason Burke, *Al Qaeda: The True Story of Radical Islam*, p. 308.

12. Jeffrey H. Norwitz (ed), *Armed Groups: Studies in National Security, Counterterrorism and Counterinsurgency* (Newport, RI: U.S. Naval War College, 2008), pp. xv–xvi.

13. Peter Curry, "Small Wars are Local: Debunking Current Assumptions about Countering Small Armed Groups," in Jeffrey H. Norwitz (ed), *Armed Groups: Studies in National Security, Counterterrorism and Counterinsurgency*, pp. 158–159.

14. See, for instance, his explanation for the Anbar Awakening, in David Kilcullen, "Anatomy of a Tribal Revolt," *Small Wars Journal* Blog, August 29, 2007, http://smallwarsjournal. com/blog/2007/08/print/anatomy-of-a-tribal-revolt

15. P H Liotta, "Takin' It to the Streets: Hydra Networks, Chaos Strategies, and the 'New' Asymmetry," in Jeffrey H. Norwitz (ed), *Armed Groups: Studies in National Security, Counterterrorism and Counterinsurgency*, pp. 419–430.

16. Gareth Evans, "The Global Response to Terrorism," 2005 Wallace Wurth Lecture, University of New South Wales, Sydney, September 27, 2005, p.13.

17. Seth G. Jones and Martin C. Libicki, *How Terrorist Groups End: Lessons for Countering Al Qaeda* (Santa Monica, CA: RAND, 2008), p. xvii.

18. Thomas Mockaitis, "Counter-Terrorism," in Andrew T. H. Tan (ed), *The Politics of Terrorism* (London: Routledge, 2006), p. 110.

19. Bruce Hoffman, "Combating Al Qaeda and the Militant Islamic Threat," p. 14.

20. Jason Burke, *Al Qaeda: The True Story of Radical Islam*, p. 313.

21. Philip H. Gordon, "Winning the Right War," *Survival*, 49(4), Winter 2007–8, 38–39.

22. See the Executive Summary of David Kilcullen, "Countering Global Insurgency", *Small Wars Journal*, November 30, 2004, http://www.smallwarsjournal.com/documents/ kilcullen.pdf

23. Thomas R Mockaitis, "Conclusion: The Future of Terrorism Studies," *Small Wars and Insurgencies*, 14(1), March 2003, 211.

24. Thomas R Mockaitis, "Conclusion: The Future of Terrorism Studies," pp. 211–212.

25. "All Change at the Pentagon," *Strategic Comments*, 14(6), August 2008, 1–2.

26. National Defense Strategy, June 2008, p. 4, http://www.defenselink.mil/news/2008%20 National%20Defense%20Strategy.pdf

27. National Defense Strategy, June 2008, p. 8.

28. National Defense Strategy, June 2008, p. 8.

29. National Defense Strategy, June 2008, pp. 8–9.

30. National Defense Strategy, June 2008, p. 9.

31. National Defense Strategy, June 2008, p. 21.

32. National Defense Strategy, June 2008, p. 18.

33. National Defense Strategy, June 2008, p. 20.

34. Gwynne Dyer, *After Iraq: Where Next for the Middle East?* (New Haven, CT: Yale University Press, 2008), p. 78.

35. Daniel Byman, *The Five Front War: The Better Way to Fight Global Jihad* (Hoboken, NJ: John Wiley and Sons, 2008), p. 228.

36. *Global Trends 2025: A Transformed World*, pp. 29–37.

37. *Global Trends 2025: A Transformed World*, p. 37.

BIOGRAPHY

Andrew T H Tan is an associate professor and Convenor, International Studies, at the University of New South Wales, Australia. Supported by the university's Strategic Priority Fund, he does research on defence and security issues, including terrorism. He was previously senior lecturer in defence studies, King's College London, and taught at the Joint Services Command and Staff College, UK. Educated in Singapore, Cambridge, and Sydney (where he obtained his PhD), his advice on security issues is sought by governments, armed forces, universities, and research institutes. He has published 10 books (with another two forthcoming) and many internationally refereed journal articles and book chapters. His recent sole-authored and edited books include: *Security Perspectives of the Malay Archipelago* (Cheltenham, UK: Edward Elgar, 2004), *A Political and Economic Dictionary of South-East Asia* (London: Europa, 2004), *The Politics of Terrorism* (London: Routledge, 2006), *A Handbook of Terrorism and Insurgency in Southeast Asia* (Cheltenham, UK: Edward Elgar, 2007), *The Politics of Maritime Power* (London: Routledge, 2007), and *The Global Arms Trade* (London: Routledge, forthcoming).

BIBLIOGRAPHY

"A Decade of Deception and Defiance: Saddam Hussein's Defiance of the United Nations," White House Background Paper, September 12, 2002, http://webharvest.gov/ peth04/20041101060918/www.whitehouse.gov/news/releases/2002/09/iraqdecade.pdf

ABC News

Afghan Bonn Agreement, http://www.afghangovernment.com/AfghanAgreementBonn.htm (accessed June 1, 2009).

"Afghan Insurgency Still a Potent Force," United States Institute of Peace Briefing, February 2006, http://www.usip.org/pubs/usipeace_briefings/2006/0223_afghan.html

"Afghanistan in the Crosshairs: Broad Agreement on the Problems, No Consensus on the Solutions," United States Institute of Peace, April–May 2006, http://www.usip.org/ peacewatch/2006/april_may/afghanistan.html

"Afghanistan: The Taliban Resurgent and NATO," The Brookings Institute, February 25, 2008, http://www.brookings.edu/opinions/2006/1128globalgovernance_riedel.aspx

AFP

"After the Abadan Fire," *Time*, September 4, 1978.

"Al Qaeda Denies Link to Iraq Blasts as US Says Group Responsible," Muslim American Society, March 4, 2004, http://www.masnet.org/news.asp?id=1011

"Al Qaeda in 2008: The Struggle for Relevance," *STRATFOR*, April 2, 2008, http://www. stratfor.com/weekly/al_qaeda_2008_struggle_relevance

"Al Qaeda in Southeast Asia: The Case of the Ngruki Network in Indonesia," Asia Briefing No. 20, August 8, 2002, International Crisis Group, http:/www.crisisgroup.org

"Al Qaeda Strikes in Algeria," *The Long War Journal*, April 11, 2007, http://www.longwarjournal.org/archives/2007/04/al_qaeda_strikes_in.php

"All Change at the Pentagon," *Strategic Comments*, 14(6), August 2008.

Allawi, Ali A, *The Occupation of Iraq: Winning the War, Losing the Peace* (New Haven, CT: Yale University Press, 2007).

Al-Shishani, Murad Batal, "The Salafi-Jihadist Movement in Iraq: Recruitment Methods and Arab Volunteers," in *Terrorism Monitor*, 3(23), December 2, 2005.

"America's Image Further Erodes, Europeans Want Weaker Ties," Pew Research Center for the People and the Press, March 18, 2003, p. 1, http://people-press.org/reports/display. php3?ReportID=175

Annual Threat Assessment of the Intelligence Community for the Senate Armed Services Committee, February 27, 2008, pp. 4–5, http://armed-services.senate.gov/statemnt/2008/ February/McConnell%2002-27-08.pdf

Arab News (Saudi Arabia)

Army Doctrine Publications: Land Operations (UK)

Ashour, Omar, "De-Radicalizatio of Jihad? The Impact of Egyptian Islamist Revisionists on Al Qaeda," *Perspectives on Terrorism*, 2(5), March 2008.

Associated Press

Background Note: Australia, US State Department, http://www.state.gov/r/pa/ei/bgn/2698.htm

BBC News

Beckett, Ian, "Forward to the Past: Insurgency in Our Midst," *Harvard International Review*, Summer 2001.

"Behind the Walls of Abu Ghraib," *Newsweek*, May 22, 2004, http://www.truthout.org/cgi-bin/artman/exec/view.cgi/9/4598

Bell, Coral, *The End of the Vasco da Gama Era: The Next Landscape of World Politics* (Sydney: Lowy Institute, 2007).

"Beneath the Hoods: Many of the Tortured at Abu Ghraib Were Common Criminals, Not Terrorists," *Newsweek*, July 19, 2004, http://www.newsweek.com/id/54447

Bennett, Christopher, "Combating Terrorism," *NATO Review*, Spring 2003, http://www.nato.int/docu/review/2003/issue1/english/art2.html

Betteridge, Anne H, A Case Study in Higher Education International and Foreign Area Needs: Changes in the Middle East Studies Association Membership from 1990 to 2002, http://www.jhfc.duke.edu/ducis/globalchallenges/pdf/betteridge1.pdf

Bhalla, Revi, "Beyond the Post 9/11 World," *STRATFOR*, October 8, 2008.

Biddle, Stephen, *American Grand Strategy After 9/11: An Assessment*, Monograph, April 2005, Strategic Studies Institute, U.S. Army War College, http://www.strategicstudiesinstitute.army.mil/pdffiles/PUB603.pdf

Bilmes, Linda J. and Joseph E. Stiglitz, "The Iraq War Will Cost Us $3 Trillion, and Much More," *Washington Post*, March 9, 2008, http://www.washingtonpost.com/up-dyn/content/article/2008/03/07/AR2008030702846.html

Bin Laden's Fatwa, http://www.pbs.org/newshour/terrorism/international/fatwa_1996.html

Bjorgo, Tore, (ed.), *Root Causes of Terrorism: Myths, Reality and Ways Forward* (New York: Routledge, 2005).

Bloomberg.com

Blumenthal, Sidney, "Washington's Chalabi Nightmare," Salon.com, May 27, 2004, http://dir.salon.com/story/opinion/blumenthal/2004/05/27/chalabi/index.html

Boot, Max, "The New American Way of War," *Foreign Affairs*, July–August 2003, http://www-stage.foreignaffairs.org/20030701faessay15404-p10/max-boot/the-new-american-way-of-war.html

Bowman, Steve, "Iraq: US Military Operations," CRS Report for Congress, Updated May 9, 2006, http://italy.usembassy.gov/pdf/other/RL31701.pdf

Brigadier Nigel Aylwin-Foster, "Changing the Army for Counterinsurgency Operations," *Military Review*, November-December 2005.

Burke, Jason, *Al Qaeda: The True Story of Radical Islam* (London: Penguin, 2007).

Burton, Fred, and Scott Stewart, "Grassroots Jihadists and the Thin Blue Line," *STRATFOR*, February 27, 2008.

Byman, Daniel, *The Five Front War: The Better Way to Fight Global Jihad* (Hoboken, NJ: John Wiley and Sons, 2008).

"Can Anyone Govern This Place?" *Time*, May 26, 2003.

Cassidy, Robert M., *Counterinsurgency and the Global War on Terror: Military Culture and Irregular War* (Westport, CT: Praeger, 2006).

"Casualties in Iraq," Antiwar.com, http://www.antiwar.com/casualties

CBS News

Cetron, Marvin J., "Defeating Terrorism: Is it Possible? Is it Probable?" *The Futurist*, May–June 2007, http://www.versaterm.com/about_vtm/advisory/DefeatingTerrorism18-25_MJ2007_Cetron.pdf

Chandler, Micheal, and Rohan Gunaratna, *Countering Terrorism: Can We Meet the Threat of Global Violence?* (London: Reaktion Books, 2007).

Channel Four News

Chomsky, Noam, *9–11* (Seven Stories, 2001).

Christian Science Monitor

CNN.com

"Commanding General Biography," U.S. Army Combined Arms Center, http://www.dodig.osd.mil/IGInformation/archives/LTG_Petreaus.pdf

Condemnation of Terrorist Attacks in the United States, United Nations General Assembly, September 12, 2001, http://www.un.org/documents/ga/docs/56/agresolution.htm

"Confessions of an Al Qaeda Terrorist," *Time*, September 15, 2002, http://www.time.com/time/world/article/0,8599,351169,00.html

Cordesman, Anthony H., and Nawaf Obaid, "Al-Qaeda in Saudi Arabia: Asymmetric Threats and Islamist Extremists," Center for Strategic and International Studies, Washington, January 26, 2005.

Corum, James S., *Fighting the War on Terror: A Counterinsurgency Strategy* (St. Paul, MN: Zenith Press, 2007).

Counterinsurgency Field Manual 1–20 to 1–24 FM 3–24/MCWP 3–33.5, December 15, 2006, Headquarters, Department of the Army, http://www.fas.org/irp/doddir/army/fm3-24.pdf

Cronin, Audrey K., *Ending Terrorism: Lessons for Defeating Al Qaeda*, Adelphi Paper 394, International Institute for Strategic Studies, London, 2008.

Department of Defense Dictionary of Military Terms, http://www.dtic.mil/doctrine/jel/doddict/data/t/05488.html

Dyer, Gwynne, *After Iraq: Where Next for the Middle East?* (New Haven, CT: Yale University Press, 2008).

Echevarria, Autolio J., *Toward An American Way of War*, Strategic Studies Institute Monograph, March 2004, http://www.strategicstudiesinstitute.army.mil/pdffiles/PUB374.pdf

Evans, Gareth, "The Global Response to Terrorism," 2005 Wallace Wurth Lecture, University of New South Wales, Sydney, September 27, 2005.

Fact Sheet: Extraordinary Rendition, June 12, 2005, American Civil Liberties Union, http://www.aclu.org/safefree/extraordinaryrendition/22203res20051206.html

"Failure to Find Weapons in Iraq Leads to Intelligence Scrutiny," *McClatchy*, June 2, 2003, http://www.mcclatchydc.com/128/story/9706.html

Financial Times

"Follow the Yellow Cake Road," *Newsweek*, July 28, 2003.

Freedman, Lawrence, "The Revolution in Strategic Affairs," Adephi Paper No. 318 (London: International Institute for Strategic Studies, 1998).

Friedman, George, "War Psychology and Time," *Strategic Forecasting*, September 11, 2007.

Fukuyama, Francis, "Self-Defeating Forays," *The Straits Times*, October 25, 2007.

Fukuyama, Francis, "The End of History?" *The National Interest*, Summer 1989, http://www.wesjones.com/eoh.htm

Fukuyama, Francis, "The Neoconservative Moment," *The National Interest*, July 1, 2004, http://www.tvo.org/goingglobal/readings/The_Neoconservative_Moment.pdf

Galbraith, Peter W., *The End of Iraq: How American Incompetence Created a War Without End* (New York: Simon & Schuster, 2006).

Gallis, Paul, "NATO in Afghanistan: A Test of the Transatlantic Alliance," Congressional Research Service Report for Congress, May 6, 2008.

Gallup Center for Muslim Studies, http://www.gallup.com/tag/Muslim%2bWorld.aspx

General David H. Petraeus, Testimony to Senate Armed Services Committee, April 8, 2008, http://www.realclearpolitics.com/articles/2008/04/gen_petraeus_testimony_to_the.html

General David Petraeus, "Report to Congress on the Situation in Iraq," September 10–11, 2007, http://www.defenselink.mil/pubs/pdfs/Petraeus-Testimony20070910.pdf

Gistaro, Ted, "Assessing the Fight Against Al Qaeda," The Washington Institute for Near East Policy, August 12, 2008, http://www.washingtoninstitute.org/print.php?template=C07&CID=414

Glennon, Michael F., "Why the Security Council Failed," *Foreign Affairs*, May/June 2003.

Global Trends 2025: A Transformed World, National Intelligence Council, November 2008, http://www.acus.org/files/publication_pdfs/3/Global-Trends-2025.pdf

Gordon, Philip H., "Winning the Right War," *Survival*, 49(4), Winter 2007–8.

Grant, Greg, "Analyst Warns of Third Islamic Terrorist Wave, Enabled by Internet," Government Executive.com, February 25, 2008, http://www.govexec.com/dailyfed/0208/022508g1.htm

Gunaratna, Rohan, *Inside Al Qaeda* (London: Hurst, 2002).

Gurr, Nadine, and Benjamin Cole, *The New Face of Terrorism: Threats from Weapons of Mass Destruction* (London: IB Taurus, 2000).

Hashim, Ahmed S., *Insurgency and Counterinsurgency in Iraq* (London: Hurst, 2006).

Hoffman, Bruce, "Al Qaeda Dangerous as Ever," *The National Interest*, September 10, 2008, http://www.nationalinterest.org/Article.aspx?id=19846

Hoffman, Bruce, "Combating Al Qaeda and the Militant Islamic Threat," Testimony Before the Committee on Armed Services Subcommittee on Terrorism, Unconventional Threats and Capabilities, United States House of Representatives, February 16, 2006, http://www.globalsecurity.net/security/library/congress/2006_h/060216-hoffman.pdf

Hoffman, Bruce, "Combating Terrorism: In Search of a National Strategy," Testimony Presented to the Subcommittee on National Security, Veterans Affairs, and International Relations, House Committee on Government Reform, March 27, 2001, http://www.rand.org/pubs/testimonies/2005/CT175.pdf

Hoffman, Bruce, "Terrorism's Twelve Step Program," *The National Interest*, January 13, 2009, http://www.nationalinterest.org/Article.aspx?id=20592

Hoffman, Bruce, "The Congruence of International and Domestic Trends in Terrorism," *Terrorism and Political Violence*, 9(2) (Summer 1997).

Hoffman, Bruce, *Inside Terrorism* (New York: Columbia University Press, 2006).

Hoffman, George F. and Donn Albert Starry (eds.), *Camp Colt to Desert Storm: the History of US Armoured Forces* (Lexington: University Press of Kentucky, 1999).

"How Much of Al Qaeda's Leadership has been Captured or Killed," News Center for the Study of Terrorism and Political Conflict, http://www.borrull.org/e/noticia.php?id=40842 (accessed February 1, 2008).

Hoyle, Russ, *How Misinformation, Disinformation, and Arrogance Led America into Iraq* (New York: Thomas Dunne Books, 2008).

Hussain, Zahid, *Frontline Pakistan: The Struggle Within Militant Islam* (London: IB Taurus, 2007).

"In the Spotlight: The Special Purpose Islamic Regiment," Center for Defence Information, Terrorism Project, May 2, 2003, http://www.cdi.org/terrorism/spir.cfm

International Herald Tribune

International Security Assistance Force, http://web.archive.org/web/20070628124507/http://www.nato.int/isaf/media/pdf/placemat_isaf.pdf

Interview with Lee Hamilton, Council on Foreign Relations, September 7, 2006, http://www.cfr.org/publication/11319

"Iran's Continuing Programs for Weapons of Mass Destruction," National Intelligence Estimate, October 1, 2002, http://homepage.ntlworld.com/jksonc/docs/nie-iraq-wmd.html

Iraq Coalition Casualty Count, http://icasualties.org/oif/

"Iraq's Provincial Elections: The Stakes," Middle East Report No. 82, International Crisis Group, January 27, 2009, http://www.crisisgroup.org/library/documents/middle_east___north_africa/iraq_iran_gulf/82_iraqs_provincial_elections___the_stakes.pdf

"Iraq's Repairman," *Newsweek*, July 5, 2004, http://www.newsweek.com/id/54322/

"Jemaah Islamiyah in Southeast Asia: Damaged But Dangerous," Asia Briefing, No. 63, August 26, 2003, International Crisis Group, http:/www.crisisgroup.org

Joint Resolution to Authorize the Use of United States Armed Forces Against Iraq, October 16, 2002, http://www.c-span.org/resources/pdf/hjres114.pdf

Jones, David Martin, and Carl Ungerer, "Delusion Reigns in Terror Studies," *The Australian*, September 15, 2006, http://www.theaustralian.news.com.au/story/0,20867,20413449-7583,00.html

Jones, Seth G., *Counterinsurgency in Afghanistan* (Santa Monica, CA: RAND, 2008).

Kagan, Frederick W., "Choosing Victory: A Plan for Success in Iraq," American Enterprise Institute, January 5, 2007, http://www.aei.org/publications/pubID.25396,filter.all/pub_detail.asp

Kalicki, Jan H., and David L. Goldwin (eds.), *Energy and Security: Toward a New Foreign Policy Strategy* (Washington, D.C.: Woodrow Wilson Center Press, 2005).

Keaney, Thomas, and Eliot Cohen, *Revolution in Warfare?* (Annapolis: Naval Institute Press, 1995).

Kegley, Charles W, Jr., *The New Terrorism: Characteristics, Causes and Controls* (Englewood Cliffs, NJ: Prentice Hall, 2003).

Kilcullen, David, "Anatomy of a Tribal Revolt," *Small Wars Journal* Blog, August 29, 2007, http://smallwarsjournal.com/blog/2007/08/print/anatomy-of-a-tribal-revolt

Kilcullen, David, "Countering Global Insurgency," *Small Wars Journal*, November 30, 2004, http://www.smallwarsjournal.com/documents/kilcullen.pdf

Kilcullen, David, "Counterinsurgency Redux," *Survival*, 48(4), December 2006, http://smallwarsjournal.com/documents/kilcullen1.pdf

Kilcullen, David, "Religion and Insurgency," *Small Wars Journal* Blog, May 12, 2007, http://smallwarsjournal.com/blog/2007/05/religion-and-insurgency/

Kilcullen, David, "Twenty-Eight Articles: Fundamentals of Company-level Counterinsurgency," http://www.au.af.mil/info-ops/iosphere_summer06_kilcullen.pdf

Klein, Joe, "David Petraeus," *Time*, December 17, 2007, http://www.time.com/time/specials/2007/personoftheyear/article/0,28804,1690753_1695388_1695379,00.html

Krauthammer, Charles, "Democratic Realism: An American Foreign Policy for a Unipolar World," February 27, 2004, American Enterprise Institute, http://www.aei.org/books/bookID.755,filter.all/book_detail.asp

Krauthammer, Charles, "The Unipolar Moment Revisited", *The National Interest*, Winter 2002/2003.

Krauthammer, Charles, "The Unipolar Moment", *Foreign Affairs*, 70(1), 1990/91.

Krepinevich, Andrew, "Cavalry to Computer: The Pattern of Military Revolutions," *The National Interest*, August 1994.

Lacqueur, Walter, *The New Terrorism: Fanaticism and the Arms of Mass Destruction* (New York: Oxford University Press, 1999).

Leventis, Evagoras C., "The Waziristan Accord," *The Middle East Review of International Affairs*, 11(4), December 2007.

Lia, Brynjar, "Al Qaeda's Appeal: Understanding its Unique Selling Points," *Perspectives on Terrorism*, 2(8), May 2008.

Lim Joo Jock and S. Vani (eds), *Armed Separatism in Southeast Asia* (Singapore: Institute of Southeast Asian Studies, 1984).

Long, Austin, *On "Other War": Lessons from Five Decades of RAND Counterinsurgency Research* (Santa Monica, CA: RAND, 2006).

"Lost in Translation," Government Executive.com, May 1, 2002, http://www.govexec.com/features/0502/0502s4.htm

Mackay, Donald, *The Malayan Emergency, 1948–60: The Domino That Stood* (London: Brassey's, 1997).

Mandelbaum, Michael, "The Inadequacy of American Power," in *Foreign Affairs*, Sep–Oct 2002.

Marc Sageman, "Leaderless Jihad: Radicalization in the West," New America Foundation, http://www.newamerica.net/files/Microsoft%20PowerPoint%20-%20Sageman.pdf

McFate, Montgomery, "The Military Utility of Understanding Adversary Culture," in *Joint Forces Quarterly*, Issue 38, July 2005, http://www.au.af.mil/au/awc/awcgate/jfq/1038.pdf

Mearsheimer, John J., "E.H. Carr vs. Idealism: The Battle Rages On," *International Relations*, 19(2), 2005.

Mearsheimer, John J., and Stephen M Walt, "Can Saddam be Contained? History Says Yes" (Occasional Paper, Belfer Center for Science and International Affairs, Kennedy School of Government, Harvard University, 2002).

Mearsheimer, John, and Stephen Walt, "The Israel Lobby and US Foreign Policy," *Middle East Policy*, 13(3), Fall 2006.

"Measuring Stability and Security in Iraq," Report to Congress, June 2008, http://www.defenselink.mil/pubs/pdfs/Master_16_June_08_%20FINAL_SIGNED%20.pdf

Memo from Secretary of Defense Donald H. Rumsfeld to Gen. James T. Hill, "Counter-Resistance Techniques in the War on Terrorism," April 2, 2003, http://texscience.org/reform/torture/rumsfeld-hill-2april03.pdf

Memo of Alberto R. Gonzales, Counsel to the President, to President George W. Bush, "Decision Re Application of the Geneva Convention on Prisoners of War to the Conflict with al Qaeda and the Taliban," January 25, 2002, http://texscience.org/reform/torture/gonzales-bush-25jan02.pdf

Merriman, Rima, "Middle East Studies Seen as Against American Interests," *Jordan Times*, March 11, 2004, http://www.arab2.com/n/newspaper/jordan-jordan-times.htm

Metz, Steven, "Learning from Iraq: Counterinsurgency Strategy in American Strategy," Monograph, Strategic Studies Institute, January 2007, http://www.strategicstudiesinstitute.army.mil/pdffiles/PUB752.pdf

Metz, Steven, "New Challenges and Old Concepts: Understanding 21st Century Insurgency," *Parameters*, Winter 2007–8.

Mindanao Times Interactive News

Mockaitis, Thomas R., "Conclusion: The Future of Terrorism Studies," *Small Wars and Insurgencies*, 14(1), March 2003.

Mockaitis, Thomas R., and Paul B Rich (eds), *Grand Strategy in the War Against Terrorism* (London: Frank Cass, 2003).

Mockaitis, Thomas, *The "New" Terrorism: Myths and Reality* (Westport, CT: Praeger, 2007).

MSBC.com

Multi-National Force-Iraq Commander's Counterinsurgency Guidance, Headquarters, Multi-National Force—Iraq, Baghdad, June 21, 2008, http://www.mnf-iraq.com/images/CGs_Messages/080621_coin_%20guidance.pdf

"Myers Thanks Mongolians for Iraqi Freedom Help," Armed Forces Press Service, U.S. Department of Defence, January 13, 2004, http://www.defenselink.mil/news/news-article.aspx?id=27505

National Defense Strategy, June 2008, http://www.defenselink.mil/news/2008%20 National%20Defense%20Strategy.pdf

National Strategy for Combating Terrorism, February 2003, http://www.globalsecurity.org/security/library/policy/national/counter_terrorism_strategy.pdf

National Strategy for Victory in Iraq, November 30, 2005, http://www.globalsecurity.org/military/library/policy/national/ns-victory-iraq_051130.htm

NATO in Afghanistan: Factsheet, http://www.nato.int/issues/afghanistan/040628-factsheet.htm

"Neocons on the Line", *Newsweek*, June 23, 2003.

New York Times

News.com

North Atlantic Treaty Organisation—Chronology Update, September 10–16. 2001, http://www.nato.int/docu/update/2001/0910/e0119a.htm

Norwitz, Jeffrey H. (ed.), *Armed Groups: Studies in National Security, Counterterrorism and Counterinsurgency* (Newport, CT: U.S. Naval War College, 2008).

NPR News

Nye, Joseph S, Jr., "US Power and Strategy After Iraq," *Foreign Affairs*, July/August 2003.

Obama, Barack, "My Plan for Iraq," *The New York Times,* July 14. 2008.

Omand, David, "Countering International Terrorism: The Use of Strategy," *Survival*, Winter 2005–6.

Osama bin Laden, "Declaration of War Against the Americans Occupying the Land of the Two Holy Places," http://www.pbs.org/newshour/terrorism/international/fatwa_1996.html (accessed March 1, 2008).

Osborne, Milton, "Getting the Job Done: Iraq and the Malayan Emergency," *Perspectives*, Lowy Institute, February 2005, http://www.lowyinstitute.org/Publication.asp?pid=215

"Overselling the World on War," *Newsweek*, June 9, 2003.

"Pak Army Protests US Drone Attack in Bajaur," The Indian.com, May 17, 2008, http://www.thaindian.com/newsportal/health/pak-army-protests-us-drone-attack-in-bajaur_10049702.html

Pakistan Elections 2008 Summary, http://www.elections.com.pk/summary.php (accessed June 1, 2008).

"Pakistan: Al Qaeda Claims Bhutto's Death," Adnkronos International, December 27, 2007 http://www.adnkronos.com/AKI/English/Security/?id=1.0.1710322437

PBS Frontline

Phares, Whalid, *The War of Ideas* (New York: Palgrave Macmillan, 2007).

Pirnie, Bruce R., and Edward O'Connell, *Counterinsurgency in Iraq: 2003–2006* (Santa Monica, CA: RAND, 2008).

Prados, Alfred B., and Christopher M. Blanchard, "Saudi Arabia: Current Issues and US Relations," *CRS Report for Congress*, August 2, 2006, http://www.fas.org/sgp/crs/mideast/RL33533.pdf

"President Addresses Nation, Discusses Iraq, War on Terror," June 28, 2005, http://merln.ndu.edu/MERLN/PFIraq/archive/wh/20050628-7.pdf

"President Bush Announces Major Combat Operations in Iraq Have Ended," May 1, 2003, http://www.americanrhetoric.com/speeches/wariniraq/gwbushiraq5103.htm

"President George Bush, Address to a Joint Session of Congress and the American People," September 20, 2001, http://www.historycentral.com/documents/Bushjoint.html

"President George W. Bush's Address to the Nation," October 7, 2001, http://www.johnston-sarchive.net/terrorism/bush911d.html

"President's Remarks at the United Nations General Assembly," September 12, 2002, http://www.johnstonsarchive.net/terrorism/bushiraqun.html

"Presidential Address to the Nation," *The White House*, October 7, 2001, http://www.white-house.gov/news/releases/2001/10/20011007-8.html (accessed February 1, 2008).

Project for the New American Century, http://www.newamericancentury.org/

"Public Diplomacy After September 11," Charlotte Beers, Under Secretary for Public Diplomacy and Public Affairs, Remarks to the National Press Club, Washington, December 18, 2002, http://www.state.gov/r/us/16269.htm

"Radicalization in the West: The Homegrown Threat," New York City Police Department, August 2007, http://www.nyc.gov/html/nypd/downloads/pdf/public_information/NYPD_Report-Radicalization_in_the_West.pdf

Radio Address of the President to the Nation, September 15, 2001, http://www.americanrheto-ric.com/speeches/gwbush911radioaddress.htm

Radio Free Europe

Raman, B., "Bin Laden's Fatwa Against Musharraf and Pakistani Army," South Asia Analysis Group, Paper No. 2388, September 22, 2007, http://www.southasiaanalysis.org/papers24/paper2388.html

Rapoport, David C., "The Fourth Wave: September 11 in the History of Terrorism," *Current History*, December 2001.

Record, Jeffrey, "The American Wary of War: Cultural Barriers to Successful Counterinsurgency," Cato Institute Policy Analysis No. 577, September 1, 2006, http://www.cato.org/pubs/pas/pa577.pdf

Remarks by the President at U.S. Naval Academy Commencement, U.S. Naval Academy Stadium, Annapolis, MD, May 25, 2001, The White House, http://www.whitehouse.gov/news/releases/2001/05/20010525-1.html (accessed June 1, 2008).

"Remarks by the President," September 12, 2001, http://www.americanrhetoric.com/speeches/gwbush911cabinetroomaddress.htm

Reuters

Ricks, Thomas E., *Fiasco: The American Military Adventure in Iraq* (London: Penguin, 2007).

Roman Kupchinsky, "Who Downed The Russian Jets," Radio Free Europe, August 30, 2004, http://www.rferl.org/featuresarticle/2004/08/76A7767C-540C-4626-9AD6-549DC-C8F4BD3.html

Rumsfeld, Donald H., "Transforming the Military," *Foreign Affairs*, May–June 2002;

Sageman, Marc, *Leaderless Jihad: Terror Networks in the Twenty-First Century* (University of Pennsylvania Press, 2007).

Scowcroft, Brent, "Don't Attack Saddam," Editorial, *Wall Street Journal*, August 15, 2002.

"Sheikh Sattar, Leader of the Anbar Awakening, Killed in Bombing," *The Long War Journal*, September 13, 2007, http://www.longwarjournal.org/archives/2007/09/sheikh_sattar_leader.php

Smith, Hugh (ed), *The Strategists* (Canberra: Australian Defence Force Academy, 2001).

Smith, Julianne, "NATO Battles the Taliban and Tests Its Future in Afghanistan," *China and Eurasia Forum Quarterly*, 4(4) (2006).

Stiglitz, Joseph, and Linda Bilme, "The Three Trillion War," *The Times*, February 23, 2008, http://www.timesonline.co.uk/tol/comment/columnists/guest_contributors/article3419840.ece

Straits Times (Singapore)

Stubbs, Richard, *Hearts and Minds in Guerilla Warfare: The Malayan Emergency 1948–1960* (Singapore: Oxford University Press, 1989).

Summary of Case Against Jemaah Islamiah in Singapore, NEFA Foundation, http://nefafoundation.org/miscellaneous/FeaturedDocs/SingMHA_JISummary.pdf

Summary of Findings, "A Year After Iraq War," Pew Research Center for the People and the Press, March 16, 2004, http://people-press.org/reports/display.php3?ReportID=206

Summers, Harry, *On Strategy: A Critical Analysis of the Vietnam War* (Novato, CA: Presidio, 1982).

Sydney Morning Herald

"Taking on the Doubters," *The Economist*, September 2, 2002.

Tan, Andrew T, H, (ed), *A Handbook of Terrorism and Insurgency in Southeast Asia* (Cheltenham: Edward Elgar, 2007).

Tan, Andrew T. H. (ed), *The Politics of Terrorism* (London: Routledge, 2006).

Tan, Andrew T. H., *A Political and Economic Dictionary of Southeast Asia* (London: Europa, 2004).

Tan, Andrew T. H., *Security Perspectives of the Malay Archipelago* (Cheltenham: Edward Elgar, 2004).

Tan, Andrew T.H,, and Kumar Ramakrishna (eds), *The New Terrorism: Anatomy, Trends and Counter-Strategies* (Singapore: Times Academic / Eastern Universities Press, 2003).

"Targeting Thailand," *Time*, January 19, 2003.

Text of Bush's Order on Treatment of Detainees, February 7, 2002, http://www.kron.com/global/story.asp?s=1962000&ClientType=Printable

The 9/11 Commission Report, http://www.gpoaccess.gov/911/pdf/fullreport.pdf

"The Abu Ghraib Photos," http://www.cnn.com/interactive/world/0405/gallery.iraq.prison.abuse/frameset.exclude.html

The Afghanistan Compact, London, January 31–February 1, 2006, http://www.nato.int/isaf/docu/epub/pdf/afghanistan_compact.pdf

The Age

The Australian

The Guardian

The Independent

"The Insurgency," Operation Iraqi Freedom, August 20, 2007, http://www.mnf-iraq.com/index.php?option=com_content&task=view&id=729&Itemid=45

The Iraq Study Group Report, http://www.usip.org/isg/iraq_study_group_report/report/1206/iraq_study_group_report.pdf

The National Security Strategy of the United States of America, September 2002, http://www.lib.umich.edu/govdocs/pdf/nss02.pdf

"The President's State of the Union Address," January 29, 2002, http://www.johnstonsarchive.net/policy/bushstun2002.html

The Secretary-General Address to the General Assembly, New York, September 23, 2003, http://www.un.org/webcast/ga/58/statements/sg2eng030923.htm

"The Situation in Afghanistan and its Implications for International Peace and Security," Report of the Secretary-General, March 6, 2008, http://daccessads.un.org/doc/UNDOC/GEN/NO8/255/80/PDF/NO825580.pdf

"The Situation in Afghanistan: A Re-evaluation Needed," United States Institute of Peace Briefing, April 2007, http://www.usip.org/pubs/usipeace_briefings/2007/0419_koenigs_afghanistan.html

The Telegraph

"The Terrorist Threat to the US Homeland," National Intelligence Estimate, July 2007, http://www.dni.gov/press_releases/20070717_release.pdf

"The Thai Connection", *Al Ahram Weekly*, Issue No. 689, May 6–12 2004, http://weekly.ahram.org

The Times

The Times of India

"The Twelve Year Itch," *Newsweek*, March 31, 2003.

Thompson, Robert, *Defeating Communist Insurgency: Experiences from Malaya and Vietnam* (London: Chatto and Windus, 1972).

Transcript: Bin Laden Accuses the West, Aljazeera.net, April 25, 2006, http://english.aljazeera.net/English/archive/archive?ArchiveId=22235

"U.S. Attorney General Says Terrorist Threats to U.S. Very Real," GlobalSecurity.org, December 2, 2005, http://www.globalsecurity.org/security/library/news/2005/12/sec-051202-usia01.htm

UN Security Council Counter Terrorism Committee, http://www.un.org/sc/ctc

UN Security Council Resolution 1386, December 20, 2001, http://daccessdds.un.org/doc/UNDOC/GEN/N01/708/55/PDF/N0170855.pdf?OpenElement

UN Security Council Resolution 1390, January 16, 2002 http://daccessdds.un.org/doc/UNDOC/GEN/N02/216/02/PDF/N0221602.pdf?OpenElement

UN Security Council Resolution 1401, March 28, 2002, http://daccessdds.un.org/doc/UNDOC/GEN/N02/309/14/PDF/N0230914.pdf?OpenElement

United Nations Security Council Resolution 1373, September 28, 2001, http://www.un.org/Docs/scres/2001/sc2001.htm

United Nations Security Council Resolution 1441, November 8, 2002, http://daccessdds.un.org/doc/UNDOC/GEN/N02/682/26/PDF/N0268226.pdf?OpenElement

US and Coalition Casualties, CNN.com, http://www.cnn.com/SPECIALS/2004/oef.casualties (accessed on January 29, 2009).

USA Today

"Views of a Changing World 2003: War With Iraq Further Divides Global Politics," June 3, 2003, Pew Research Center for the People and the Press, http://people-press.org/reports/print.php3?PageID=712

VOA News

von Clausewitz, Carl, *On War* (Plain Label Books), http://books.google.com.au/books?id=fXJnOde4eYkC

Washington Post

Washington Times

Weigley, Russell R., *The American Way of War: A History of United States Military Strategy and Policy* (Bloomington: Indiana University Press, 1973).

Weinberger, Casper W., *Fighting for Peace: Seven Critical Years in the Pentagon* (New York: Warner, 1990).

Weisser, Rebecca, "Strategist Behind War Gains," *The Australian*, August 18, 2007, http://www.theaustralian.news.com.au/story/0,25197,22263435-31477,00.html

"Why the War on Terror Will Never End," *Time*, May 20, 2003.

"Will Petraeus Strategy be the Last?" The Atlantic.com, September 17, 2007, http://www.theatlantic.com/doc/200709u/petraeus-bing-west

Wilson, Isaiah, *New Thoughts on War and Peace*, Prologue, http://www.thinkbeyondwar.com/Documents/Prologue_New_Thoughts_on_War_and_Peace.pdf (accessed February 1, 2008).

Wolfowitz, Paul, "Iraq, What Does Disarmament Look Like?" Council on Foreign Relations, January 23, 2003, http://www.cfr.org/publication.html?id=5454

"Working Group Report on Detainee Interrogations in the Global War on Terrorism: Assessment of Legal, Historical, Policy, and Operational Considerations," Department of Defense, March 6, 2003, http://texscience.org/reform/torture/dod-detainee-interro-6mar03.pdf

World Tribune.com

INDEX

9/11 Commission
  See National Commission on
      Terrorist Attacks

Abadan theater attack, 2
Abu Ghraib, 56, 94–95, 127, 174
Afghanistan
  Al Qaeda and, 24, 40–42, 57,
      58–59, 73, 83–84, 97–98
  Baker-Hamilton report and, 60
  bin Laden and, 81
  CIA and, 93
  COIN and, 11, 12
  GWOT and, 27
  insurgency, 135, 139, 148,
      149–154, 155, 157–158, 167,
      171, 177–181
  JI and, 32
  post-cold War, 8
  post-invasion issues, 115, 123, 183,
      185, 188, 189
  RMA and, 109–112
  Soviet Union and, 32–33, 34, 40
  Taliban and, 40–41, 100
  U.S. invasion, 2–3, 20–24, 37,
      48, 52, 75–76, 78,
      106, 133
Ahmed, Hashim, 10, 56
Al Da'wah party, 68, 91
Al Jazeera, 2, 37, 82

Al Qaeda
  9/11 attacks, 1–2
  Afghanistan and, 15, 24, 40–42,
      57, 58–59, 73, 83–84,
      97–98
  GCOIN and, 139, 145, 148–151, 153,
      154–164, 166–169, 171, 173
  globalization and, 73–74
  goals, 74
  GWOT and, 19–43, 60, 75–76, 79–80,
      85, 88, 93, 118–121, 122–123,
      130–131, 190
  Iraq and, 16, 45, 47, 48–50, 54, 57–59,
      61–65, 69, 92, 113, 188
  jihad and, 81–85, 135
  Middle Eastern view of, 94–95,
      125–128
  National Strategy for Combating
      Terrorism and, 118–121
  post-9/11 attacks, 41–43
  study of, 7, 11–12
  Taliban and, 109
  transformation to global threat,
      177–181, 182, 184
  U.S. and, 3–4, 97–100, 106–107, 113
  See also AQI (Al Qaeda in Iraq)
Al Tawhid Wal Jihad, 38
Algeria, 38–39, 73, 133
Ali, Ahmad Omar Abu, 29
Al-Islambouli, 36
Al-Kadhimiya mosque, 58

Allawi, Ali A., 10
American Way of War
  COIN and, 142
  failure of GWOT and, 102–111
  Gates and, 184–185
  GCOIN and, 173, 187
  Rumsfeld and, 16
  unilateral foreign policy and, 129
Amrozi bin Nurhasyim, 31
Annan, Kofi, 89
annihilation, strategy of, 102–103
Anti-Ballistic Missile Treaty, 88
ANZUS Treaty, 19
AQI (Al Qaeda in Iraq), 57–58, 62–65,
  68, 81–82, 97–98, 110, 145–146,
  149, 178
  See also Al Qaeda; Iraq
*Armed Groups: Studies in National
  Security, Counterterrorism and
  Counterinsurgency* (Norwitz), 180
As-Sahad, 40
Atef, Mohammad, 20
Atta, Muhammad, 47
Aum Supreme Truth, 7, 8, 134–135
Aylwin-Foster, Nigel, 111

Ba'ath Party, 54–55, 57, 81, 90
Baer, Robert, 93
Baker-Hamilton study, 59–61
Bali, terrorist bombing of (2002), 20,
  31–32, 35, 37, 85, 159, 179
Baradei, Mohamad El, 51
Barayev, Arbi, 33
Barayev, Movsar, 33
Basayev, Shamil, 33, 37
Bashir, Abu Bakar, 32, 160
Beers, Charlotte, 127
Bell, Coral, 14
Bentizi, Taeb, 34
Bhutto, Benazir, 24, 41, 155–157
Biddle, Stephen, 131
Bilmes, Linda, 13
bin Al-Shibh, Ramzi, 20

bin Laden, Osama
  9/11 and, 2
  Al Qaeda and, 38–41,
    81–82, 98
  fatwa against U.S., 74, 125–128
  insurgencies and, 158–161, 163
  Iraq and, 122, 136
  Pakistan and, 106
  Saudi Arabia and, 34, 100
  Spain and, 34
  support for, 50, 72, 85, 112, 184
  Taliban and, 21–22, 109
  U.S. pursuit of, 24, 58
Biological Weapons Convention, 88
Blix, Hans, 86
Bolton, John, 89
Boot, Max, 108
Bremmer, Paul, 55
Brigades of the Martyr Abu Hafz
  al-Masri, 35
Burke, Jason, 9, 72, 125, 127, 166,
  180, 182
Bush, George H.W., 92
Bush, George W.
  Al Qaeda and, 29
  Allawi on, 10
  "Axis of Evil" and, 90, 111
  conflation of terror threat, 75–76
  Fukuyama on, 101
  GCOIN and, 174–175
  invasion of Iraq, 46, 48–50, 51, 53,
    54, 56, 59–61, 63, 80, 123,
    136, 142
  loss of legitimacy, 92–95
  misdiagnosis of terror threat, 71–75,
    78–80
  National Strategy for Combating
    Terrorism, 118, 120–121
  neoconservatives and, 105–108
  Obama and, 108, 187
  Operation Enduring Freedom and,
    21, 150
  Pakistan and, 155, 157
  Southeast Asia and, 159

strategic failures of, 13–16, 101–102, 131, 142, 171
troop surge and, 144
unilateral foreign policy, 105–108, 113, 166, 182, 189–190
U.S. grand strategy and, 2–4
war on terror and, 1, 85–86, 115, 127–129
Byman, Daniel, 11, 74, 83, 165–166, 188

Central Intelligence Agency (CIA), 45, 47, 79, 91, 93
Cetron, Marvin J., 99
Chalabi, Ahmed, 53
Chandler, Michael, 11, 165
Chechnya, terrorism and, 32–34, 36–37, 42, 63, 72–73, 139, 157, 170, 183
Cheney, Dick, 47, 78, 79
Chirac, Jacques, 52, 87
Choosing Victory: A Plan for Success in Iraq (Kagan), 60
Clausewitzian, Carl von, 102–103, 110, 112, 129
Clinton, Bill, 88
Cohen, Eliot, 105
COIN, 11–12, 17, 117–137, 139–175
COIN (counterinsurgency)
Afghanistan and, 11, 12–16
American Way of War and, 142
Great Britain and, 132–133, 139–140, 144, 146–147, 166, 171
jihad movement and, 169–171
unilateralism and, 165–166
Cole, Benjamin, 7
Corum, James, 11, 166–167
Counter Terrorism Committee (CTC), 19–20
counterinsurgency, See COIN (counterinsurgency)
Cronin, Audrey, 11
Curry, Peter, 180

Dahab, terrorist bombing of, 38

Darul Islam rebellion, 32, 160, 167
Department of Homeland Security, 3, 26, 131
Depuy, William, 103
disaggregation, 12, 61, 170, 173–174, 183–185
drug trade, 23, 180
Dyer, Gwynne, 187–188

Echevarria, Autolio J., 102
Egypt, 36, 37–38, 50, 63, 81, 93, 128
End of Iraq, The (Galbraith), 10, 123
Ending Terrorism: Lessons for Defeating Al-Qaeda (Cronin), 11
ETA, 36, 134
Evans, Gareth, 75, 181
explosively formed penetrators (EFPs), 91

Farouq, Omar Al-, 20
fatwa, 40, 74, 125
Federally Administered Tribal Areas (FATAs), 27, 97
Fiasco: The American Military Adventure in Iraq (Ricks), 10
Fighting the War on Terror: A Counterinsurgency Strategy (Corum), 11
Flight 11 (American Airlines), 1
Flight 175 (United Airlines), 1
Flight 77 (American Airlines), 1
Flight 93 (United Airlines), 1
four Ds of combating terrorism, 4
four waves of terrorism theory, 7, 24–25
Freedman, Lawrence, 105
Friedman, George, 115
Fukuyama, Francis, 76, 77, 100–101

Galbraith, Peter W., 10, 54, 123
Gallis, Paul, 152
Garner, Jay, 53, 55

Gates, Robert, 6, 136–137, 151, 181, 184, 186
GCOIN (global counterinsurgency), 164–175, 182–185
  Al Qaeda and, 139, 145, 148–151, 153, 154–164, 166–169, 171, 173
  American Way of War and, 173, 187
  Bush, George W. and, 174–175
  jihad movement and, 164–165, 173–174, 183–184
  multilateralism and, 17, 165
Geneva Conventions, 93
Getting the Job Done: Iraq and the Malaysian Emergency (Osborne), 146–147
Ghailani, Ahmed Kahalfan, 20
Glennon, Michael, 87
global counterinsurgency, *See* GCOIN (global counterinsurgency)
Global Trends 2025, 24–25, 177, 189–190
Global War on Terror (GWOT)
  Al Qaeda and, 24–27, 41–43
  initial successes, 19–24
  Pakistan and, 39–41
  post-9/11 terror attacks, 41–43
  terrorist attacks around world, 31–39
  terrorist plots in U.S. homeland, 28–31
globalization, 7–8, 12–14, 25, 72–73, 119, 124, 128, 132, 158, 168, 171, 173, 180–181, 189
Gonzales, Alberto, 29, 93
Gordon, Philip H., 183
Great Britain
  COIN and, 132–133, 139–140, 144, 146–147, 166, 171
  global influence, 13, 190
  Gulf War and, 80
  GWOT and, 29–30, 84
  insurgency and, 91, 135
  Iraq and, 52–53, 55
  ISAF and, 150
  Malaysia and, 146–147
  Middle East studies and, 124

support for U.S. invasion of Iraq, 21–23, 87–88, 108–109
  terror attacks on, 26, 35, 37
Guantanamo Bay, 13, 93–94, 120, 127, 166, 174, 179
Guerbouzi, Mohamed, 34
Gulf Air War Survey, The, 105
Gulf War, 46, 49, 51–53, 74, 78, 80, 87, 90, 92, 104–105, 108
Gunaratna, Rohan, 11, 165
Gurr, Nadine, 7

Hakim, Abdul Aziz Al, 67
Hakim, Ayatollah Sayyid Mohamed Baqir Al, 57, 67
Hamas, 25, 42, 120, 135
Hambali, 20, 32, 159, 163
Hamilton, Lee, 30, 59–61
Harethi, Qaed Salim Sinan Al, 20
Hashim, Ahmed S., 10, 56
Hawsawi, Mustafa Ahmed, 20
Hindi, Abu Issa Al, 20
Hizbollah, 25
Hoffman, Bruce, 2, 7–8, 12, 25, 27, 43, 73, 98, 117, 118, 122–123, 131, 132, 136, 164–166, 178, 185
Hussein, Saddam
  Al Qaeda and, 3, 46–50, 81–83
  Gulf War and, 105
  GWOT and, 129–130, 159
  instability of Iraq following overthrow, 53–57, 56,68–69, 188
  Iran and, 45–46, 68–69
  Mehdi Army and, 66
  overthrow, 10, 15–16, 52, 86, 115, 129–130
  Reagan and, 45–46
  regional security and, 90–92
  U.S. case against, 45–50, 78–79
  WMDs and, 3, 46–50, 76

improvised explosive devices (IEDs), 42, 58, 83, 110–111, 150, 179–180
Inside Terrorism (Hoffman), 7

insurgency
  Afghanistan, 135, 139, 148, 149–154,
      155, 157–159, 167, 171, 177–181
  Iraq, 17, 42–43, 100, 102, 105,
      108–111, 122, 187
  Pakistan, 157–158
  See also COIN (counterinsurgency);
      GCOIN (global
      counterinsurgency)
Insurgency and Counterinsurgency in Iraq
  (Hashim), 10
Integrated National Asymmetric Threat
  strategy, 5
International Atomic Energy Agency
  (IAEA), 48, 51, 90
International Security Assistance Force
  (ISAF), 22–23, 150, 154
Internet, 8, 26, 30, 48, 73, 84, 98–99,
  126, 133, 168, 180
Iranian Revolution, 7, 46, 91
Iran-Iraq War, 45, 92
Iraq
  Abu Ghraib and, 127
  AQI (Al Qaeda in Iraq), 26, 38,
      57–58, 62–65, 68, 81–82,
      97–98, 110, 145–146,
      149, 178
  case against, 45–51
  COIN and, 139–149, 167–168,
      170–174
  conflation with terrorism, 3, 12–14,
      75–80
  Great Britain and, 37
  GWOT and, 27, 80–86, 99, 113–115,
      120–121, 129–133, 135–136,
      150–151, 159, 179–180,
      189, 190
  impact on U.S., 86–87
  implications for international system,
      87–90, 95
  implications for regional security,
      90–92, 112
  insurgency, 17, 42–43, 100, 102, 105,
      108–111, 122, 187
  loss of U.S. legitimacy and, 92–95
  misdiagnosis of terror threat from,
      71–75
  Shiite power struggle, 66–69
  Sunnis and, 163
  unexpected challenges in, 53–57
  U.S. invasion of, 3, 9–15, 46, 48–50,
      51, 53, 54, 56, 59–61, 63, 80,
      123, 125–126, 136, 142
  U.S. occupation, 100–101, 183
  U.S. offensive against, 51–53
  U.S. strategy in, 59–66, 187–188
Iraq Study Group, 59–60
Islamic Supreme Council of Iraq (ISCI),
  67–68, 91

Jaish-e-Mohammad (JEM), 39, 155
Jama'at al-Tawhid wal-Jihad (JTJ), 57,
  81
Jemaah Islamiah (JI), 26, 31, 159
jihad movement
  Al Qaeda and, 34, 139
  Chechnya and, 37
  COIN and, 169–171
  disaggregation and, 12
  GCOIN and, 164–165, 173–174,
      183–184
  globalization and, 31–32, 73, 74
  GWOT and, 113–114, 135–136, 179
  Internet and, 99
  Iraq and, 45, 54–55, 57–58, 81–84,
      188
  Pakistan and, 40
  propaganda, 29–31, 123–127
  Southeast Asia and, 159, 163–164
Jones, James, 149
Jones, Sidney, 160
Jordan, 30, 38, 57, 65, 85, 93, 98

Kagan, Frederick, 60, 144
Karzai, Hamid, 22–23, 109, 149–150
Kashmir, 40, 72, 139, 157, 183
Keaney, Thomas, 105
Khan, Mohammed Siddique, 37
Khoei, Imam Abdul Majid Al, 67

Khomeini, Ayatollah, 46
Kilcullen, David, 11–12, 61, 63, 132,
    136, 141, 159, 167–175, 181, 185
Kissinger, Henry, 95
Krauthammer, Charles, 76–77
Krepinevich, Andrew, 104
Kurdistan Workers' Party (PKK),
    65–66, 134
Kurds, 52, 54–56, 57, 59–60, 65–66, 68,
    90, 92, 114, 134, 146
Kyoto Protocol, 88

Lacqueur, Walter, 7
Lashkar-e-Jhangvi (LEJ), 155
Lashkar-e-Toiba, 39
Lia, Brynjar, 126
Libbi, Abu Faraj Al, 20
Liotta, P.H., 181
London bombings (2005), 26, 37, 84, 85
Long, Austin, 10, 167

Maktab Al-Khidamat, 81
Malayan Emergency, 12, 130, 132, 139,
    144, 146–147, 164–165, 172, 186
Maliki, Nouri, 61–62, 66, 67–68, 91
Mandelbaum, Michael, 78
Mazar-I-Sharif, 22, 96
McCain, John, 115
McConnell, Mike, 65
McFate, Montgomery, 170
Mearsheimer, John, 49, 79, 124,
    129–130
Mehdi Army, 62, 66–68, 91–92, 109,
    145, 171
Mehsud, Baitullah, 24, 154–155, 156
Metz, Steven, 109–110, 111, 132–134,
    136
Middle East Studies Association
    (MESA), 123
Mockaitis, Thomas, 11, 112–113,
    130–134, 136, 139, 146, 164–166,
    168, 182, 184–185
Mohammed, Khalid Sheikh, 20, 28
Moltke, Helmuth von, 102

Moroccan Islamic Combatant Group,
    34, 39
Mosaed, Khaled, 38
Motassadek, Mounir Al, 20
Mubarak, Hosni, 50
multilateralism
    Bush's rejection of, 46, 79, 88
    GCOIN and, 17, 165
    GWOT and, 129, 181–182, 189–191
    Krauthammer and, 76–77
    loss of U.S. legitimacy and, 94
    National Strategy for Combating
        Terrorism and, 121
    NATO and, 152
    Rumsfeld and, 107
    United Nations and, 14
    U.S. National Defense Strategy and,
        6, 185–186
    See also unilateralism
Mumbai, terrorist bombing of, 39
Musharaff, Pervez, 40–41, 154, 156

Nashiri, Abd Al-Rahim Al, 20
National Commission on Terrorist
    Attacks, 3, 30
National Intelligence Estimate (NIE),
    47, 79
National Security Strategy, 3–4, 117
National Strategy for Combating
    Terrorism, 4, 16, 117–122
NATO (North Atlantic Treaty
    Organization), 13, 19, 22–23, 41,
    109, 150–152, 154, 187
North Korea, 13, 48, 50, 76, 79, 87,
    89–90, 110–111, 187, 189
Northern Alliance, 2, 21, 106
Norwitz, Jeffrey, 180
Nye, Joseph, 95

Obama, Barack, 15, 27, 94–95, 108,
    113–115, 136–137, 148, 154,
    157–158, 174, 178, 187
Occupation of Iraq, The (Allawi), 10
Office of Special Plans (OSP), 47

Omand, David, 113
Omar, Mohammed, 3, 22, 23, 106, 153
Operation Bojinka, 30, 158
Osborne, Milton, 146–147
Owens, William, 104

Pakistan
  Al Qaeda and, 22, 42, 95, 109, 178
  GWOT and, 20, 39–41, 115, 148,
      150–151, 153
  insurgency, 157–158
  Islamic radicalism in, 154–157
  Mumbai terrorist bombings, 39
  Pashtun tribes, 106
  post-9/11 attacks and, 42, 85
  Taliban and, 3, 22–24, 27, 30, 109
  See also Federally Administered Tribal
      Areas (FATAs)
Palestine, 42, 72, 85, 120, 134, 168, 183
Pashtun, 3, 21–23, 41, 106, 123,
      153, 156
Patriot Act, 3, 4, 120
Petraeus, David, 61–64, 140–141,
      144–145, 148, 153, 157, 171
Phares, Whalid, 124, 125–126
postpositivism, 124, 174
Powell, Colin, 51, 103, 134
preemption, 4, 6, 13, 46, 77–78, 87, 88,
      101, 105, 107, 111, 118, 123, 127,
      136, 188
Putin, Vladimir, 52

RAND studies, 10–11, 182
Rapoport, David, 7, 25, 132
Reagan, Ronald, 45, 91–92
Record, Jeffrey, 111
Red Mosque, seizure of, 155
Reid, Richard, 29
renditions, 13, 93, 94, 120, 166, 174, 179
Revolution in Military Affairs (RMA),
      53, 78, 104–106, 108, 110, 134
Ricks, Thomas E., 10, 108
Riyadus–Salikhin Reconnaissance and
      Sabotage Battalion of Shahids, 33, 37

rogue states, 5, 13–15, 46, 76, 78, 80, 87,
      89, 101, 115, 120–121, 129, 133, 159,
      188, 189
Rumsfeld, Donald, 6, 16, 22, 46–47, 53,
      78, 79, 86, 93, 105–108, 137, 142,
      184, 186

Sadat, Anwar, 36
Sadr, Ayatollah Mohammed Sadeq Al,
      66
Sadr, Muqtada al, 62, 66–67, 91, 109,
      145, 171
Sageman, Marc, 26, 84, 99, 180
Salafist Group for Prayer and Combat
      (GSPC), 39
Sattar, Sheikh Abdul, 63–64
Saudi Arabia, 24, 29, 34, 36, 42, 46, 58,
      63, 74, 84, 85, 91, 99–100,
      114, 177
Scowcroft, Brent, 49, 50
Sears Tower, 29, 99
Shared Values Initiative, 127
sharia, 48, 67, 72, 84, 126, 128, 155, 169
Sharif, Nawaz, 40, 156
Shiites
  Al Qaeda and, 57–60
  insurgency and, 81
  Iran and, 114, 188
  Iran-Iraq War and, 45–46
  Iraq and, 16, 54–57, 114, 148
  power struggle among, 66–69
  regional security and, 90–92
  Saddam Hussein and, 49
  Sunnis and, 63–64, 123, 146
Shinseki, Eric, 107–108, 142
Shishani, Murad Batal Al-, 83
Shock and Awe strategy, 52, 108, 115
Sistani, Grand Ayatollah Ali Al, 67
Slahi, Mohamedou Ould, 20
Southeast Asia, 20, 26, 28, 31–32, 35,
      72, 157–164, 169, 172, 179
Spain, 35–36, 88
Special Purpose Islamic Regiment, 33
Stiglitz, Joseph, 13

Stubbs, Richard, 140

subprime housing loan crisis, 13,
  113, 167

suicide bombings
  Al Qaeda and, 83, 98–99, 110, 146,
    179
  attempted, 28–29
  Bali attacks, 31
  Iraq, 23, 57–58
  Jordan, 65
  Pakistan, 23, 40–41, 150, 155
  post-9/11 attacks, 41–43
  worldwide, 31–38

Sungkar, Abdullah, 32, 160

Sunnis, 10, 26, 54–60, 62–66, 81, 90,
  92, 114, 123, 136, 145–146, 148,
  163, 171, 188

Super Ferry bombing, 35

Syria, 55, 56, 60–61, 81, 93, 99, 130

Taliban
  Afghanistan and, 40–41, 100,
    148–151, 153
  Al Qaeda and, 21, 27, 28, 40–41, 60,
    75, 128, 177
  GWOT and, 92–93, 106, 179
  Operation Enduring Freedom and,
    2–3, 15, 21–24, 84, 115
  Pakistan and, 148, 154–156, 158
  resurgence of, 13, 23–24, 97, 100,
    109–110, 115, 178
  Zarqawi and, 57

Tamil Tigers, 42

Tehrik-e-Taliban Pakistan (TTP), 154

Tehrik-e-Nifaz-Shariat-e-Mohammadi
  (TNSM), 155

terrorism, analysis of, 7–14

terrorism, four waves of, 7, 24–25

Tora Bora, 22

torture, 13, 37, 56, 93–94, 120, 166,
  174, 179

traditional counterinsurgency, *See*
  COIN

UN Resolution 1373, 19–20

UN Resolution 1441, 51

UN Resolution 1510, 22

unilateralism
  Bush and, 13–14, 75
  GWOT and, 182–183
  impact on international community,
    88–89, 112–113, 190–191
  Krauthammer and, 77–78
  loss of U.S. legitimacy and, 94–95,
    100, 120
  Mockaitis on, 130–131
  National Defense Strategy and, 185
  Pakistan and, 157
  Rumsfeld and, 46, 106–107
  U.S. National Defense Strategy and, 6

"Unipolar Movement, The"
  (Krauthammer), 76

United Nations Assistance Mission for
  Afghanistan (UNAMA), 22

Viera de Mello, Sergio, 35

Vietnam War, 78, 103–104, 107, 147

Walt, Stephen, 49, 79, 129–130

Weigley, Russell F., 102

Weinberger, Casper, 103

Wilson, Isaiah, 10, 54, 102, 133

WMDs, 3–5, 7–8, 14–16, 45–51, 53, 65,
  118, 120–121

Wolfowitz, Paul, 47, 78, 79, 108

Yazid, Mustafa Abu Al, 41

Yousef, Ramzi, 30, 161

Zammar, Mohammed Haydar, 20

Zarqawi, Abu Musab Al, 38, 57–58, 65,
  81, 98

Zawahiri, Ayman Al, 24, 37, 41, 83, 98,
  122, 162

Zubaydah, Abu, 20